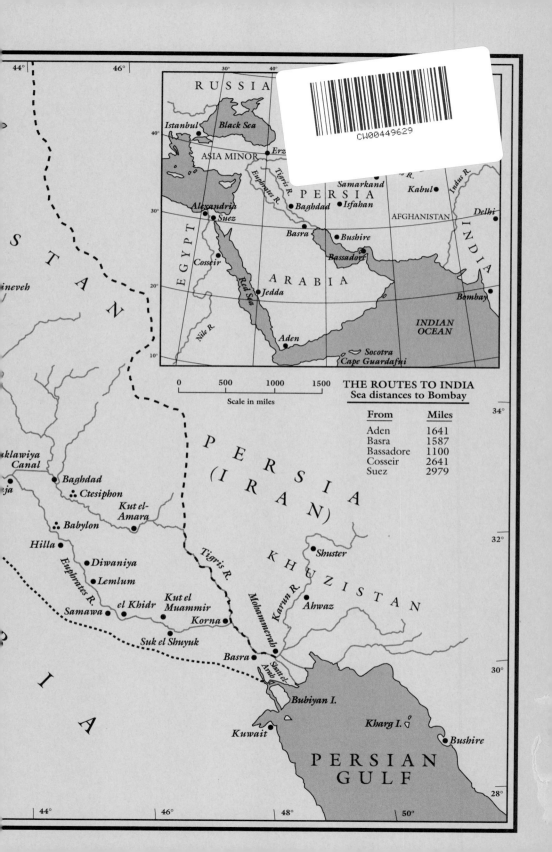

RUSSIA

Istanbul *Black Sea*

ASIA MINOR *Erz—*

Alexandria
Suez

Cosseir

EGYPT

Nile R.

Red Sea

Jedda

Aden

ARABIA

Euphrates R. *Tigris R.*

Baghdad

P E R S I A

Isfahan

Basra

Bushire

Bassadore

Samarkand *Kabul*

AFGHANISTAN

Indus R.

Delhi

INDIA

Bombay

INDIAN
OCEAN

Socotra
Cape Guardafui

0   500   1000   1500

Scale in miles

THE ROUTES TO INDIA
Sea distances to Bombay

From	Miles
Aden	1641
Basra	1587
Bassadore	1100
Cosseir	2641
Suez	2979

34°

—ineveh

—S T A N

—klawiya
Canal

—ja

Baghdad
Ctesiphon

Kut el-
Amara

Babylon

Hilla

Euphrates R.

Diwaniya

Lemlum

el Khidr

Samawa

Kut el
Muammir

Korna

Suk el Shuyuk

P E R S I A
(I R A N)

K H U Z I S T A N

Tigris R.

Shuster

Karun R.

Mohammerah

Ahwaz

Basra

Shatt el-
Arab

Bubiyan I.

Kuwait

Kharg I.

P E R S I A N
G U L F

Bushire

32°

30°

28°

44°   46°   48°   50°

44°   46°

30°   40°

40°

30°

20°

10°

The
Euphrates
Expedition

By the same author

The Yezidis: A Study in Survival

The
Euphrates
Expedition

John S. Guest

KEGAN PAUL INTERNATIONAL
London and New York

First published in 1992 by
Kegan Paul International Ltd
PO Box 256, London WC1B 3SW, England

Distributed by
John Wiley & Sons Ltd
Southern Cross Trading Estate
1 Oldlands Way, Bognor Regis
West Sussex, PO22 9SA, England

Routledge, Chapman & Hall Inc
29 West 35th Street
New York, NY 10001, USA

© *John S. Guest 1992*

Set in 10/12pt Baskerville
by Intype, London

Printed in Great Britain by T. J. Press

British Library Cataloguing in Publication Data
Guest, John S,.
   The Euphrates expedition.
   1. Great Britain. Soviet Union. Middle East. Foreign
     relations, history
   I. Title
   327.41047

   ISBN 0–7103–0429–3

Library of Congress Cataloging-in-Publication Data
Guest, John S.
   The Euphrates expedition / John S. Guest.
   182pp. 244cm.
   Includes bibliographical references and index.
   ISBN 0–7103–0429–3
   1. Euphrates River Valley–Discovery and exploration–British.
2. Steam navigation–Euphrates River–History–19th century.
I. Title.
DS48.2.G86 1991
956.7–dc20

91–8581
CIP

TO
ELIZABETH

Contents

Illustrations

Maps

Plan

The maps were made by Tom Pretnar and Brad Howe, Waterbury, Connecticut, USA, adapted from original maps published in Chesney's *Reports on the Navigation of the Euphrates* and his *Expedition for the Survey of the Rivers Euphrates and Tigris*.

Figure 1 is taken from Chesney's *Narrative of the Euphrates Expedition*, facing p. 255. The artist's name is not given.

Introduction

This book invites the reader to cast the mind a hundred and fifty years back to a short span of time between 1829 and 1842. This was an exciting period when Britain's might, demonstrated to the world at Trafalgar and Waterloo, was fortified by leadership in steam technology and was given a new direction by the liberal philosophy that British statesmen, thinkers and poets proclaimed at home and abroad.

From the material point of view it was a prehistoric age, when a letter from England took three months to reach India and live sheep were embarked on ships to provide fresh meat for the voyage. But despite changes in ways of life and forms of expression, the spirit of the times was not unlike the world we live in today.

The Euphrates expedition was an attempt by well intentioned British governments to achieve a geopolitical end by a technological means. The objective was to halt Russian expansion in the Near East, where some observers saw a threat to Britain's control of India. The instrument would be a flotilla of iron-hulled paddle-wheel steamboats that would patrol the long stretch of the river Euphrates from the Anatolian mountains to the Persian Gulf. Two steamers were sent out from England in early 1835 to confirm that the river was navigable for such vessels.

New technologies, which in one way or another extend the reach of man, beguile politicians with a prospect of instant, relatively effortless results that can bring fame and favour to their sponsors. More cautious men are wary of new-fangled inventions until the test of time has shown their limitations as well as their powers. Even when a technology appears proven its application in a new environment often creates unanticipated problems that call for quick decisions by the managers of the project in which the technology is employed.

Britain's efforts to navigate the Euphrates provide a case history for these truisms. The steamers, assembled in a makeshift shipyard in a primitive country, functioned well. Technical failures occurred, not because of faulty equipment, but due on one occasion to exposure to the unimagined stress of hurricane winds and on another to overworking the engine. After a third attempt had proved that the design of the vessels was inappropriate to the conditions along the river, the entire experiment was abandoned.

In the present age of instant communication, it is hard to imagine a project of national importance being undertaken when it required two or three months for reports from the scene of action to reach London or for the ministry in charge of the project to issue new instructions to the people in the field. The men on the spot were, inevitably, blamed for failing to achieve the desired results; but it is clear from the dates on which various letters were sent and received that the managers of the project made little provision for contingencies that might have been foreseen.

Politicians from both of the leading parties in Britain had been in charge of the Euphrates project. Consequently, after its abandonment there was no grand inquest but a tacit understanding that the project should pass quietly into oblivion. Historians have accepted this verdict and an occasional reference to the Euphrates expedition dismisses it as an irrelevant sideshow.

Yet sideshows are conducted by real people of flesh and blood who reveal their strengths and weaknesses at each step of the story. In this instance, a wealth of official papers and correspondence, supplemented by some published material and a meagre but rewarding file of contemporary prints and private letters, enables the reader to participate in the triumphs and tribulations of what one member of the expedition termed 'no mean undertaking'.[1]

I am most grateful for the access to official documents granted by the Public Record Office, the India Office Library and Records and the Public Record Office of Northern Ireland, as well as for the helpfulness of the staff at these institutions. Transcripts/translations of Crown copyright records in the Public Record Offices and unpublished Crown copyright material in the India Office Records reproduced in this book appear by permission of the Controller of Her Majesty's Stationery Office. I am also grateful for similar permission from the French Ministère des Affaires Étrangères, Division Historique des Archives Diplomatiques.

I am much obliged to the authorities in the Turkish and Syrian republics whose kindness enabled me in 1988–90 to retrace the route of the expedition from the Mediterranean coast to Birecik and to travel along the roads that run parallel to the Euphrates from Rumkale to Abu Kemal. Regrettably, I was unable to follow the course of the expedition to Iraq and the Persian Gulf, though parts of that region were familiar to me from previous visits.

In addition to the libraries in Britain, Germany and the United States which have granted me access to their collections and their photocopy facilities, I should express my special thanks to the Gloucestershire Records Office, which holds the Estcourt Papers, and to the Royal Artillery Institution, where Chesney's uniform may be seen.

I should also acknowledge my gratitude for the encouragement and advice I have received from many kind individuals (none of whom bears any responsibility for the contents of this book). Among them I am pleased to cite: Major H. C. Blosse-Lynch; Frank O. Braynard; Dr. J. F. Coakley; Rev. Christian Dienel; Dr Nuri Eren; David H. Finnie; my cousin Desmond FitzGerald, Knight of Glin; Mihai H. Handrea; the late Dr W. J. Hanna; Sir Donald Hawley, KCMG; F. William Hulton; Prof Nicholas A. Joukovsky; Mrs Pamela Linton; Dr Ertuğrul Zekâi Ökte; Mr and Mrs Morris Reilly; Sarah Searight; Prof. David Shoenberg FRS; A. M. Smith and Sigrid Tröger.

Special thanks are due to Mr Fred M. Walker of the National Maritime Museum, who looked over the manuscript of Chapters 1, 2 and 9 and made a number of useful suggestions. As regards the remainder of the text, I hope that sailors and steamboaters will pardon the mistakes of a writer whose nautical experience is limited to windsurfing.

Perhaps my greatest debts of all are owed to my wife, who tolerated my frequent absences from home in pursuit of elusive records, and to our dear daughter Cornelia, who edited my entire manuscript and put it in shape for publication.

John S. Guest

Fishers Island, New York
July 1990

Chapter 1

Peacock's Dream

Thomas Love Peacock, civil servant and man of letters, was born in 1785, the only child of a London glass merchant, who died when the boy was still quite young. His mother, Sarah Love, moved with her son to Surrey to live with her father, who had retired from the Royal Navy with the rank of Master after losing a leg at the battle of The Saints in 1782.

Peacock was educated at a small private school near his home. At the age of thirteen he went to work in London as a clerk. But as he grew up he discovered that his real interests were poetry and the study of Greek and Roman civilization.

His first volume of poetry, *Palmyra, and other Poems*, was published when the author was twenty years old. The title poem, revised, shortened and reissued in 1812, is an ode in memory of the ancient city in the Syrian desert that once handled the flow of merchandise from India and the Far East to Mediterranean ports. In its heyday (the third century AD) Palmyra was a wealthy buffer state between the Roman and Persian empires; its queen, Zenobia [Zeineb], maintained a lavish court and a school of Greek philosophy. But Zenobia's attempt to conquer Egypt and other provinces in the Near East led to her defeat by the Roman emperor Aurelian. Captured in flight to a fortress on the Euphrates, she was taken to Italy and died in captivity. The emperor accepted the submission of Palmyra, but when the inhabitants revolted the Romans sacked the city, much of which still stands in ruins.

Later, Peacock dismissed *Palmyra* as a 'juvenile production'.[1] But most reviews were favourable and when the revised version appeared the poet Shelley wrote to the publisher that 'the conclusion of *Palmyra* [is] the finest piece of poetry I ever read'.[2] Shelley and Peacock first met towards the end of 1812. Their friendship, sometimes warm, sometimes cool, lasted as long as they both lived and Peacock was named (with Byron, who declined) one of Shelley's executors.

In his twenties Peacock is described as 'a fine, tall, handsome man, with a profusion of bright brown hair, eyes of fine dark blue, massive brow, and regular features, a Roman nose, a handsome mouth which, when he laughed, turned up at the corners, and a complexion, fair as a girl's.'[3] Exposure to the brilliant, headstrong, idealistic Shelley and his circle of friends quickened Peacock's immature personality. Always an observer rather than a participant, he found his role as the amiable, witty foil to Shelley's enthusiasms and ensured his place in literary history as a pioneer of the satirical novel rather than as one of many minor poets.

Peacock's last long poem was published in 1818. Two years earlier *Headlong Hall* had appeared, the first of his humorous novels in which absurdly exaggerated characters bear many traits resembling Shelley, Byron and other writers of the day. Here and in his critical essays Peacock compared the current literary scene unfavourably with the poetic legacy of Greece and Rome.

The happy days of floating like a butterfly in Shelley's lively world ended in 1818, when the poet and his wife left England to live in Italy. About this time Peacock's financial situation, often precarious, changed for the better through the good offices of Peter Auber, a literary friend who was also Assistant Secretary of the Honourable East India Company. Peacock was thirty-three years old when, upon Auber's suggestion, he applied for and was soon appointed to the post of an Assistant to the Examiner of Indian Correspondence at the East India House, the imposing building in the City of London from which the Chairman and Deputy Chairman (known as the Chairs), the Court of Directors and a handful of the Company's 'servants', as its employees were styled, directed the affairs of Britain's empire in the East.

The East India Company was chartered by Queen Elizabeth I in 1600 to trade with the East Indies. Throughout its long life the Company's philosophy was that of a commercial concern.

Half way through the eighteenth century the genius of Robert Clive and Britain's victories in two wars with France thrust upon the Company the rewards and burdens of governing the richest province of the decaying Moghul empire in India. Calcutta, hitherto a trading 'factory', became the capital of the Presidency of Bengal, whose Governor-General also supervised the governors of the two smaller presidencies of Madras and Bombay.

Further wars and annexations enlarged the British possessions; when

Peacock entered the East India House the Company ruled over one hundred million people and the rest of the sub-continent was under its protection. The Company's administrative budget (which excluded trading operations) was close to twenty million pounds a year – one third of the comparable figure for Great Britain. For many years the Company had held the exclusive right to trade between Britain and India; this was terminated in 1813, but a monopoly of the valuable China trade was still retained.

To administer this vast realm with its diversity of peoples, faiths and laws the Company established a Civil Service recruited from among its European employees, with promotion depending on experience as well as merit. (In 1821 Peacock was obliged to explain these regulations to Shelley when the poet, allured by some visitors' stories of life in India, sought his friend's help in obtaining a position as advisor to a maharajah.) The authority of the civil servants, who at this time numbered only about 2,500, was backed by the Company's army of Indian troops led by British officers, reinforced by regiments of the British army, while the shores of India were guarded by vigilant British men of war.

Inevitably the British government, which provided for the defence of the Company's territories, began to assert its power over an entity that derived its existence from a royal charter renewable from time to time by act of Parliament. From 1784 onwards the home government's approval was required for appointments to the posts of Governor-General or governor of a presidency and for certain army commands. In that year a Board of Commissioners for the Affairs of India (often called the India Board or the Board of Control) was established as a branch of the government, with authority to review and, if necessary, to override policy decisions of the Company's directors.

Surprisingly, this system of dividing responsibility between Whitehall, the East India House and Calcutta worked tolerably well – mainly because time and distance limited the ability of anyone in London to influence the course of events in India. The splendid three-masted East Indiamen that carried the Company's cargoes between England and the East handled all its massive correspondence with India. Copies of important despatches were also sent overland by messenger to Istanbul (referred to in those days as Constantinople); from there mounted Ottoman couriers known as 'tartars' would carry them to Aleppo and onward by the so-called 'Direct Route' to Baghdad and down to Basra at the head of the Persian Gulf, where the Company had maintained a trading post for many years. But communication by this mode was expensive, vulnerable to robbers and unavailable in times of war. It was better to rely on the Company's own ships, which sailed regularly throughout the year and could complete the voyage between London and Calcutta in four or five months.

The directors kept a close hand on administrative expense and, as the volume of matters referred home mounted, some letters did not receive an answer for two years. The occasion for Peacock's engagement, along with two other assistants, was an effort to improve the efficiency of the Examiner's office, which received incoming correspondence and drafted replies to be approved by the directors and the Board of Control. Peacock was placed in charge of correspondence concerning public works.

Peacock's first few years with the Company passed agreeably. He married and lived comfortably in London, finding time to write another novel and to deal with Shelley's tangled affairs after the poet's death in 1822.

The atmosphere at the East India House was lethargic, reflecting the directors' lack of vigour and their presentiment that, when the Company's charter came up for renewal in 1833, the China trade would be opened to all. A victorious but costly war with Burma in 1824–6 increased the administrative deficit and after it was over instructions were sent out to India to cut back on every item of expense.

In September 1828 the Duke of Wellington, then Prime Minister, selected Lord Ellenborough, an ambitious thirty-eight-year-old politician, to be President of the India Board. Ellenborough was determined that his department, which was responsible to Parliament for the affairs of India, should take over many of the powers exercised by the directors of the Company, which he regarded as a clubby, inefficient vestige of the past. But the India Board's own staff was small and it depended for information on the files at the East India House, which were far from current. One particularly aggravating practice, carried down from the days when voyages to and from India were less frequent, required incoming despatches to be answered, paragraph by paragraph, in the order in which they had been received, regardless of their relative importance.

An Ellenborough's urging the Company adopted some improvements in its procedures and after ten months in office he tackled the root of the whole problem. His diary for 28 July 1829 records: 'I recommended to the Chairs the establishment of steam communication with India by the Red Sea.'[4]

In the Company's existing plight the directors were in no mood to commit it to a large-scale capital-intensive project. But at the same time they could not turn down outright a request from a minister on whose favour their future might depend. Peacock, who had recently become interested in steam, was instructed to prepare a report. His *Memorandum respecting the Application of Steam Navigation to the internal and external Communications of India* was submitted to Ellenborough in September 1829.[5] (The memorandum is quite concise. A modern reader requires some knowledge of background material, included below but omitted by Peacock because it was familiar to his readers.)

Peacock began by reviewing the improvements in river transport within India, where two locally built steamboats, equipped with British engines, had recently been placed in service on the Ganges between Calcutta and Allahabad. He then turned to the more glamorous topic of the three routes of communication between Britain and India: the ocean route around the Cape of Good Hope; the 'Overland Route' by ship to Alexandria, then overland across Egypt and then by ship again to India; and a new route, first proposed by Peacock, by ship to Syria, then overland to the upper Euphrates and by river boat to Basra, and from there by ship to India.

The first route considered by Peacock was the traditional route around the Cape of Good Hope regularly used by the Company's merchantmen. Facilities for water and other supplies were available at its way station at St Helena and at Ascension, Cape Town and Mauritius, British possessions since 1815. Only two steam-propelled vessels, the *Enterprize* and the *Falcon*, had ever made this voyage from England to India and none had attempted the westbound voyage home.

The *Enterprize* was a 470-ton* paddle steamer built in 1824 and specially designed for the ocean voyage. She was powered by two 60 hp engines and could carry thirty-five days' supply of coal. In addition, she carried three masts and was rigged fore and aft. Her captain, Lieutenant J. H. Johnston, was a naval officer on half pay.

The owners had laid down only one depot of coal, at Cape Town, and had reckoned that the combination of steam and sail would take the vessel from England to India in less than seventy days. Their hopes were disappointed. The *Enterprize* left Falmouth on 16 August 1825, and reached Cape Town fifty-six days later after an unscheduled maintenance stop at São Tomé. The vessel had steamed two-thirds and sailed one-third of the time. On the Cape Town–Calcutta leg of the voyage the *Enterprize* used steam and sail equally. She arrived at Diamond Harbour in the Hooghly river on 8 December 1825 – 113 days after leaving England – having consumed all her coal; as a result the captain was obliged to buy wood to steam the last forty miles up the river to Calcutta.

---

* Tonnages referred to here are 'Builders Old Measurement', a calculation based on length and beam of a sailing ship. Since the middle of the nineteenth century tonnage has been calculated by reference to a vessel's interior capacity.

A few weeks later another steamship, the 170-ton *Falcon*, a converted yacht, reached Calcutta after a four months' voyage, mostly under sail.

After remarking that some steam enthusiasts still favoured the Cape route, Peacock turned to the Red Sea route suggested by Lord Ellenborough. This second alternative was known as the 'Overland Route' because it required land and river travel through Egypt – either by canal and river boat from Alexandria to Cairo and from there across the desert to Suez, or by taking a boat up the Nile all the way to Luxor and then crossing the desert to Cosseir [Quseir], a now insignificant port on the Red Sea. This route was used by occasional antiquarians and Company servants and at certain seasons for despatches to and from Bombay.

Egypt was one of the richest provinces of the Ottoman empire and Britain had maintained a consulate at Alexandria for over twenty years. The country had been occupied by the French from 1798 to 1801. Napoleon commanded the expeditionary force and ruled Egypt for the first thirteen months, but after his departure the invaders were cut off from France by a British blockade and finally surrendered to a British force, which restored the province to the Sultan. Since 1805 Egypt had been governed by Mehemet Ali, a wily Albanian who consolidated his power by massacring the Mameluke* warlords who had fought the French. After defeating the Wahabis (ancestors of the present Saudi rulers) in 1818, Mehemet Ali had extended his authority to Mecca, Medina and down the Arabian coast as far as Jedda.

Mehemet Ali, now generally called 'the viceroy', welcomed foreigners, especially the French, and employed them to modernize the economy of Egypt. Law and order prevailed in his territories and the only hazard faced by foreign travellers was the plague, which appeared in the Nile delta every spring and required them to be detained in quarantine upon their return to European ports.

Peacock pointed out in his memorandum that the use of steamers for mail communication between London and Bombay by way of Egypt had been proposed in 1823 and again in 1826 by Mountstuart Elphinstone, a far-sighted governor of Bombay. He noted without comment that the Court of Directors 'were not disposed to act on the suggestion'.

Early in 1829 Elphinstone's successor, Sir John Malcolm, had renewed the same proposal and actually laid down depots of coal at Red Sea ports in preparation for a trial voyage by the *Enterprize*. The directors rejected Malcolm's overall plan but did not forbid the experiment. Peacock's memorandum stated tersely that 'Sir John Malcolm has recently announced his

---

* Mamelukes were Caucasian slave-boys who rose to become a caste in the Ottoman army and the effective rulers of Egypt and Iraq.

intention of sending the *Enterprize*, on the 15th November, from Bombay to Suez.'

This would be a bold venture. In the days of sail the Red Sea, fringed with uncharted coral reefs that limited navigation by night, was a dangerous trap. In the lower part south-easterly winds blow constantly from October to June, while for ten months of the year strong north-westers blow down the Gulf of Suez to Cosseir. One old India hand had said: 'There is one half the year you cannot get in, and you can get out; and the other half you can get in, and cannot get out of the Red Sea.'[6]

In addition, between June and September the south-west monsoon in the Indian Ocean forced ships sailing from Bombay to the Red Sea to make a long detour south to the equator 'line', cross over to the coast of Africa and then work their way around Cape Guardafui (the 'Cape of Burial') to the straits of Bab el-Mandeb (the 'Gate of Lamentation'), where Africa and Asia almost touch.

Peacock noted that the *Enterprize* would be crossing the Indian ocean at a favourable season, but doubted whether she could get up the northern part of the Red Sea against the wind. He judged that more powerful steam vessels should be able to navigate the Red Sea at all seasons, but were unlikely to prevail against the south-west monsoon.

The memorandum also examined the possibilities of building a canal to connect the Red Sea with the Mediterranean – a project considered by Napoleon when he was in Egypt. But the French engineers had measured a thirty-foot difference between the levels of the two seas and Commander Tuckey, a leading British geographer, had declared in 1815 that:

> If the Isthmus of Suez was cut through, the waters of the Red
> Sea would rush with rapidity into the Mediterranean, while
> those of the Atlantic running in through the Strait of Gibraltar,
> an accumulation and concussion would take place, the
> consequences of which are incalculable.[7]

In his memorandum Peacock cited Tuckey several times, but he did not quote the foregoing passage, remarking only that a difference in levels could be compensated for by the modern invention of locks.

The third alternative route was Peacock's own conception. Elphinstone had suggested in 1823 that, if disturbances in Egypt were to interrupt communications by the Red Sea route, steamers could deliver the mail to Syrian ports for onward delivery by the 'Direct Route' to Basra, where another steamer could carry it to Bombay. Peacock brought a new dimension to this idea by proposing that the Euphrates should become a commercial waterway like the Mississippi, with steamboats plying between Basra and Bir [Birecik], a town on the river only 120 miles from the Mediterranean Sea.

The Euphrates rises in the mountains of eastern Anatolia and flows south-westward through rocky gorges to Rumkale, a strategic point where an old Crusader castle guards an open stretch where the river makes a wide bend. For thirty miles below Rumkale the stream runs between steep cliffs and finally emerges into the Syrian Desert plain at Bir. From Bir, another Crusader strongpoint, its course runs initially to the south as far as the ruins of Beles [Meskene], but then turns sharply to the south-east for its long descent to the Persian Gulf. Today there are dams across the river, but before they were built the water level varied with the season; normally the highest was in June and July, when the snow melted in the mountains, and the lowest from November through February.

Two two extremities of Peacock's proposed route were familiar territory for British travellers. At the western end the Ottoman province of Syria possessed several harbours well known to British mariners. The Levant Company had traded here since the days of Queen Elizabeth I and after its dissolution in 1825 its consular agents in Aleppo and elsewhere became representatives of the British Crown. The approaches from the Syrian coast to the interior are guarded by mountain ranges, except where the Orontes river cuts its way from Antioch to the sea. Peacock's memorandum, repeat-ing the long unchallenged opinion of Major John Taylor, author of a 1789 handbook of the routes to India, stated that 'the Orontes, it is said, might easily be made navigable, up to Antioch, for vessels of considerable burthen'.

Inland, the country is a rolling plain. For centuries caravans from Aleppo to Baghdad had ferried across the Euphrates at Bir to head east by way of Urfa (now named Sanliurfa) and Mardin to Mosul on the Tigris. (Those starting from Damascus took the 'Little Desert Route' past Palmyra to cross the river at Felluja, twenty-five miles from Baghdad; while a few bold travellers to the Persian Gulf would take the 'Great Desert Route', a string of wells that led direct to Basra.)

At the farther end of Peacock's proposed route the long arm of the East India Company already stretched from Bombay to the province of Baghdad. For many years the Persian Gulf had been a British lake, surveyed and patrolled by the Bombay Marine – the Company's private navy that pro-tected the sea lanes to its 'factories' at Bushire, which handled the Persian trade, and at Basra, where the Company purchased dates and Arabian horses. A few months before Peacock wrote his memorandum the much maligned directors had sent out from England two 80-hp engines for instal-

lation in a new 411-ton steam cruiser to be built in the local shipyard for
the Bombay Marine.

Iraq (then known as Turkish Arabia) was ruled in the name of the Sultan
by the governors of Baghdad, Mosul and Basra. In practice, power had
long been concentrated in a group of local Mamelukes headed by the
governor of Baghdad, whose appointment was ritually confirmed by the
Sultan. Daud Pasha, a Georgian by birth, had become governor in 1817 by
murdering his predecessor. Peacock could state with confidence that 'the
Pacha of Bagdad would no doubt do all in his power to facilitate this mode
of communication', because Daud had already discussed the idea of forming
a steamboat flotilla in his talks with the East India Company Resident at
Baghdad.

The Euphrates, known as the Shatt el-Arab below Korna [Qurna] where
the Tigris flows in from the north, was the usual route between the Persian
Gulf and Baghdad (which lies on the Tigris but was connected by road
with Hilla on the Euphrates). The Shatt el-Arab is a tidal waterway, while
the lower Euphrates had long been navigated as far as Hilla by river boats,
either sailing in mid-channel with the current or being dragged upstream
by organized relays of towpath 'trackers' like Volga boatmen. (Tracking
was more arduous on the direct route to Baghdad up the faster-flowing
Tigris.) But two hundred and fifty miles above Korna the broad, placid
river, lined with date palms, changed its character. The traveller now
entered the strange, watery world of the Lemlum marshes (now largely
reclaimed), where for fifty miles the river twisted below low banks that
barely separated the stream from a panorama of bulrushes, rice paddies
and swamp.

Peacock reported that 'the marshes of Lemlum are said to interrupt the
common navigation in the floods, by spreading out the waters to such an
extent that the channel is "lost in the immensity of the fluid hollow".' But
he observed pithily that 'a steam boat would scarcely be impeded by too
much water' and suggested that buoys could be placed to mark out the
channel along the ten miles most prone to flooding.

Above the marshes the river was once more a broad waterway, passing
Hilla and the nearby ruins of Babylon. A few miles upstream from Felluja
an ancient canal led from the Euphrates to the Tigris at Baghdad. This
well settled stretch of country ended at Hit, a town famed for its fountains
of tar that was used to caulk the river boats.

Little was known about the upper part of the Euphrates route, where the
river flows for 650 miles through the Syrian desert, at that time a no-man's
land infested by marauding Arab tribes, past the old fortress towns of
Ana, Deir ez-Zor and Rakka. But the East India House library contained

narratives by English and other European merchants who had sailed down
the river from Bir to Felluja in flat-bottomed boats. These voyages had been
made between 1563 and 1600, at various seasons of the year. Even more
convincing for Peacock – and for many of his contemporaries who had been
brought up to revere the technical achievements of classical times – was the
well documented experience of two Roman emperors who had sent fleets
down the Euphrates in support of their campaigns. (Alexander the Great,
the most celebrated conqueror of all, had crossed the river near Rakka but
had then marched north to follow the caravan road to the east; after winning
the decisive battle of Arbela [Erbil] in the Tigris valley, he had advanced
through Persia and Afghanistan to invade India.)

Peacock's memorandum, which the Duke of Wellington read with interest,
recalled that Trajan, who reigned from AD 98 to 117, had led his army
down the Euphrates valley, supported by a fleet of boats, as far as Babylon.
He had later sailed down the Tigris to the Persian Gulf. In the spring of
AD 363 the emperor Julian assembled 1,100 vessels to carry stores and
heavy equipment for his Persian campaign. Despite the loss of many vessels
in a hurricane near Ana, the fleet accompanied the Roman army down the
Euphrates and along an old canal to the Tigris near Ctesiphon, the Persian
capital a few miles below the present Baghdad. Unable to storm that city,
Julian burned his boats and was killed while retreating up the Tigris valley.

At the close of his memorandum Peacock considered the risk that a
foreign power might threaten Britain's interests by repeating the triumphs of
Alexander and Trajan. Russian expansion in the Caucasus, cemented by
the absorption of Georgia in 1801, had recently been resumed. A brief,
victorious war with Persia in 1826–8 had enabled Russia to annex Armenia.
In April 1828 war broke out between Russia and Turkey. The decisive
action took place in the Balkans, where the Turks held the line of the
Danube despite the loss of the Black Sea fortress of Varna in October 1828.
But in the summer of 1829 the Russians swept past the Ottoman armies
and captured Adrianople [Edirne], only 150 miles from Istanbul, forcing
Sultan Mahmud to sue for peace. The peace treaty required no significant
surrenders of Ottoman territory in the east. But before withdrawing back
to its bases in Transcaucasia a Russian army had penetrated into Anatolia
as far as Erzurum and had occupied the mountain valleys where one branch
of the Euphrates river rises.

These startling events aroused concern in Britain, where Ellenborough
was among the first to see the threat to India. Peacock surmised that a
more likely invasion route would be by way of Turkestan, since an advance
through Iraq could be blocked by British seapower in the Persian Gulf. But
he conceded that the Russians might come down the two great rivers and

suggested that if that were imminent, Britain should 'pre-occupy' Korna. He remarked that 'an interest in the navigation of the Euphrates would give us a reasonable ground for resisting innovations.'

Many things were necessary for Peacock's dream to become a reality: a willingness to consider the idea; availability of suitable vessels; a survey on the spot; agreement with local authorities; choice of a good leader for the first experiment; and a policy decision to proceed.

Ellenborough still preferred the Red Sea route. But he was intrigued by the strategic potential of an alternative route through Iraq. Peacock was asked to prepare a questionnaire to be circulated to British embassies and consulates in the Near East. Among the questions to be answered were the condition of the Overland Route between the Red Sea and the Mediterranean, the incidence of plague in various regions, and the navigability of the Euphrates river.

Chapter 2
The State of the Art

Peacock's doubts as to the *Enterprize*'s ability to get up the Gulf of Suez against the wind reflected the primitive state of marine engineering in 1829 and the little that was known of steamship performance on the open sea.

The age of steam dates back to the classic inventions of Newcomen, Watt and others during the eighteenth century. For a long time, however, their application was limited to stationary engines that drove pumps and mill machinery.

Around the turn of the century the idea of using steam-powered paddles to propel vessels was developed in France, Scotland and the United States. The first experiments took place in rivers, which offered smooth surfaces and plenty of fresh water for the boiler. Commercial service began in 1807, when Robert Fulton's *Clermont* steamed up and down the Hudson between New York and Albany; in 1812 Henry Bell's smaller *Comet* carried passengers on the Clyde between Glasgow and Helensburgh, a resort twenty-five miles down the river.

Steam navigation spread rapidly in the United States, particularly along the forest-lined Mississippi and Ohio rivers. American steamships were mostly driven by 'high-pressure' engines with circular boilers that developed pressures up to 150 pounds per square inch (similar to the engines soon to be used in railway locomotives). These engines were small and fuel-efficient but often unsafe. Their greatest drawback, however, was the impossibility of using sea water in their boilers.

In Britain, where the rivers are short, steamers were in demand for use in the coasting trade and in ferry services to Ireland and the Continent. Accordingly the conventional 'low-pressure' engine was preferred. These engines, developed by Watt, Maudslay, Field and others, were powered by steam from large rectangular boilers made of wrought iron or copper, producing a little above atmospheric pressure. The vacuum in the cylinder was created by a condenser and was maintained by an air pump which drew off air and water. Leakage in a boiler was kept under control by plastering weak spots with oatmeal, potatoes or dung.

Boilers for low-pressure engines could use salt water as well as fresh water. When they required descaling, the engines were stopped, the paddles were unshipped and the vessel continued on her way with the aid of sails. Later models were designed to 'blow off' encrustations while still operating. The low-pressure engine was a heavy consumer of boiler fuel. Fortunately, Britain was blessed with large, easily accessible reserves of high-grade coal that was mined for domestic and foreign markets. Coaling facilities quickly became an essential feature of every European port.

The marine engine, one of the glories of Britain's engineering trade, developed rapidly in power and reliability. A 4 hp engine had driven the *Comet* and a 20 hp engine had been brought from England for the *Clermont*; both of them were single-engined ships. By 1829 many steamers had two engines, each capable of driving both paddle wheels, with combined ratings approaching 200 horse power.

Meanwhile, shipbuilders were discovering by trial and error how to design paddle-wheel steamers and what ratios of size, power and coal storage space were most efficient in different kinds of service. Steam vessels were seen along the rivers and seacoasts of Europe. The poet Shelley invested money in a project, never completed, to build a steamer that would ply between Leghorn, Genoa and Marseilles. Peacock's memorandum mentioned that '[the Russians] have now steam boats on the Volga and the Caspian Sea.'[1] A more humdrum use of steam power was for tugs to tow sailing ships, including men of war, into and out of harbours.

By 1829 there were over 300 steam vessels registered in Great Britain, mostly in the coasting trade. Several joint stock companies were already assembling fleets of steamers for regular service to Irish and Continental ports.

The Admiralty, responsible in those days for oversea mails, had operated cross-Channel steamers to France since 1822. Steam packet service was extended in 1830 to the Mediterranean, with a monthly departure from Falmouth to Gibraltar, Malta and Corfu (then in British hands).

Britain also exported steamships and marine engines to other countries. Some vessels, such as the river boat ordered by Mehemet Ali in 1828, were sent out 'in frame'. In these cases the steamer would be built, launched and tried out at the shipyard, then taken apart into sections that were crated and loaded on to a sailing ship for re-assembly at its destination.

13

All of the early steamers were made of wood, a material that was becoming more costly as European supplies decreased. By the 1820s British iron-masters had improved the precision of wrought iron manufacture to the point where it became feasible and economical to use iron plates, ¼ or ⅜ inch thick, instead of wood for a vessel's hull. The edges of the plates were fastened to strips of bar iron by riveters, who hammered red-hot iron bolts from the inside through holes in the strip and in the plates, which were countersunk on the outside to permit the tail of the bolt to be hammered flush with the surface of the hull. Riveting was an ancient skill known to medieval armourers and revived when boilers came into fashion.

The advantages of greater strength and lighter draught provided by iron vessels were soon perceived by river boat operators, particularly on the Continent. On the other hand, for voyages where position fixing by compass was required, iron ships were little used before the 1840s when reliable magnetic compass correctors came into use and Britain's Astronomer Royal published a set of correction tables.

In contrast with the proven technology and reliable service provided by steam vessels on the rivers and narrow seas of Europe, ocean navigation by steam was still the domain of inventors, promoters and intrepid pioneers.

Initially, steam engines were treated as an auxiliary means of propelling sailing ships. The American-built *Savannah*, which crossed the Atlantic in 1819, used her engine for 85 hours in the course of a 27-day voyage; finding no purchaser in Europe, she returned to the United States under sail. Two years later the twin-engined *Rising Star* was built in England for Lord Cochrane's Chilean expedition, incorporating enclosed paddle wheels of the owner's design; she is believed to have used steam for part of her voyage across the Atlantic and around Cape Horn. The *Victory*, flagship of Sir John Ross's 1829–33 Arctic expedition, carried auxiliary steam engines, but the explorer found the machinery so troublesome that he took them out of his ship and left them on the ice.

Peacock's memorandum cited Ross's dictum that 'steam navigation sets at defiance the monsoons, the currents, and the calms.'[2] But for an ocean-going vessel the use of steam as the prime source of power, even if supplemented by sail, failed to meet the commercial yardsticks that ruled at the East India House.

In contrast to sailing ships, steamers had to 'buy their wind' with the fuel they carried on board, which needed replenishment at prearranged times and places. Coal was readily available at ports where British ships brought it out in ballast. But the early steamships required frequent refuelling and ocean navigation involved much wastage and expense in establishing chains of coal depots at faraway places, transporting the coal there in local vessels, storing it where the carbon would not evaporate and loading it from a lighter on to the waiting steamship.

The revenue side of the steam equation was discouraging. An owner could not expect to earn much from carrying merchandise, because the movement of ocean freight is seldom time-sensitive. In addition, the cargo space in the early steamships was filled with coal, leaving little room for payload.

Passengers would one day provide a great source of revenue. But in 1829, when Ellenborough urged the East India Company to start a steamship line, most of the prospective passengers would have been the Company's own servants or army officers going to or from their stations. No private travellers could visit India without permission from the East India House. Moreover, the regulations for home leave allowances encouraged long sea voyages.

The remaining source of revenue was mail, where the benefits of speed are most apparent. Here the British government itself held the key, since the rates of postage and the compensation paid to the steamship company could only be fixed after negotiation with the General Post Office, a department then engaged in establishing a profitable monopoly in its field.

But poets, politicians and men of trade could all see that the age of steam had arrived. The constraints and uncertainties that caused the East India Company directors to act so cautiously were treated as phantoms by the promoters in London and Calcutta who eyed the rewards of steam navigation to India and assumed that public or private funds would be found to underwrite the risks. The citizens of Calcutta were so sanguine that in 1823 they formed a 'Steam Committee' which agreed to award a prize of 100,000 rupees (then worth £10,000) to the first British ship owner 'making a double voyage by steam out and home, not averaging above seventy days each, between a port in England and Calcutta, by either route of the Cape or the Red Sea; to be performed before the expiration of the year 1826.'[3] The Governor-General of Bengal contributed one-fifth of the prize fund.

The rashest and unluckiest adventurer to be tempted by this offer was James Taylor, a Calcutta merchant whose brother was the East India Company's Resident at Basra and later at Baghdad. He hastened to London and became the original promoter of the *Enterprize* project. But while the vessel was still under construction he sold his interest in the syndicate in order to develop an ambitious scheme of his own whereby a fleet of powerful steam tugs, each towing a sailing ship carrying passengers and extra coal, would ply between England and Egypt and between Suez and Calcutta. The first two vessels proved defective and were sent out to India under sail.

Taylor's resources were by then exhausted and he moved to the Continent to escape his creditors.

The voyage of the *Falcon* disappointed her backers, although after her engines and boiler were removed she earned the reputation of being 'one of the prettiest and fastest opium traders belonging to the port of Calcutta'.[4]

The *Enterprize* venture was deemed a failure because her outbound voyage fell short of the award conditions. The syndicate was fortunate to recover most of their investment by selling the vessel to the Bengal government for use in the Burmese war. Under Johnston's command the steamer made several voyages between Calcutta and Burmese ports, contributing significantly to the success of British arms. After the war was over the Calcutta Steam Committee awarded Johnston 36,000 rupees out of the prize fund in recognition of his seamanship. A motion to grant a similar sum to James Taylor was voted down.

One of the many who watched the *Enterprize* carrying out her duties was Thomas Fletcher Waghorn, a midshipman in charge of piloting vessels in Akyab harbour on the Burmese coast. At that time Waghorn was twenty-six years old. The son of a Chatham butcher, he had joined the Royal Navy as a midshipman and had served in the West Indies before transferring to the Bengal Pilot Service. He had volunteered for the Burmese war, where he commanded a cutter and is said to have once manhandled a 12-pounder gun from the deck of his ship to the top of a 220-feet high rock on the Arakan river, long known as 'Waghorn Rock'.[5]

A man of limited education, uncouth manners and no technical or commercial skills, Waghorn possessed the vision to perceive what steam navigation could mean for the British empire in the east. Endowed with immense energy and self-confidence, he was a natural publicist born a hundred years too soon. In the colonial world of British India he was always well regarded, but when he came to London later he was out of his depth. One of his close associates noted sadly that 'he had an unfortunate gift for quarrelling with people, his energy was unqualified by tact.'[6]

After talking with Johnston and making at least one trip on the *Enterprize*, Waghorn conceived the idea of a fast mail packet steamer to carry letters at a premium rate of postage between Britain and India around the Cape. At the end of the Burmese war he was granted leave to go to England to promote his scheme.

Waghorn was in London from June 1827 until February 1828. Despite good recommendations from Calcutta officials, his stay was unproductive. Hugh Lindsay, Chairman of the East India Company, offered to lend him two engines, but the Post Office declined to negotiate with an unknown person. Private investors were wary, in the light of Taylor's bankruptcy and the near-fiasco of the *Enterprize* attempt. Never a man to admit defeat, Waghorn returned to Calcutta and with Johnston's support persuaded the Steam Committee to promise him the balance of the prize fund if it remained unclaimed by the end of February 1829. He promptly sailed home in August 1828, arriving in December to renew his efforts with somewhat greater credibility than before.

A few weeks earlier the *Enterprize* had conveyed a new Governor-General, Lord William Bentinck, from the mouth of the Hooghly for his official entry into Calcutta. In February 1829 Bentinck, a steam enthusiast, took the *Enterprize* for an inspection trip to Penang and Singapore.

In October 1827 General Sir John Malcolm, a veteran of Wellington's Indian campaigns, arrived as the new Governor of Bombay, to be joined a few months later by his brother, Captain Sir Charles Malcolm, who was appointed to be Superintendent of the Bombay Marine.

The child of a Dumfriesshire sheep-farmer, six feet six inches tall, extravagant and brave, Sir John Malcolm looks off calmly into the future from his statue in Westminster Abbey. A pioneer in the art of geopolitics, he was one of the first to understand the 'Great Game' by which Britain strove to keep Russia away from India. He had negotiated twice with the Shah of Persia and had met Mehemet Ali when returning home in 1822 by the Red Sea. During his next few years in Britain he had watched the growth of steam navigation and had foreseen its importance for Britain and India.

In September 1828 Malcolm asked Bentinck to lend the *Enterprize* for a trial voyage in the following year, after the south-west monsoon was over, from Bombay to Suez or Cosseir. The Governor-General recognized that, although Calcutta was the capital and chief seaport of British India, well placed for sailing ships rounding the Cape of Good Hope or trading with China, Bombay was the port best situated for steam navigation to the Persian Gulf and the Red Sea. Bentinck agreed to lend the steamer and Malcolm arranged for coals to be laid down at Aden, Jedda, Cosseir and Suez. The collier was wrecked on her way back, prompting the Bombay Marine to start a thorough survey of the Red Sea.

The *Enterprize*, commanded by Johnston's successor, left Calcutta in May 1829, only five weeks after returning from Singapore. Mechanical problems forced the steamer to put in at a port in Ceylon and when she finally reached Bombay in November her boilers were found to be too weak to attempt the voyage to the Red Sea.

This dismaying turn of events was not known in London for several weeks. In the meantime Waghorn, still frustrated by the Post Office, had prevailed upon the East India House and Lord Ellenborough to appoint him a special courier to carry despatches to Sir John Malcolm by way of

Egypt, taking the *Enterprize* from Suez to Bombay. He was also entrusted with a supplemental questionnaire from Peacock, addressed to John Barker, the British Consul-General at Alexandria.

Waghorn left London at the end of October 1829 and reached Alexandria a month later. A chartered vessel lay in the harbour ready to take the Indian mail on to Corfu, but there was no news of the steamer. As a bearer of official despatches, Waghorn was not disposed to wait around. He pressed on to Cairo to obtain travelling papers for the onward journey. Here he encountered an unexpected competitor – James Taylor, who had somehow made his peace with his creditors and was now on his way to India to promote yet another Red Sea steamship scheme. Although this project would hurt Waghorn's own plan to send fast steamers around the Cape, he reluctantly allowed Taylor to travel with him to Suez, where there was still no sign of the *Enterprize*.

Waghorn decided that – as Peacock had feared – the vessel had been unable to steam against the strong north-west wind that was blowing down the Gulf of Suez. In that case it was essential to get to Cosseir before the *Enterprize* returned to India. Hiring an open sailing boat with a surly crew, the two adventurers endured a rough passage to Cosseir, waited there vainly for a few days and then sailed on to Jedda, 660 miles from Suez, where a Bombay Marine survey ship informed them that the *Enterprize* was not coming at all.

After hiring another boat to go on to the next port down the Arabian coast, Waghorn and Taylor were picked up by a brig of war which Malcolm had sent to the Red Sea with the much delayed mail for England. They reached Bombay in March 1830 – 144 days after Waghorn had left London – and learned that the Bombay Marine's new steam cruiser had just left on her maiden voyage, bound for Suez.

The teak-hulled *Hugh Lindsay*, named after the chairman on whose initiative she was built, was designed for service along the west coast of India and the Persian Gulf. She could carry little more than five days' supply of coal, about half the amount needed to steam to the *Enterprize*'s first depot at Aden. Resourceful and determined, Sir John Malcolm and his brother ordered the passenger cabins and saloon to be filled with coal. When she left Bombay on 20 March 1830, with one passenger and 306 pieces of private mail, her decks were almost awash and her paddles could hardly turn around. Sceptical observers called her 'the Water Lily'.[7]

Eleven days later, aided by favourable winds, the *Hugh Lindsay* reached Aden with six hours' coal remaining. After refuelling there and again at Jedda, the steamer anchored off Suez on 22 April, thirty-two days after leaving India. The return voyage was equally successful and she was back in Bombay by the end of May.

Lord Ellenborough was delighted, but he noted with scorn that '[the East India Company Chairs] are dissatisfied with Malcolm for sending a steam vessel into the Red Sea, because he had no important intelligence to communicate!'[8]

Many years later the Birkenhead shipbuilder John Laird, who with his brother MacGregor Laird built many of the early iron steamers, acclaimed Peacock's role in promoting steam navigation. But in his first few years at the East India House Peacock showed little interest in the new technology. Nor is there any record of him commenting on Shelley's involvement in a steamboat project between 1818 and 1820, though ironically it was from the engineer's workshop that the poet wrote the much-quoted lines on Peacock in his *Letter to Maria Gisborne*:

> his fine wit
> Makes such a wound, the knife is lost in it;
> A strain too learned for a shallow age,
> Too wise for selfish bigots; let his page
> Which charms the chosen spirits of the time,
> Fold itself up for the serener clime
> Of years to come, and find its recompense
> In that just expectation.

Peacock knew MacGregor Laird, who combined exploration with shipbuilding. In *Crotchet Castle*, published in 1831, the novelist poked fun at his friend's obsession with distant rivers.

It was Waghorn, a Dickensian character too large to fit into one of Peacock's books, who was responsible for his introduction to steam. In 1834 Peacock was asked at what point he had first turned his attention to the subject of steam navigation between India and Europe. He replied: 'Since the beginning of the year 1829, when Mr. Waghorn was in England. The [East India Company] Chairman of that day spoke to me upon the subject, and asked me to look into the whole question.'[9]

Peacock had no naval experience, apart from a few months' service in 1808–9 as a clerk on a British warship blockading the Dutch coast. But as a child he had been steeped in naval tradition and he soon became the East India Company's expert in steam vessel technology and design. After Peacock retired from their service, a cousin who had made his career in the Royal Navy declared: 'Mr Peacock was meant for an Admiral.'[10]

Peacock was forty-four years old when Waghorn's petition and Ellenborough's command first impelled him to 'look into the whole question'. One side of his character relished the mental challenge of taming the steam genie and fitting it to the actual world. But Peacock's instincts warned him against the motives of Bentinck and a new generation of reformers who welcomed better communications as a means for hastening the introduction of English laws and education into India.

In the summer of 1837 Peacock, now promoted to be Examiner at the East India House, testified before a committee of the House of Commons that was reviewing the arrangements whereby the Company and the government had agreed to finance a regular steamer service between Britain and India. When asked whether India would not benefit from easier intercourse with the mother country, Peacock replied: 'I am not sure that it would be of any benefit to the people of India to send Europeans amongst them.'[11] He agreed that the new service would bring more Europeans to India, but predicted that the effect 'on the morals and domestic happiness of the people of India [would be] a bad one'. Except for this one occasion, Peacock never publicly discussed the consequences of the progress he was helping to bring about. Perhaps, like others have, he salved his conscience by reasoning that change was inevitable and that it was better for his own country rather than an enemy to be in the lead.

On 21 December 1829 Ellenborough sent Peacock's memorandum to the Duke of Wellington. The India Board had already requested the Admiralty and the Foreign Office to gather the information sought by Peacock. In March 1830, at Ellenborough's insistence, the East India Company asked Bentinck and Malcolm to report on the feasibility of the Red Sea and Euphrates routes.

Chapter 3

The Chesney Reconnaissance

The first attempt to survey the Euphrates route was tragically cut short.

Sir John Malcolm, the Governor of Bombay, shared Ellenborough's concerns about the Russian threat to India and the possibility of a Russian advance through Iraq to the Persian Gulf. Hoping to strengthen the local government in Iraq, Malcolm encouraged Major Robert Taylor, the East India Company Resident at Baghdad, to build up a close friendship with Daud Pasha. It was agreed that Daud's bodyguard and cavalry should be trained by the Resident's son and an Englishman named Littlejohn. In the spring of 1830 Taylor encouraged the pasha's plans to patrol the Euphrates and Tigris with a steam flotilla by engaging a former naval officer who was passing through Iraq to undertake a survey of the two rivers.

William Bowater, who had been a lieutenant in the Bombay Marine, was available for this assignment because he had recently been discharged from the service for insubordination. Upon arrival in Baghdad he composed a long memorandum on steam navigation of the Indian Ocean, the Persian Gulf and the Red Sea (already partly outdated by the experience of the *Hugh Lindsay*, which returned to Bombay after Bowater had left).[1]

Major Taylor arranged with Daud Pasha that Bowater would go up the Tigris to Mosul, travel west to Bir on the upper Euphrates and descend that river down to the Felluja-Baghdad canal. He would be accompanied as far as Bir by the Resident's brother, James Taylor, who had arrived empty-handed from Bombay but had just obtained from Daud Pasha a concession to run steamboats along the two rivers. James Taylor planned to go on to London to raise capital for this scheme, which granted the concession-holder land along the rivers to cultivate sugar and indigo.

21

(Waghorn, no more fortunate in his endeavours in Bombay, returned home a convert to the Overland Route through Egypt and published a widely read account of his travels.)[2]

Arrangements were made for James Taylor and Bowater, together with their interpreter William Elliot and three other Englishmen, to join a caravan from Mosul to Bir that was carrying treasure for the Sultan and consequently was escorted by an armed guard. On 15 August 1830, the caravan was attacked by Yezidi robbers from the Sinjar hills. The escort fled and the caravan dispersed. Taylor, his servant and Bowater were surrounded. In a foolhardy attempt to rescue them, one of their companions killed a Yezidi chief, whereupon all four of them were slain. Elliot and the other Englishmen escaped to Mosul.

Bowater's mission, like James Taylor's project, expired in the desert sand far short of the Euphrates. But unknown to the authorities in London, Baghdad or Bombay, another ripple from Peacock's historic memorandum was bringing to Syria a self-appointed explorer, intent on going down the great river that would dominate his life.

In 1830 Francis Rawdon Chesney, captain in the Royal Artillery, was forty-one years old. Born in Ballyveagh, County Down (now in Northern Ireland), he was the third of nine children born to Alexander Chesney, a coast guard officer, by his second wife, Margaret Wilson.

Alexander Chesney had been taken to South Carolina in his youth when his family migrated there from Ulster. During the American Revolutionary War he had fought with the Loyalists and attracted the attention of the local British commander, Francis Lord Rawdon. Towards the end of the war, after his first wife died, Alexander Chesney had returned to Ireland, where he ultimately obtained a steady but dangerous job foiling smugglers along the coast of Mourne.

As a child Francis Chesney had been strictly brought up, with a military career always in view. With the help of Lord Rawdon (now Earl of Moira), he had been admitted to the Royal Military Academy at Woolwich to be trained as an artillery cadet. Although the Napoleonic War had already resumed when Chesney was gazetted lieutenant in 1805, he did not see active service overseas. The artillery, along with the Corps of Sappers and Miners (as the Royal Engineers were then called), belonged to the Ordnance Department, at that time a separate branch of the armed forces more involved in coastal defence than in the field. Chesney had been stationed first at Portsmouth and later from 1808 to 1814 in Guernsey, off the coast of France.

Chesney in his prime was described as 'a small,* wiry man, with very small hands and feet, a broken nose and a mobile mouth, showing his teeth a good deal when laughing and talking.' His dark brown hair was 'very fine and soft'; in his youth he wore it 'brushed straight up, perhaps under the idea that it would give him height'. Years later another friend remembered that:

> [he] was a little man, who insinuated himself quietly into a
> room, made his bow, and sat down. He smiled a refined smile,
> stammered a little, and it was only after some conversation that
> you perceived the talent, careful research, and detailed
> knowledge, which made him propose things which needed his
> energy and perseverance to prove as he seemed to think that
> 'nothing was impossible'.[3]

Upon arrival in Guernsey Chesney fell in love with Everilda Fraser, the daughter of the garrison second in command. She left the island soon afterwards when her father was transferred, but for years he wrote to her and called on her when he was on leave. Once, when she was in Tunbridge Wells to 'drink the waters' and her family were thinking of moving on to Brighton, the frugal Chesney walked there and back in one day, a distance of fifty-nine miles, to inspect the place where she would stay. In 1814 and again in 1818 she refused his proposals but remained single.

Chesney was promoted to the rank of captain in 1815, but the end of the war with France was followed by tedious years of peacetime soldiering with periods of half pay and extended leave. In 1821, when the coast guard needed his father's house for other purposes, the young Chesney built, largely with his own hands, a new house for him at nearby Ballyardel named Packolet in memory of the South Carolina river valley where he had first settled. The following year Chesney married Georgette Forster, a girl he had known from his Guernsey days who had a lively disposition and was related through her mother to the Gledstanes shipping family. A three-year tour of duty in Gibraltar – his first offshore posting – was ended by his wife's death in childbirth.

The year 1829 marked the turning point in Captain Chesney's hitherto commonplace career. Turkey, then at war with Russia, had placed an order in London for Congreve rockets, a lethal device developed during Britain's wars with France. Chesney, who had just been turned down for the third

---

* The coatee of Chesney's uniform is preserved at the Royal Artillery Institution, Woolwich, with a notation that Chesney was only four feet nine inches tall.

23

time by Everilda Fraser (herself no longer young), volunteered to go to the Balkans as a military observer and to organize covertly a Turkish rocket corps that would defend mountain passes too precipitous for guns.

In June 1829 a fast sailing clipper left England for Istanbul with Chesney and the missiles; but bad weather off North Africa delayed his arrival until September, by which time the fighting was over. Chesney stayed on, hoping the war might start again. During the winter he toured the Balkan battle-fields and wrote a report on the campaign for the British Ambassador Sir Robert Gordon, a brother of the Foreign Secretary Lord Aberdeen.

The peace treaty with Russia was ratified and the rocket corps was never formed. But there were still many uncertainties and in the spring of 1830 the Ambassador, well satisfied with Chesney's Balkan report, arranged for him to make a trip around the Near East – Syria, Egypt, Iraq and Anatolia – where the provincial governors' loyalty to the Sultan was in doubt.

Before he left Istanbul Chesney was shown one of Peacock's question-naires concerning the routes to India by the Red Sea and the Euphrates. In his travel notes he recorded that:

> With regard to the latter, my busy imagination pictured my descent of the stream on a double boat to be carried across from Alexandria [Alexandretta, also called Iskenderun or Scanderoon] with a shed raised thereon and shooting Lions from my boat.[4]

Chesney arrived in Egypt at the end of April. In Alexandria he noted 'extensive Naval and Military preparations'[5] and when he met Mehemet Ali, the viceroy inquired as to the state of the Sultan's battered army. John Barker, the British Consul-General, reviewed with Chesney the Peacock questionnaires, especially the one brought by Waghorn, which called for detailed information on the Euphrates route. (Barker had long served as Consul in Aleppo and still owned a villa at Suedia [Samandağ], on the Mediterranean coast near the mouth of the Orontes.)

Among other personalities in Egypt, Chesney met Mehemet Ali's son Ibrahim Pasha, the conqueror of Arabia; Colonel Andrew Campbell of the Bombay Artillery, who had just arrived on the *Hugh Lindsay*; and Rev. Joseph Wolff, a German Jew ordained in the Protestant Church who trav-elled fearlessly through the Near East preaching the Christian faith.

As he pondered over the routes to India, papers from Paris brought Chesney news of a much-loved brother's death. At that moment he resolved to put aside the boredom and frustration of his former life and seize the chance to explore the beguiling uncharted lands and seas and rivers of the East.

The first part of his decision was simple. The Royal Artillery was overstaffed and willing to grant extended leaves. His five-year-old daughter was being brought up by relatives. Most important, his rejection by Everilda Fraser chilled the thought of returning home.

For a man approaching middle age the vocation he was choosing was fraught with risk. Chesney's sound health and Spartan habits fitted him for the hardships of travel – which he could always mitigate by using his diplomatic ties or his own private means. But he had never travelled in the Orient and had no conception of what dangers he might face. His military training had included astronomy and survey, but he had no knowledge of navigation and his engineering skills related principally to guns. Worst of all, he knew no Arabic.

But Chesney's mind was made up. On 9 May 1830, he informed Sir Robert Gordon that, in addition to carrying out his political assignments, he proposed to conduct a personal reconnaissance of the two alternative routes to India. Assuming correctly that there would be no objection, he took off on a trip to Suez, Sinai, Cosseir and the Nile valley.

Chesney's report on the Red Sea route to India added only one new fact to what was contained in Peacock's memorandum. For some reason Chesney did not refer to the voyage of the *Hugh Lindsay*, which had been at Suez only a few days before he had arrived in Egypt. But he was the first to correct the French engineers' estimates of the relative levels of the Mediterranean and Red Seas and to suggest that a sea-level canal could be built.[6]

From September through mid-December Chesney travelled around Palestine and Syria, sight-seeing and exploring desert trails while he awaited the Ambassador's approval of his plans. Sir Robert Gordon's reply advised against Chesney's original idea of building two boats at Iskenderun and transporting them to the Euphrates, but encouraged him to take the 'Little Desert Route' to Baghdad.

On 10 December 1830, Chesney left Damascus in Arab garb with an interpreter and a slave-boy to join a caravan headed for Baghdad. His spirit of adventure had been whetted by garbled reports of the recent Sinjar incident and a rumour that a wounded Englishman was awaiting succour in Palmyra.

Like every land or sea convoy, a desert caravan hopes for a trip free from incidents. Chesney's first journey passed this test. In the mornings there was great bustle as tents were struck and camels loaded. But once each animal took its place in line to plod on for hours across the treeless plain, Chesney noted that 'the Desert Journey . . . had a good deal of sameness'[7]

25

(and in his case much discomfort caused by 'a particular ailment'[8] that was intensified by riding camelback). On various pretexts the caravan leader skirted Palmyra (where in fact there was no wounded traveller) and after thirteen days of travel the caravan approached the Euphrates at El Kaim, seventy miles above Ana.

For some time the broad river had been visible in the distance, but Chesney's first real sight was on a moonlit evening after the camels had lain down and the travellers had retired to their tents. The night air was filled with the creak of water-wheels and the roar of lions as Chesney and his guide walked through underbrush to the river edge, where he recalled later that 'the stream was much below its banks but it had a placid silvery appearance'.[9] The next day he hastened to Ana, a straggling, picturesque village where he sold his camel and ordered a raft to take him down the river.

From prehistoric times until a few decades ago the traditional means of navigating the Euphrates and the Tigris has been the 'kelek' – a rectangular raft supported by inflated sheepskins, with a clay fireplace at one corner for cooking food. A portion of the aft deck was left open to form a well that the crew could descend to re-inflate a skin. The kelek was steered by two men with fan-shaped date-tree oars.

The captain of Chesney's raft was an experienced river pilot named Mohammed Gedgut (Anglicized by Chesney to 'Getgood'). Under his guidance Chesney, his two attendants and the two oarsmen left Ana on 2 January 1831. For five days they floated down the river, while Chesney made sketches, took compass readings and measured the depth of the river by putting a ten-foot pole down the well. At night the raft was moored at a mid-stream island or by the bank. One misty morning they saw a lion drinking from the river fifteen feet away. Chesney raised his gun but did not fire, 'as the people in the Raft believed that the animal could spring on board between the flash of the pan and the discharge.'[10]

Farther downstream the kelek's leisurely descent was disturbed by shots from Arab robbers, easily repelled. But when they reached Hit, Chesney exchanged his raft for a swifter river boat caulked with local tar. Three days later he reached Felluja, where he hired a donkey to take him to Baghdad. He arrived there on 16 January.

In Alexandria and Cairo Chesney had seen the dawn of modern Egypt. Baghdad in 1831 resembled Belshazzar's Babylon near its end.

For thirteen years Daud Pasha had ruled his province with cunning, ostentation and caprice. A person admitted into his presence dismounted in an outer courtyard where the palace guard presented arms and brilliantly uniformed courtiers led him through an inner court to a gateway adorned with the three horse-tails of office. The visitor next entered the hall of audience, where the curtains and the cushions were crimson and the gilded woodwork of the walls was inlaid with mirror glass. Two lines of guardsmen stood motionless with folded arms as he was ushered across rich carpets to salute the governor, who sat in cushioned splendour in a corner of the room. Daud's piety, munificence and greed were as famous as his stable of Arabian broodmares, too valuable for anyone to ride.

Having no dress uniform with him, Chesney was unable to accompany Major Taylor on his official visit to the palace. A private audience was arranged and Chesney reported to Sir Robert Gordon that 'There is little doubt that Daoud Pacha sincerely desires to see steam navigation established, because it would bring his cherished idol, money.'[11]

But for the Pasha and his riches the handwriting was already on the wall. In October 1830 a special envoy from Istanbul, sent to enforce stricter obedience, was murdered by Daud's agents. He was said to have died from cholera, but the Sultan was not deceived. In February 1831 Daud was ordered to yield his post to a new governor, Ali Riza Pasha, who advanced with an army from Aleppo to take charge of Iraq.

No Daniel rose up to prophesy, but a dedicated group of Plymouth Brethren lived quietly in Baghdad, trying to save souls in a benighted land. Anthony Norris Groves, a missionary, had arrived from England at the end of 1829 with his family and his boys' tutor John Kitto – a gifted Biblical scholar despite being deaf and almost dumb from childhood – and had started a children's school.

Between these two worlds stood a spacious building flying the British flag – the East India Company residency, guarded by Sepoy sentinels with the Resident's yacht moored nearby. Major Taylor, who had served the Company in Iraq since 1818, had only recently moved permanently from Basra to Baghdad. In appearance a typically short, slight Indian Army officer in his forties, he was also a man of culture who knew several European and Oriental languages and collected Arabic and Persian manuscripts. His wife was an Armenian from Shiraz. The Resident was known as a kind, genial host who welcomed visitors officially and also in his leisure hours, when one missionary observed with some surprise that:

> [his] indoor dress is like that of an English cricketer – loose
> white pantaloons, white waistcoat, open neck, and little jacket
> (like a footman's) of the same material as the waistcoat.[12]

Soon after Chesney's arrival Major Taylor informed him that the Bombay government had recently instructed him to complete the survey of the Euphrates and Tigris rivers. Before his death Bowater had surveyed the upper Tigris. The remainder of the work would be carried out by Lieutenant Ormsby, a young officer of the Bombay Marine (renamed Indian Navy since May 1830), assisted by Bowater's interpreter William Elliot.

Henry Alexander Ormsby, born in 1811, probably overstated his age when he joined the Bombay Marine in 1823. But after a few years he tired of naval life. His biographer records that he 'voluntarily quitted that service' to travel for three years among the Arabs – a life that brought out his 'buoyancy of spirit, . . . his courage, and zealous perseverence, . . . and the facility with which he filled up the variety of characters it was necessary he would assume.'[13] Towards the end of 1830 he was in Basra, passing as an Arab, when Major Taylor called him to Baghdad to undertake the survey.

In February 1831 Ormsby and Elliot sailed down the Tigris to Korna and thence back up the Euphrates to the Lemlum marshes. After various adventures with river tribesmen they got up as far as Hilla and returned to the Baghdad Residency at the beginning of March. Their next assignment would be to complete their project by surveying the upper Euphrates between Bir and the Felluja-Baghdad canal.

Chesney, who was writing out a report of his journey and making a large-scale map of the river between Ana and Felluja, was uncertain about continuing down the Euphrates and perhaps duplicating the work Ormsby and Elliot had done. Taylor, on the other hand, urged him to go on to Basra 'on the ground that a comparative statement was always advantageous to the cause of truth.'[14]

Suddenly, at the end of March 1831, the British community in Baghdad was dispersed. Bubonic plague broke out in the city and all who could do so fled – except for Groves and Kitto, who stayed to care for their flock and record the catastrophe that ensued. Major Taylor took his family and staff by boat to Basra. Ormsby and Elliot left hurriedly across the desert for Damascus. Chesney made his way on foot to Felluja, hiring donkeys to carry his baggage and his incomplete report. Upon reaching the Euphrates he found his boat destroyed by a storm and Getgood anxious to go home.

A new boat was procured and Chesney resumed the survey. At Hilla he transferred to Major Taylor's little schooner, which brought him to Basra by the end of April. Chesney's voyage down the river was full of incident – the schooner was once overturned by a squall but soon refloated – but he had time to make a thorough survey that took in the Felluja-Hilla portion not covered by Ormsby and Elliot. According to Chesney, the swift, winding passage through the Lemlum marshes was no worse than the Firth of Forth below Stirling, though he warned of the unfriendly Khezail tribe of Arabs on the banks.

Chesney was now anxious to get back to Syria to survey the upper part of the river from Bir to Ana. In his report to the Ambassador, despatched in June 1831 from Shuster (a Persian town on the Karun river, which flows into the Shatt el-Arab), he described this upper stretch of the Euphrates in as much detail as Getgood and other river boatmen could provide.[15]

To avoid plague-stricken Iraq, Chesney returned to Syria by way of Persia and Anatolia, a 3,000-mile detour that earned him his laurels as a traveller but required eight months to complete.

Chesney was in Aleppo in February and March 1832. Here he discovered that Ormsby had given up his planned survey owing to warfare among the desert Arabs and was on his way back to India. (Elliot had actually walked along the river bank from Bir to El Kaim, dressed as an Arab and accompanied by two dervishes, and had made many sketches and a map; but the draughtsman's office in Bombay had called his material valueless 'as it contains neither meridian, nor any directing line or mark whatever by which the work can be connected'.)[16]

The turmoil among the Arabs reflected the collapse of law and order in Iraq. Plague raged throughout the province and Baghdad became a city of the dead. From his palace, half ruined by a flood that swept away whole buildings, Daud Pasha watched his court and his garrison melt away, while his brood mares, untended, roamed the streets and galloped off into the desert. Plague and floods gave way to famine and in September 1831 Baghdad surrendered to Ali Riza. But the new governor could barely maintain his army against the Arab marauders who gathered outside the city to intercept supplies of food.

In Syria conditions were better, though half of the pilgrimage to Mecca was said to have died of the plague. But here the feeble Ottoman regime faced a different kind of threat. In October 1831 Mehemet Ali, alleging jurisdictional disputes, had invaded Palestine. The Sultan's forces still held Acre; but, as Chesney had seen in 1830, the Egyptian army, led by the viceroy's son Ibrahim Pasha, was well equipped and trained by French veterans of Napoleon's campaigns.

Under these circumstances there was little Chesney could accomplish. He inspected the Euphrates at Bir and Rumkale and made his way to Urfa, fifty miles east of Bir. But no guides would take him down to Kalat Jaber, the ruined fortress on the left bank of the river where he might cross over to Beles and return to Aleppo by road. Once again, he had to glean information from others, including Vincent Germain, a French engineer in the

Sultan's service who shared Chesney's interest in developing the Euphrates route.

Before leaving Syria for the final overland journey to Istanbul, Chesney examined the three main harbours on the coast. In his opinion Iskenderun was the best port and had a good road to Aleppo; but malaria was endemic and foreigners were loath to go ashore. Latakia was healthier, but the roads inland were poor.[17]

The ancient port of Seleucia on the Bay of Antioch was in ruins, but anchorage was possible a few miles farther down where the Orontes river flows into the sea. Chesney reported that 'this river is of considerable size and depth, but making a most tortuous course, at a slow rate along the valley of the Orontes and subsequent plain; it is very muddy, and free from any other obstructions than those occasioned by the mill-dams, fish-weirs, and three bridges with narrow arches.' He predicted that one day there would be a canal from a point on the Orontes above Antioch to the Euphrates and noted that 'by merely enlarging one arch in each bridge over the river, and opening a passage through the wooden fish-dams, the Orontes would serve at all times, for small steamers, from its point of junction with the canal to the sea.' He also stated that 'with a little preparation' the road from the mouth of the Orontes could take loaded wagons to Aleppo.

Chesney reached Istanbul in April 1832 and wrote up his Syrian experiences as a supplement to his main report. His overall conclusion, presented with much supporting detail, was that the Euphrates should be navigable for suitably designed steamers. During the high-water season from March through October they should be able to navigate day and night, but only by day between November and February, when the river is low. Chesney was concerned about rock ledges at various points above Ana, but pointed out that they could be blasted with the aid of diving bells. The greatest hazard was Arab hostility, which should yield to greater fire power and the lure of trade.

Sir Robert Gordon was no longer the British Ambassador, but Chesney and his project received a cordial welcome from Sir Stratford Canning, a diplomat on special assignment who was temporarily in charge of the embassy. Chesney left Turkey with Canning on a Royal Navy frigate and returned home on 26 September 1832. Much had changed in England during the three years Chesney had been away. The once ignored captain of artillery was now a celebrity.

Chapter 4

The Balance of Power

King George IV, an odious reprobate derided by Byron, Shelley and their friends, died in June 1830. He was succeeded by his more innocuous brother William IV, an elderly man of limited intellect who had spent much of his life in the Navy.

For over a century Britain had enjoyed constitutional government, with the monarch's role more evident in patronage than in the field of policy. But tradition still required that upon a sovereign's death the House of Commons was automatically dissolved and that new elections should be held.

The spirit of reform was in the air and the 1830 election returned a majority of Whigs and their allies, who forced the Duke of Wellington's Tory administration to resign. In 1831 Lord Grey's new Whig ministry determined to reform the House of Commons by re-apportioning the obsolete constituencies and increasing the number of voters. The bill was narrowly defeated in the House of Commons, but after a new election returned a stronger Whig majority it was passed and sent to the Tory-dominated House of Lords, which threw out the bill. The House of Commons thereupon passed a second bill, which was rejected in May 1832 by the Lords. At this point William IV agreed, if necessary, to create enough new Whig peers to pass the bill. The Tories gave in and the Reform Bill became law.

This protracted crisis left a legacy of bitterness and mistrust. The new House of Commons, elected by the re-drawn constituencies in December 1832, was described by one Whig as 'the most enlightened generation of the most enlightened people that ever existed'. But the Tories, who were still well represented in the new chamber, were determined to fight back.

Wisely, the Tories did not battle over the renewal of the East India

Company charter. The leaders of both parties desired to terminate the China trade monopoly and give more authority over Indian affairs to the Board of Control. The Charter Act of August 1833 achieved these ends and effectively converted the East India House into an administrative branch of the British government.

This legislation followed lengthy hearings, interrupted by two elections, held by a select committee of the House of Commons between 1830 and 1832. Peacock testified in March 1832 and reviewed the status of steam communication in India and between India and Britain.[1] The East India Company had placed orders for a new generation of Ganges steamers – iron boats fitted with bulkheads for greater strength and safety – and would soon send them out to India in frame. As regards steam communication between India and Britain, Peacock had little to report. A new coaling station had been set up on the south coast of Arabia, enabling the *Hugh Lindsay* to make two more voyages to Egypt. The first of these, in December 1830, had carried Sir John Malcolm to his retirement. His successor, Lord Clare, had met him at Cosseir and steamed on to Bombay – a trip that took eighty days owing to mis-allocation of coal at the Red Sea depots. The most recent voyage of the *Hugh Lindsay* in early 1832 had reached Suez a month after she left Bombay (and the return trip, about which Peacock was not yet informed, took approximately the same time).

There were good reasons for Peacock to be reticent about the Red Sea route. Lord Clare had pressed the East India Company directors to start a regular service between Bombay and Suez, but shortly before Peacock testified the Court advised Clare that his project was too expensive and should be deferred. There was much criticism of the directors when their decision became generally known. Waghorn, for some time out of sight, seized the opportunity to contact merchants in Britain and also in Calcutta, where a new 'Steam Committee', supported by the Governor-General and the Bishop of Calcutta, was seeking public and private funds to start a new service between Calcutta and Suez.

The first public mention of the Euphrates project was in Peacock's testimony before the select committee. He urged that this route, while still 'all matter of speculation at present', should be considered because steam navigation by river was cheaper than by sea. When asked whether this line of communication would be safe against a Russian attack, Peacock replied that 'with the co-operation of the people in the country, which is implied in the supposition of our being there at all, I think we could easily retain a military possession of the upper part of the river.' He pointed out that 'if we commanded it at Roomkala', an enemy from the north could not force a passage. Peacock minimized the Arab threat and made no comment on the latest developments in Iraq.

Ellenborough's successor at the India Board was Charles Grant, a painstaking, indecisive bachelor who had inherited Evangelical principles and a large fortune from his father, a three-time chairman of the East India Company. Although Grant's main interest was the spread of Christian faith and morals in India, he was also concerned about conditions in Iraq, where the weakness of Ali Riza Pasha's government invited interference by other powers.

Major Taylor, promoted Lieutenant-Colonel in 1831, returned to Baghdad after the new governor was installed and soon became his close advisor. Ali Riza warmly supported the idea of steam navigation on the Euphrates and Tigris rivers once the Arab tribes had been subdued. But in 1832, while England was still torn by party strife, a great international crisis began to loom. Events in Syria threatened to bring about the collapse of the Ottoman empire and a change in the European balance of power.

The post-Napoleonic era was dominated by five 'Great Powers' – Britain, France, Prussia, Austria and Russia – who had agreed in 1815 to maintain peace and security for the peoples of Europe. But as with the tectonic plates beneath the earth, strains among the powers brought on frictions that called for resolution by diplomacy or arms.

One such tremor, now long forgotten, disturbed England shortly before Lord Palmerston, Foreign Secretary in the new Whig administration, took office at the end of 1830. The July revolution in France, which created a parliamentary regime, was followed by an uprising in Flanders, then part of the kingdom of the Netherlands. French troops crossed the border in support of an independent Belgium and the situation remained tense until a peaceful settlement was reached in 1833.

The Royal Navy enabled Britain to rule the waves and to exert pressure when foreign policy required. But a concentration of force at one or two points – such as along the Dutch coast or off Portugal, a British ally menaced by Spain – made it more difficult to reinforce elsewhere. Insufficient naval power in the Mediterranean, rather than mistakes in judgment or preoccupation with home affairs, explains Britain's weak posture in the 1832–3 Near East crisis. In this first round of the 'Great Game' with Russia the British Mediterranean fleet would not be risked to call the other player's bluff.

Acre fell to Ibrahim Pasha in May 1832. Within a few weeks his army entered Jerusalem and Damascus and defeated an Ottoman army at the battle of Homs. Aleppo surrendered to him in mid-July and at that point it became clear that Mehemet Ali was bent on establishing an independent Arab state or possibly seizing control of the whole Ottoman empire for himself.

When Stratford Canning left Istanbul for home in August, he bore with him a plea from the Sultan for British naval aid. But in November the Whig cabinet declined to intervene – a fateful decision confirmed at the end of January 1833, after the election was over and after news had reached London that Ibrahim had defeated a new Ottoman army at Konia and that its commander, the Grand Vizier Reshid Pasha, had been taken prisoner.

While the Egyptian army advanced toward Istanbul, Tsar Nicholas of Russia made his move. He had already sent an envoy to Alexandria in January to warn Mehemet Ali not to go too far. In February he accepted an invitation from the Sultan to send a Russian squadron to the Bosporus and a Russian army that was soon encamped on the Asiatic shore.

The crisis ended after the Sultan agreed that Mehemet Ali and his son might keep Palestine, Syria and Cilicia. The Russians withdrew in July 1833 after signing a treaty of alliance with Turkey.

These untoward happenings shifted the balance of power in Russia's favour and endangered Britain's communications with India. Unless they took some remedial action, the Whig ministers would face harsh criticism from the Tory opposition and the press.

Lord Palmerston proposed a bold new policy whereby Britain would shore up the Sultan's crumbling empire and would seek by quiet diplomacy to draw Turkey away from the Russian embrace. Support for the Sultan would require Britain to resist Mehemet Ali's ambitions; but at the same time it was essential to restrain the Sultan from using force against him, since a new conflict would give the Tsar a pretext for sending the Russian army and navy back to Istanbul.

The reformers who brought the Whigs to power had long regarded the Ottoman regime as a cruel, corrupt obstacle to progress. Many of them had supported Greece's fight for independence, in which Turkish and Egyptian soldiers showed no mercy and Lord Byron died of fever. But Palmerston was able to convince his colleagues that his policy was the soundest way to counter the Russian moves.

Lord Ponsonby, the new Ambassador to Turkey, and Colonel Patrick Campbell, who replaced John Barker as Consul-General in Alexandria, were carefully instructed along these lines. Sultan Mahmud soon saw the advantage of playing Britain off against Russia; while in Egypt Mehemet Ali hoped that by encouraging the Overland Route to India he might win Britain to his side. (Even at the height of the crisis the *Hugh Lindsay* had been allowed to enter and leave Suez on her fourth voyage from Bombay, and in May 1834 Mehemet Ali gave an audience to Waghorn, who was seeking a concession to transport mail and passengers between Alexandria and Suez.)

Chesney returned to England in September 1832, just as affairs in the Near East began to unravel. Stories of his travels and hairbreadth escapes had preceded him and a London publisher offered a thousand pounds for his rough journals and maps. Chesney replied that they were government property and devoted the next few weeks to completing his reports and supervising the reproduction of his maps.

Chesney first met Peacock on 1 January 1833. His diary records:

> I found that he was deeply versed in the ancient history of the
> Euphrates and that he had not only been the first to bring this
> line of communication with India forward, but that he had
> collected in a thick book every private notice he could find of
> that river, whether contained in Gibbon, Balbi, or any other
> work.[2]

The two enthusiasts thereupon started a campaign to persuade the government to undertake a trial experiment of the Euphrates route. When Chesney learned that the East India Company was planning to publish only the Red Sea portion of his report, Peacock urged him to publish the entire document in February 1833 at his own expense. Copies were sent to Sir Stratford Canning and other influential people, including the aged but well connected John Sulivan, a member of the Board of Control who had descended the Tigris by kelek in 1781.

In normal times there would have been little support for a new rival to the Overland Route. The Red Sea survey was now complete and the *Hugh Lindsay*'s voyages had proved the feasibility of this route. Merchants in India had already formed a steam committee in London to press for a regular service to begin. In contrast, critics of the Euphrates project could point out that the most hazardous part of that river was still unsurveyed and that the seasonal flows of its water were not precisely known. Opinions differed as to the best type of river steamer to use. Meanwhile, the desert Arabs were warring and the river tribes were more inclined to larceny than trade.

But these were not normal times. Chesney's reports, his detailed survey and, most of all, his passionate conviction began to persuade his listeners that this project was more than a desk-bound writer's dream. An interview with King William IV, arranged in April 1833 by Sulivan, gave Chesney great satisfaction and some publicity. More important, as the Near East crisis worsened, the Euphrates route gained support from some senior cabinet members – Lord Lansdowne, president of the council; Lord Ripon, the lord privy seal and a former prime minister; and Charles Grant at the Board of Control, who saw possibilities for introducing Christianity among the Arabs.

The concept, as it developed in the latter part of 1833, was for the British government to obtain permission from the Sultan to establish a commercial steamboat service along the Euphrates between Bir and Basra and to undertake an experimental voyage forthwith. It was contemplated that initially two vessels would be used and that they would carry naval guns for self-defence. Coal depots would be sited at Bir, Hit, Hilla, Korna and Basra, some of them floating depots, others ashore, but all well protected; at Korna, it was thought, an old man-of-war or an Indiaman might be fitted with some guns to serve as a floating battery for the defence of the river. Martello towers would be erected at the northern terminus near Bir and at the fortress of Rumkale.

These arrangements were deemed sufficient to protect the vessels and their supplies from unfriendly Arab tribes. In any case, as Chesney pointed out, even if the Arabs caused the service to be abandoned, 'we shall have secured two stations, useful for ordinary purposes of commerce and sufficient to defend the river for a time against a descent of Russia.'[3]

Herein lay the covert essence of the project and the reason why statesmen, diplomats and staff officers supported a venture so filled with risk and offering such meagre commercial rewards. Peacock had alluded to the Russian menace in 1829 and 1832. This time he was more explicit; when asked in June 1834 whether 'the establishment of steam along the Euphrates would serve in any respect to counteract Russia', he replied: 'I think so, by giving us a vested interest and a right to interfere.'[4]

For a long time Palmerston refused even to see Chesney. He knew that the Russians would oppose the project and thereby upset his policy of subtly gaining the Sultan as a friend. In addition, its advocates took for granted the co-operation of Mehemet Ali, who controlled the right bank of the Euphrates from the Anatolian foothills opposite Bir down to Deir ez-Zor; his forces also still occupied the provinces of Urfa and Rakka on the left bank, despite his agreement to restore them to the Sultan.

But political pressures were increasing and the survival of the Whig administration began to be in doubt. On 30 January 1834, a cabinet committee approved the Euphrates project as one of several measures to restore the balance of power in the east.

The next four months were consumed in the bureaucratic wrangling common among government projects of this kind. William Cabell, senior clerk at the India Board, worked closely with Peacock and Chesney in the planning of the project. But the East India Company directors, penny-pinchers to the end, refused to pay for any part of the Euphrates project on the grounds that they had already spent between £60,000 and £70,000 on the *Hugh Lindsay* trials of the Red Sea route, now subordinated to another scheme. Naval assistance was essential for the project, but John Barrow, the senior civil servant who had ruled the Admiralty since the days of Nelson, was vehemently opposed to the Euphrates route and had even written an unsigned magazine article to that effect.[5] Grant was forced to apply to the Treasury for all the finance and to agree with the Admiralty that as part of its assignment the expedition would complete a survey of the Cilician coast commenced by Captain Beaufort in 1810–12.

After weighing the diversity of departmental views, the need for public funds and the uncertainties of parliamentary debate, the government decided that a select committee of the House of Commons should hold hearings in June 1834 on the whole question of steam navigation to India. As President of the India Board, Charles Grant would be chairman, but Sir Robert Peel and other Tory leaders were also named as members. (The author's great-grandfather, Josiah John Guest, an ironmaster from South Wales who supported the Whigs, served on this committee.)

The select committee documents are a mine of historical information, but the hearings were mainly for show. In a private letter to Lord William Bentinck the secretary of the East India Company, Peacock's old friend Peter Auber wrote: 'It is rather more with a view of watching and forestalling Russia on the borders of the Euphrates etc. than anything else, but this is of course not avowed.'[6]

Peacock and Chesney, the first witnesses, reviewed the problems and prospects involved in the transition from sail to steam and made a case for the Euphrates route to be examined as a possible alternative to the Red Sea route during the period of the south-west monsoon.[7]

A plan of action had already been prepared. Two iron vessels would be built and tried out in England; six months after placing the order they should be ready to be shipped off in frame. The larger one would measure 100 tons and would be powered by two 25 hp engines, while the smaller, designed for the low-water season, would measure between 60 and 70 tons with two 8 hp engines. If they were shipped to the Syrian coast, as Chesney recommended, the voyage would take about fifty days. Five days would be required for unloading the crates and tracking them up the Orontes to a point near Antioch, whence camels and heavy wagons could transport the entire 300-ton load in three journeys to Bir, only fifty miles distant, in a week. Allowing forty days to reassemble the vessels, the initial 1,100-mile trip down the Euphrates, which would also require time for negotiations with the Arabs and for laying down coal depots, should bring them down to Basra a month later – for a total elapsed time of 131 days after leaving England.

The return trip upstream to Bir was estimated at eight to ten days. Thereafter, for the duration of the experiment, assumed to be twelve months, regular trips would take eight days to go up the river and five days to go down during the high water, and two days longer in each direction during the low-water season. (These times assumed that, except on certain stretches, the vessels would steam day and night.) The actual number of voyages would depend on the arrivals of the mails.

No witnesses came forward to challenge these estimates, though two expert witnesses – MacGregor Laird and his rival Joshua Field, who had built the steamboats for the Ganges – expressed various opinions on the size, shape and power of the proposed vessels.[8] (Laird had just returned from West Africa after taking two steamers up the Niger at a heavy cost in lives).

One illuminating difference of views concerned the point at which the boats should start their voyage. Peacock and some other witnesses thought it more prudent to start at Basra and work upstream; in case of difficulty a vessel could always float back with the current. Chesney felt strongly that they should start at Bir, pointing out that if the worst Arab tribes were in the upper part of the river, the expedition should tackle them first rather than go upstream and risk putting the ships in their power. As regards repair facilities, Chesney stated: 'There are very great facilities at Bussora, in the one case, and at Aleppo in the other', adding that at Aleppo there were many skilled riveters. The real reason, which led to Peacock being overruled, was that the boats could be in the river two months sooner at Bir than if they went around the Cape to Basra.

A number of witnesses, including Waghorn, spoke in favour of the Red Sea route.[9] In its final report the committee recommended that service on that route should be started immediately, with the costs to be shared equally between the government and the East India Company.

The committee hearings were cut short by a cabinet crisis in July 1834, which resulted in Lord Grey being replaced as prime minister by Lord Melbourne. Charles Grant remained President of the Board of Control. On July 14 the Select Committee submitted its report, which endorsed the Euphrates route experiment and recommended that the entire cost, estimated at £20,000, should be paid out of public funds. On 4 August the House of Commons duly voted this amount.

Chapter 5
Getting Ready

The general plan for the Euphrates route experiment had been outlined in the Select Committee hearings. Now that Parliament had approved the project, the time had come to define its scope, determine the size and composition of the expeditionary force, settle on its starting point and destination, and draw up a timetable for everything to be done.

At the India Board Charles Grant and his capable assistant William Cabell would be responsible for selecting a commander for the expedition; arranging for qualified officers to be borrowed from other departments or hired from outside; obtaining guns, engineering stores and skilled personnel from the Ordnance Department (who would also procure weapons and consumer goods to be presented or sold to Arab tribesmen*); drawing on government stores for up to three years' supply of provisions; chartering a merchantman to take the expedition and its vessels (in frame) to the starting point; negotiating with the Admiralty for an accompanying escort; and providing information to back up the Foreign Office's requests for permits from the Sultan of Turkey and the Viceroy of Egypt.

The East India Company, against proper reimbursement, would place orders for the vessels, engines and other equipment and would also undertake to buy and deliver coal at designated points. Peacock was assigned to carry out this work and to supervise the construction and completion of the steamers; he also helped to assemble the ships' library. The Company would inform the authorities in India about the expedition and would instruct

* The principal items were shotguns, pistols, swords, knives, cutlery, rings, watches and Glasgow soft goods. The list also included musical snuff boxes and magic lanterns.

Colonel Taylor, the Resident in Baghdad, to establish coal depots along the middle and lower Euphrates.

The scope of the expedition's survey work was left vague, since the military aspect could not be openly disclosed. But the nature of the task could be perceived from the composition of the fifty-three-man group that was scheduled to sail from England by the end of 1834:

1 Commander	2 ship engineers
5 naval officers	16 artillerymen
3 military officers	5 sappers and miners
1 civilian surveyor	16 seamen
2 physicians	39
1 surgeon/geologist	
1 purser	
14 officers	TOTAL – 53

The foregoing numbers do not include nine carpenters and riveters who were to sail with the expedition and return to England after the steamers had been put together. Stokers, interpreters and possibly one or two musicians were to be recruited when the expedition reached Malta.

Selection of a commander presented some problems for the India Board. In many ways Chesney was the logical choice, but he was only a captain, whereas the responsibilities called for an officer of higher rank. When the Board of Ordnance proved unwilling to promote Chesney by two steps to the rank of lieutenant-colonel, Grant had to look elsewhere. Alexander Burnes, a noted Asiatic explorer, and Dr Gideon Colquhoun, who had preceded Taylor as Resident at Basra, were for various reasons deemed unfitted. Colonel William Colebrooke, an artillery officer who had served with the Indian army in the Persian Gulf, was offered the command but preferred to go to the Bahamas as lieutenant-governor. Finally, on 20 August Grant prevailed upon Chesney to accept the appointment; several weeks later he was given the rank of 'colonel on a particular service' for the duration of the expedition.

Lieutenant Henry Blosse Lynch was borrowed from the Indian Navy to serve as second in command of the expedition and to be captain of the smaller vessel. He was born in 1807, the third of eleven brothers, at Partry House overlooking Lough Carra in County Mayo, where his family had lived for two centuries and still resides. He joined the Indian Navy in 1823 and took part in the survey of the Persian Gulf, where he learned Arabic and Persian. In 1830 he was appointed to bring back the *Enterprize* steamer from Bombay to Calcutta. He then returned to Persia, where he undertook special missions for the East India Company and encountered Chesney in 1831. Two years later, on his way home on leave, his ship was wrecked in the Red Sea, but he managed to get ashore and made his way to safety by crossing the Nubian desert and sailing down the Nile.

After eleven years of dealing with Indians, Persians and Arabs, Lynch had become somewhat Orientalised himself. In Aleppo a German traveller noted 'that with a good English education he combined a taste for Asiatic hospitality and Oriental luxury',[1] traits that did not fit in with Chesney's Spartan ways. But Lynch's debonair exterior concealed a strong will and a keen sense of duty. A colleague later recalled him 'as an excellent observer and daring explorer . . . having those rare qualities of geniality, tact, and temper, which command the respect of the wildest, and win the confidence of the less barbarous, Orientals.'[2]

Captain James Bucknall Bucknall-Estcourt of the 43rd Light Infantry was lent by the army to take charge of the survey. Born in 1802 at the family seat in Gloucestershire and educated at Harrow and Sandhurst, Estcourt had led the comfortable but dull life of a peacetime regimental officer, including five years of garrison duty at Gibraltar. Chesney met Estcourt there and subsequently in England, where he became acquainted with Estcourt's father, a highly regarded Tory politician.

Estcourt's well balanced personality shines through his letters home; to his father he is frank, serious and respectful, to his sisters witty and affection-ate. In Gibraltar he was remembered for 'his gentle and amiable temper, his peculiarly engaging manners, combined with a manly and enterprising spirit.'[3] All of these virtues proved useful during the expedition, together with his talent for drawing, which enabled him to portray some memorable events.

Fourth in order of authority as prescribed by regulations was Lieutenant Richard Francis Cleaveland, on loan from the Royal Navy to be captain of the larger vessel. He had entered the navy in 1824; at the time he joined the expedition his most recent service had been on the 800-ton frigate *Phoenix*, one of the navy's first steam-powered warships. Beyond these meagre details little is known of this officer's antecedents, but he proved to be a skilled navigator and a tower of strength for the expedition.

Next in line was Lieutenant Hastings Fitz-Edward Murphy of the Royal Engineers, who was appointed astronomer and director of the expedition's trigonometrical survey. Born in 1798 in County Kerry, he was the second oldest member of the expedition and had already made a name for himself in the Ordnance Survey of Ireland. Upon first acquaintance Estcourt described him as 'exceedingly quiet, and quite softly amiable: wrapped up in his astronomy, constantly poking after the sun, moon, or star and forgetful of any thing of minor detail in life.'[4] Later on Murphy became more talkative, deluging his listeners with endless technical speculations.

Henry Eden, a midshipman from the Royal Navy, was quite a different type. He had joined the navy as a volunteer in 1825 and had served on several of the Mediterranean steam packets. One of his fellow officers described him as 'everlastingly growling'.[5]

Lieutenant Robert Cockburn of the Royal Artillery, who was appointed to be Murphy's chief assistant in the survey, came from an old Scottish family. His father was a wine importer with offices in Edinburgh and London. His mother, Mary Duff, had spent her childhood in Banff, where she had been much admired by Byron, then aged seven. They never met again, but the poet never forgot 'her brown, dark hair and hazel eyes; her very dress!'[6] and was greatly upset when he learned of her marriage ten years later in 1805. Robert Cockburn was recommended to Chesney by the Duke of Wellington. A member of the expedition described him as 'a most amiable and promising young officer [who] always looked kindly after the men who belonged to his branch of the service.'[7] Cockburn was also a good draughtsman.

The two most junior officers of the expedition were close friends, both of them midshipmen from the Royal Navy. Edward Philips Charlewood, twenty years old, was the son of a Staffordshire clergyman. He had been educated at the Royal Naval College at Portsmouth and had spent four years at sea off the coast of Africa before joining one of the new steam frigates. A cheerful, intelligent, hard-working officer, Charlewood was a perfect foil for his brilliant, charismatic friend James Fitzjames.

Fitzjames, six months older than Charlewood but one month his junior in the service, was destined to be one of the finest sailors of his generation. An orphan, he joined the navy in 1825 and soon attracted the notice of John Barrow at the Admiralty, who wrote later that 'by his zeal and alacrity, his good humour and ever cheerful disposition, he has made himself a universal favourite in the navy.'[8] Fitzjames's nine years of service, almost all on battleships, had taken him to Mexico, Portugal and Greece and, despite a lingering addiction to pranks and practical jokes, he was maturing into a man described by a naval historian as 'strong, self-reliant, a perfect sailor, imaginative, enthusiastic, full of sympathy for others, a born leader of men.'[9] He was also one of the expedition's best draughtsmen.

Dr Charles Frederick Staunton of the Royal Artillery had received his medical education in Dublin. A capable physician who bore a heavy load when sickness struck the expedition, he preferred the orderly routine of a doctor's office to going on the road. On one long trip Estcourt recorded that Staunton 'is unfortunately one of the slowest coaches I have met with; so full of neatness and arrangement in his own little *"traps"*, that he places and displaces his combs, medicines and brushes half a dozen times, before he can make up his mind to use them.'[10] Charles Staunton's ichthyologist brother Andrew, who had some medical training, joined the expedition as a draughtsman and made numerous drawings of places and events.

William Francis Ainsworth was appointed surgeon and geologist to the expedition. He was born in 1807, the son of an infantry officer from Cheshire. After receiving a medical degree at Edinburgh and attending the Paris School of Mines, he spent a few years editing a learned journal, lecturing on geology and practising in several hospitals during a cholera epidemic. Chesney met Ainsworth through Captain Sabine, a Woolwich classmate and lifelong friend who was now a famous explorer and astronomer.

Ainsworth's many writings* reveal a thwarted but resilient person who failed in many endeavours because his intellectual gifts were unseasoned by common sense. On the expedition he at first cut a comic figure, earning the nickname of 'Young Strabo', but Estcourt judged him 'a very good sort of young man with great good nature, which balances his vulgarity and pretense to learning'.[11] Later he became generally respected for his devotion to Chesney and his endurance of the hardships of Oriental travel, justifying Sabine's assessment of Ainsworth as 'active, courageous, indefatigable, & healthy, each in the highest degree: very amiable:- quite what the French call "bon camarade" – one who will stand by you for ever, do any thing and every thing to help.'[12]

William Taylour Thomson, second draughtsman in charge of Murphy's chronometer and other instruments, came from a Fifeshire family. He was born in Edinburgh in 1813 and was educated there. It is not known how he came to Chesney's attention, but he had volunteered to serve without pay.

Alexander Hector, the purser and store keeper, was engaged on the recommendation of MacGregor Laird, whom he had accompanied on the 1832–3 Niger Expedition in West Africa.

Arrangements were made for the members of the expedition and the gunners, sappers and miners to be trained in their new duties at the Portsmouth naval station, the Sandhurst military college and the Chatham engineering school.

Specifications for the expedition's two steamers had been developed by Peacock and Chesney in the spring of 1834. Chesney's 1831 report on the

---

* His cousin William Harrison Ainsworth wrote a number of historical novels, including *The Tower of London*.

Euphrates had recommended a trimaran design with enclosed paddle wheels, but Peacock persuaded him to accept a conventional design modelled after the iron river boats recently sent to India for use on the Ganges. After discussion with several builders, the East India Company placed the order with the Laird shipyard at Birkenhead, which had just delivered two iron steamships to customers in Ireland and the United States. Engines would be supplied by Fawcett & Preston of Liverpool.

The final dimensions of the larger vessel were: length, 105 feet; breadth, 19 feet; and tonnage, 179 tons. She was powered by two 25 hp engines. Her draught was rated at three feet.

The smaller vessel, as delivered from the yard, measured 90 feet length; 16 feet breadth; and 109 tons. She was powered by two 10 hp engines. Her draught was rated at 22 inches.

Both vessels would be well armed. The larger one would have two nine-pounder carronades (small, short-range guns that fired a heavy shot, often called 'smashers'), six one-pounder swivel guns and a Congreve rocket launcher. The smaller vessel would have one nine-pounder carronade, six one-pounder swivels and a rocket launcher. Personal weapons would include muskets, rifles, carbines, pistols, swords and cutlasses.

Chesney divided his time between London, where he worked with Peacock and Cabell on the organization of the expedition, and Liverpool, where all the material was being assembled for loading. (Charles Grant, the indolent President of the India Board, relied heavily on his staff and allowed Cabell a relatively free hand to expedite the project). On 8 September Chesney assured Lord Palmerston that the steamers should be ready by mid-November and that he expected to sail from Liverpool by 1 December and reach the coast of Syria by the middle of January 1835. Chesney was confident that, after the Arab tribes had been properly informed about the expedition, 'the vessels will begin to ply about the month of May'.[13]

(Due to Chesney's insistence on haste, there would be no trials of the completed steamers when they were ready. The sections would be crated and loaded immediately, leaving the trials to be made when the vessels were put together on the Euphrates.)

As with many such projects, the specifications were modified from time to time to provide improvements over the original design. Toward the end of November MacGregor Laird informed Peacock that the smaller vessel and her engines were nearly ready, adding that 'she is a pretty model and will go fast – possibly about 12 Miles p. Hour'.[14] The larger vessel was also ready, except for her engines, which had been delayed about three weeks due to modifications and now would not be ready until January.

Chesney was infuriated by this news and by Laird's off-hand suggestion that he should take the smaller vessel to the Syrian coast and let the shipyard send the larger vessel to Basra.[15] After threatening to call off the whole expedition, Chesney finally accepted the fact that there would be a delay.

The rest of the material was assembled in good time, due in part to the general knowledge that King William IV was taking a personal interest in the expedition. On 15 November, shortly before he learned about the shipyard delay, Chesney gave an encouraging progress report to the king.

By this time the route of the expedition had been settled. The Bay of Antioch, where the Orontes river flows into the sea, was selected as the disembarkation point because access to the interior of Syria appeared easier than from Iskenderun or Latakia. The dock site on the Euphrates would be either near Bir or at Beles, depending on the recommendation to be made by Lynch, who left for Syria at the end of November. His mission was to work with Vincent Germain, the engineer whom Chesney had met in Aleppo in 1832 and now hoped to use for digging out the dock basins.

To assist the expedition at the farther end of the line, Chesney urged Grant to have a back-up steamer available in the Persian Gulf in case the *Hugh Lindsay* were disabled. At the beginning of December the India Board learned that the Admiralty did not have a steamer available to go to India and that consequently Chesney would have to rely on the *Hugh Lindsay* for steam communication between Bombay and the mouth of the Euphrates.

Toward the middle of September Lord Ponsonby, the British Ambassador in Istanbul, received an official despatch from Palmerston, advising him that, with the object of improving communications between Britain and India, the British government planned to conduct an experimental voyage by two steamers along the Euphrates, to be followed by a regular commercial service if the experiment proved successful.*[16] The Sultan was requested to authorize the project and to instruct his officials to co-operate with the expedition.

Mehemet Ali was notified separately by a despatch to Colonel Campbell, the British Consul in Alexandria.[17] He was also sent a detailed list of proposed road and bridge improvements which Chesney would require for the transport between Antioch and the Euphrates. In addition, sketches of dock basins to be dug on the river bank, preferably by a resident foreign

---

* The original concession granted by Daud Pasha to James Taylor had contemplated using the Tigris between Korna and Baghdad and a canal between Baghdad and Felluja on the Euphrates. The new permit requested by Ponsonby mentioned only the Euphrates, but British diplomats later asserted that it also covered the Tigris between Korna and Baghdad.

engineer such as Vincent Germain, were attached, along with a request for a regiment of soldiers to protect the works until proper defences could be built.

At the same time Colonel Taylor, the East India Company Resident in Baghdad, informed Ali Riza Pasha, the provincial governor, about the proposed expedition and asked him to ensure a friendly reception from the Arab tribes along the middle and lower Euphrates.

When Lord Ponsonby communicated Palmerston's request to the Sultan's ministers, they were uncertain how to respond. They explained that in the present circumstances, where Mehemet Ali controlled the upper part of the Euphrates and large stretches farther down were infested by Arab tribes, the Turkish authorities could provide little protection for the British steamers. After the Russian ambassador expressed strong opposition to the project, the Sultan informed Ponsonby that the whole matter had been referred to Ali Riza Pasha in Baghdad and that nothing could be done until the governor had submitted his report. This was an obvious ruse to gain time, since it was generally known that Ali Riza was in favour of the expedition.

Palmerston's despatch dealing with the Euphrates project reached Alexandria on 8 October. Chesney's attachments arrived ten days later on Mehemet Ali's new, British-built steamship *Nile*. They came at an inopportune moment, since Colonel Campbell and Mehemet Ali both had more important matters on their minds. For several months Campbell and the other foreign consuls had been urging the viceroy to honour his pledge to withdraw his troops from the provinces of Urfa and Rakka on the left bank of the Euphrates. Mehemet Ali, a hard bargainer, claimed that he could not comply so long as the Arab tribes in the district were raiding peaceful villages. On 22 October, while Chesney's voluminous material was still being translated into French and Turkish, a new despatch arrived from Palmerston, demanding the immediate evacuation of the provinces.[18]

Meanwhile, Mehemet Ali had raised a far more serious issue. At the beginning of September 1834 the viceroy asked the foreign consuls to let him know how their governments would react if he were to declare himself independent of the Sultan. Campbell's report of this 'trial balloon', which could undermine Britain's carefully balanced Near Eastern policy and threaten the balance of power, reached London toward the end of October. Palmerston sent off a sharp rebuke,[19] which Campbell delivered to Mehemet Ali's minister on 23 November.

Initially Mehemet Ali had indicated a willingness to help the Euphrates project, subject to learning more about its proposed route. But after studying Chesney's material, he found its military aspects troublesome. Palmerston's two recent despatches had revealed a determination to oppose Mehemet Ali's ambitious plans. The viceroy began to wonder whether a British presence along the Euphrates valley would really be in his interest.

At the end of November Campbell was summoned to Cairo. In the course of several audiences with Mehemet Ali and his minister, Campbell was informed that Urfa and Rakka would be evacuated, except for a small portion on the right bank of the Euphrates opposite Bir. As regards the British steamer project, the viceroy regretted that he could not carry out his earlier promise to help. He explained that, since the whole Euphrates river would now be under the Sultan's direct control, only the Sultan could issue instructions in this matter, which, as Lord Palmerston had reminded him, it would be Mehemet Ali's duty to obey.

Campbell's despatches reporting these proceedings reached London on 19 January 1835.[20] By that time Lord Palmerston was no longer Foreign Secretary.

On 14 November 1834, King William IV unexpectedly dismissed the Whig administration (a rare event in British constitutional history) and called on the Tories to form a government. Since Sir Robert Peel, the party leader and prospective premier, was away on the Continent, a curious interregnum lasted for a few weeks, when the Duke of Wellington took charge of the Treasury, the Foreign Office and the Home Office, while the other departments were run by civil servants. Charles Grant remained President of the India Board pending appointment of a successor. Finally, on 15 December Peel's new administration was sworn in. The Duke of Wellington remained Foreign Secretary and Ellenborough returned to his previous post at the Board of Control.

When Ellenborough took office he found that the earliest departure date for Chesney's expedition had slipped back to 10 January 1835, due to delayed delivery of one engine. He also learned that the Admiralty steam packet *Alban*, which would escort the expedition's merchantman across the Bay of Biscay and would be available to tow her through the Mediterranean, could not be ready before 23 January. Meanwhile, replies had not yet been received from the Sultan or from Mehemet Ali.

As an early proponent of the Red Sea route, the new President of the India Board saw nothing but trouble coming out of the Euphrates expedition, which his colleague Lord de Grey, the First Lord of the Admiralty, termed 'an Arabian Nights' Tale'.[21] Ellenborough distrusted Chesney, whom he called 'a red-hot Irishman, likely to lead others to serious danger'.[22] In the short time that now remained before departure, he tried in vain to persuade Wellington to call off the whole project and later sought to change the starting point to Basra instead of the Syrian coast. On this issue the Admiralty argued for Syria, partly because Grant had agreed to complete their survey.

All this time Chesney was shuttling between London and Liverpool, assembling the expedition and expediting last-minute items. The India Board had not yet authorized him to charter a ship, but the crates and packing cases were ready to be put on board. At the end of the year Chesney was notified that his two vessels would be named *Euphrates* and *Tigris*.

On 8 January 1835, a discouraging report from Ponsonby in Istanbul caused Ellenborough to order the expedition to be broken up.[23] But on the night of 12 January a courier brought a subsequent letter from Ponsonby with a copy of an official note from the Ottoman government granting permission for the project to go forward.[24] (A *firman* from the sultan to the local authorities was issued on 29 December*).

Chesney immediately chartered the 390-ton *George Canning* and loading was completed by 1 February. On the last day of loading a customs house official fell overboard and was rescued by Fitzjames, who jumped in, caught the man (a non-swimmer) by the hair and supported him until they were picked up half a mile away.

For some reason no heed was paid to the ominous change in Mehemet Ali's attitude towards the expedition. (It is possible that Colonel Campbell's despatch, received on 19 January, was somehow mislaid, since the Foreign Office did not send a copy to the India Board until 13 February.) Chesney's instructions from Ellenborough, issued on 24 January, merely authorized him, in case he found it 'impracticable' to transport the steamers from the mouth of the Orontes to the Euphrates, to abandon the project and take them to Bombay.[25] Meanwhile, Estcourt would be detached from the expedition at Malta to go to Egypt and explain everything to the viceroy.

Gales in the Irish Sea delayed the *George Canning*'s departure until 10 February. The ship sailed first to Cork, where she took on tinned and preserved food for the expedition; fresh provisions, together with live cattle, sheep and chickens, were also loaded for the voyage. After being towed out of the Cove of Cork by the *Alban* steamer, they endured four weeks of winter gales that forced their escort to turn back.

Finally, the *George Canning* sailed past the rock of Gibraltar. Estcourt noted that the weather improved as they entered the Mediterranean and that:

---

* An addendum stated that there were two identical *firmans*, addressed to the authorities on each bank of the Euphrates.

our sheep are allowed to exercise their limbs on the forecastle,
as well as the fowls: these poor things, having been so long
confined could scarcely walk, but stretching their wings to
balance, they made a sort of walking fly.[26]

The expedition reached Malta on 12 March 1835.

Malta was at that time a British possession and the home base for the
Mediterranean fleet. The governor, General Sir Frederick Ponsonby, was a
hero of Waterloo and a cousin of the British Ambassador to Turkey. It had
been intended that the expedition should pick up stores and equipment at
Malta, as well as two large flat-bottomed boats to be used in floating the
heavier loads from ship to shore and up the Orontes river. Due to the
winter storms, no instructions had reached Malta, but the governor provided
whatever was needed. He also helped Chesney to recruit twelve Arabic-
speaking interpreters, who would work under John Bell, a local school
teacher, and Christian Rassam, a native of Mosul who had been working
as a translator with a Church of England mission in Malta. There is no
record of any musicians being engaged.

All was now prepared, though one precautionary step had to be foregone.
Upon learning that the plague had broken out again in Egypt, Chesney
decided to keep Estcourt with him for the critical landing process rather
than send him to see Mehemet Ali and risk losing his services for several
weeks of quarantine.

The *George Canning* left Malta on 21 March 1835. In the absence of the
Alban steamer, she was towed by HMS *Columbine*, a fast-sailing 18-gun sloop-
of-war. A few days earlier Chesney had written to Sir Robert Grant, the
Governor of Bombay, to inform him that he expected the expedition to
reach Basra by the end of June and that he would be able to take a mail
from India back up the river for delivery to an Admiralty packet that was
expected on the Syrian coast about the middle of July.[27]

Chesney's reminiscences, often quite selective, do not mention this letter
nor the remarkable speed with which it was conveyed. The Admiralty and
the East India Company had arranged that the Red Sea route to India
should be inaugurated by scheduling the first Malta-Alexandria steam
packet in time to connect with the *Hugh Lindsay*'s return trip from Suez to
Bombay. As a result Chesney's letter of 17 March from Malta reached
Bombay at the beginning of May.

The expedition's departure from Malta marks the end of Peacock's role
in launching the project he had conceived and worked so hard to bring
about. Once the ships reached Basra, he expected to be involved once more,

since Lord Ellenborough had determined that at that point the ownership, use and upkeep of the two vessels would be turned over to the authorities in Bombay.

It was now Chesney's task to accomplish Peacock's dream and prove to the world that Britain could match the achievements of Greece and Rome.

Chapter 6
Disappointments and Delays

Nine days after leaving Malta the *George Canning* and her escort reached the coast of Cyprus, the starting point for the Admiralty survey. Estcourt enjoyed breathing 'an air perfumed with the most delightful aromatic scents',[1] but when the vessels hove to in Larnaca harbour, a boat from the British consulate warned them that there was plague on the island and in parts of Syria as well.

Plague in Syria would oblige the expedition to return to Malta and face the prospect of going around the Cape to Basra. Leaving the *George Canning* to plough on towards the Bay of Antioch, Chesney took the *Columbine* to Beirut, where there was a British consulate, to find out for himself. In Estcourt's words:

> At Beirout we did not arrive till very late in the evening of
> Tuesday 31st: it was very dark, and not knowing the place we
> Hove to at a distance, fired a gun, burnt Blue lights, hoisted
> lanthorns & made other signals, hoping to attract attention,
> and draw out the British Consul: but all in vain. Therefore
> three of us got into the Brig's Gig and rowed for the shore: we
> rowed first one way and then another: consulted together,
> canvassed opinions as to the right way, but all in vain: we
> could find no town, no landing place. At length however after
> some time spent in this manner, we did hit off Beirout, and
> fortunately by hallooing drew some Maltese to a broken small
> projecting pier: from them we learnt there was no plague: and
> persuaded them to send for the British Vice Consul: who soon
> came down: confirmed the good news, and invited us to come

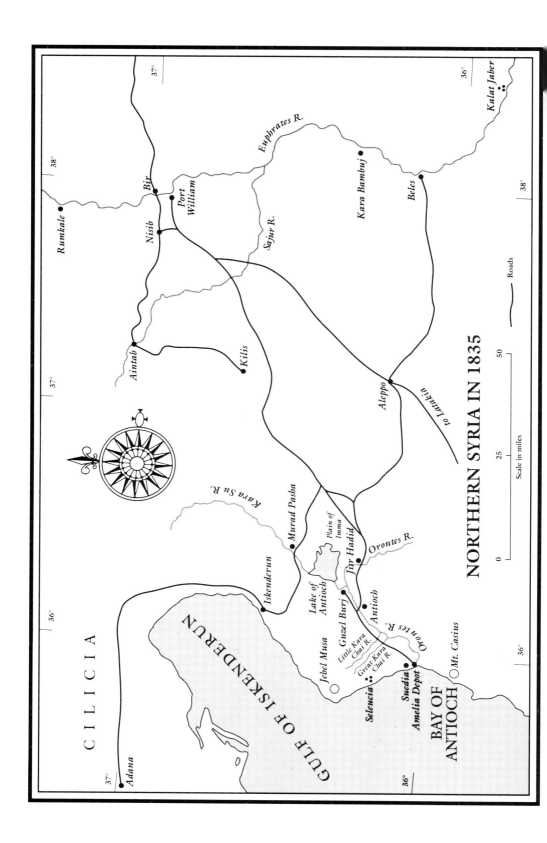

NORTHERN SYRIA IN 1835

Roads

Scale in miles

0 25 50

CILICIA

GULF OF ISKENDERUN

BAY OF ANTIOCH

Adana

Rumkale

Bir

Nisib

Port William

Aintab

Kilis

Euphrates R.

Sajur R.

Kara Bambuj

Beles

Kalat Jaber

Aleppo

to Latakia

Kara Su R.

Murad Pasha

Iskenderun

Plain of Imma

Jsr Hadid

Orontes R.

Lake of Antioch

Guzel Burj

Antioch

Jebel Musa

Little Kara Chai R.

Great Kara Chai R.

Orontes R.

Selencia

Suedia

Amelia Depot

Mt. Casius

36°

37°

38°

36°

37°

38°

36°

37°

36°

on shore without waiting for permission from the authorities, who had gone to bed! This gentleman was an old friend, at least acquaintance of Colonel Chesney's: of course they were delighted to meet, more particularly under the circumstances: we sat in his house for a couple of hours, hearing generally good reports, buying some Lebanon wine, drinking Coffee, and enjoying the strangeness of our situation: at about 12 at night we set off again and in due time, what with blue lights, flashes of pistols etc. caught sight of our *Columbine* again, got on board, and since have stood up for Orontes.[2]

The vice-consul reported that Lynch had been in Beirut and that he had made the necessary preparations at Suedia for the expedition to land.

Indeed, when the two vessels entered the Bay of Antioch a few days later, lookouts spotted what appeared to be a regiment of soldiers in red coats, drawn up on the shore. But it was only a flock of flamingoes, who flew away.

Viewed from the sea, the seven-mile-wide Bay of Antioch has magnificence and charm. At the northern end the ruins of the old Roman port of Seleucia are strewn on the foothills of a pine-clad mountain range. A few miles inland lies Suedia, where Chesney's friend John Barker had built a villa overlooking acres of mulberry groves. At the southern end of the bay the water is deep and sheer cliffs form the base of Mount Casius [Jebel Akra], whose peak is snowy until late spring. In between, the Orontes river emerges from low hills and meanders across a fertile plain to the sea. A bar at its mouth creates a surf that is treacherous in rough weather.

Early in the morning of 4 April Cleaveland was sent ashore to select a good landing place between Seleucia and the mouth of the Orontes. After picking a site described by Fitzjames as 'a nice green plat, having the river and a small creek for three of the sides',[3] he returned with the mayor of Suedia, who brought some disturbing news. The mayor, a Greek Christian, told Chesney that no official *firman* had arrived and that the camels Lynch had hired to carry the expedition's lighter loads had been discharged.

The next day a package of letters from Lynch in Aleppo made everything brutally clear. Lynch had been sent ahead to Syria to select a dock site on the Euphrates and work with Vincent Germain and others on the programme of road improvements and dock construction that Chesney expected to be completed by the time the expedition arrived. But owing to Mehemet Ali's decision to provide no help without an order from the Sultan, these works had not even been begun. In February 1835 Ibrahim Pasha, who was deputizing for his father while the viceroy was touring Upper Egypt, had learned from Colonel Campbell that the expedition was believed to be on its way. Orders were at once issued that if the British landed on the coast of Syria, local authorities should offer no opposition but should deny any assistance to their further progress.

James Farren, the British Consul-General in Damascus, who believed that the best means of communication between Syria and Iraq would be a dromedary mail service, wrote smugly to Chesney that 'I cannot suppose that you left England in ignorance of this change in Mehemet Ali which Colonel Campbell tells me he communicated to Government in December last. He requests me to tell you that he can do nothing on this point and that the whole matter rests with the Ambassador.'[4]

Ulstermen do not take such language kindly, but this unexpected turn of events gave Chesney more important matters to worry about. In his memoirs he recalls weighing the alternatives of withdrawing to Malta for further instructions, sailing around Africa to Basra, or unloading in defiance of the Egyptians.[5] He decided to go ahead with the unloading and trust that this display of British vigour would help to make Mehemet Ali change his mind.

Everyone was put to work. Cockburn and Thomson laid out and fortified the base camp on the shore, which Chesney named Amelia Depot in memory of William IV's deceased sister. Charlewood and Fitzjames, assisted by the crew of the *Columbine*, organized the unloading of the stores from the *George Canning* in the ships' boats, guided by a 3,600-foot hawser stretching from the vessel across the sandbar to the 'depot'. The heavier loads – the biggest engine weighed seven tons – were brought ashore on the flatboats Chesney had acquired in Malta.

Meanwhile, Cleaveland and Estcourt were inspecting the routes inland. Chesney had planned to use the Orontes for floating the heavier loads past Antioch to a transfer point east of the city at Jisr Hadid (the Iron Bridge), where the river turns sharply to the south. Here the loads would be put on locally built wagons for conveyance by road across the rolling plain that forms the watershed between the Orontes and the Euphrates. The lighter loads would be transported by camel caravans all the way.

Cleaveland's party, tracking two loaded boats up the Orontes against the stream, ran in to difficulties in the hilly country beyond the coastal plain. The river here descends through narrow gorges with bare rock on one side and dense vegetation on the other, rushing over waterfalls and around masses of fallen rock. Ainsworth records that 'great efforts were made to overcome these obstacles; the officers and men took off their coats',[6] but without success. The effort was abandoned and they made their way to

Antioch on foot, passing the ancient grove of Daphne and several weirs. Estcourt, who had ridden up from Suedia, reported that the arches of the bridge leading into Antioch, as well as those at Jisr Hadid, were too low for boats of any size.

In retrospect, the mistake about the Orontes is hard to explain. Peacock could be faulted for over-reliance on the Taylor guidebook and for not inquiring further from John Barker, whose villa was near the river, or from others who had visited the district. But the blame falls most on Chesney, who had been there; even if he had not surveyed the river, he had seen the bridges and should have learned at Woolwich to be wary of a stream that dropped three hundred feet in ten miles of broken ground.

Then as now, the road from the coast to Antioch runs north of the Orontes, crossing two spurs of the Jebel Musa mountain range and two valleys where tributaries flow in to the main river. Estcourt reported that 'part of the road was stony, hilly, and bad; in fact it was at best but a mere horse-track.'[7] He also warned that the two tributaries, 'which dwindle into streams in dry weather, swell again into torrents in a single night of rain.'

Meanwhile, six days of fine weather enabled Chesney to move over half of the expedition's stores to the shore. During this period Lynch arrived with a story that in March a Russian diplomat had come to Aleppo from Alexandria and, after visiting Bir, had inspected a stretch of the Euphrates downstream.[8] This Russian had talked about the British expedition, saying 'perhaps [it] might never take place at all'.

Chesney now had to decide where on the Euphrates the steamboats should be assembled and launched. The obvious choice was Bir, a town with a Turkish garrison, which offered better security than Beles, a desolate spot nearer to Aleppo but exposed to Arab raids. The real problem was that for seven miles above and below Bir there were no practical sites on the left bank because of the steep chalk cliffs (much favoured by nesting bald ibis*) that rise up from the river edge. The right bank, where the ground is flat, was still occupied by Ibrahim Pasha's troops.

In a bold gesture of defiance to Mehemet Ali, Chesney ordered Lynch to go to Bir without delay and select a site on the right bank of the river. Lynch took with him his elder brother Robert Lynch, a lieutenant in the Indian Army who was returning to his regiment from leave and had volunteered to join the expedition.

The Governor of Antioch came down to Suedia and was displeased to see how much progress had been made without any local help. In an attempt

---

* The bald ibis, a denizen of east Africa, is now an endangered species. A few nests may still be seen on the cliffs above Bir.

to forestall fresh hindrance, Chesney sent Estcourt and Charles Staunton off to Damascus with a protest to his superiors, who were themselves nervously awaiting Ibrahim Pasha's return from Egypt.

Rough seas now slowed the unloading. The captain of the *Columbine* was almost drowned when his boat overturned in the surf. But by the end of April the job was finished and Chesney was relieved to see the *George Canning* depart, as she had been chartered at considerable expense.

When Chesney learned that Ibrahim Pasha had returned to Syria, he sailed down on the *Columbine* to call on him at Tripoli. Colonel Campbell claimed later that Chesney had offended the pasha by invoking the sultan's *firman*, but Ibrahim Pasha replied courteously that he had received no new orders from his father. Estcourt, who saw Ibrahim a few days later and received the same message, describes him as 'a fat, vulgar looking, shrewd Arab'.[9]

On 3 May the *Columbine*'s 32-pounder guns fired a farewell salute that reverberated across the Bay of Antioch, attesting to the might of the Royal Navy and the impotence of the expedition on the shore.

Chesney had reported his plight to Lord Ponsonby in Istanbul and to the authorities at home. Meanwhile, the expedition stayed immobilized in its camp. Chesney tried to move things along elsewhere, but with only limited success. Murphy, Thomson and Ainsworth completed most of Beaufort's survey and caught malaria while dragging a chain through the marshes of Iskenderun. At Bir Lynch selected a site for the shipyard two miles downstream on the right bank of the river where a backwater afforded a natural slip. Since this location would be in territory occupied by the Egyptians, Chesney also prepared a fallback plan to launch the vessels farther down at Rakka, which the Egyptians had just yielded to the Sultan. Estcourt, Cockburn and Charles Staunton were sent on a six-week trip to Diyarbakir in eastern Anatolia to seek the support of Reshid Pasha, the new regional commander. The pasha was polite but noncommittal; he had only recently reoccupied Urfa and his authority was tenuous farther south.

Despite the fine weather and John Barker's hospitality, everyone at Suedia was anxious to get going. One caravan of light material passed undetected from Amelia Depot to Aleppo, but no other draught animals were available, so that nothing could be moved by land.

Chafing at forced inaction, Chesney decided to send the *Tigris* up the Orontes, thereby proving the capability of the steamer – Ibrahim Pasha had told Estcourt that an iron vessel would not even float[10] – and showing that a British expedition would not be deterred. Cleaveland dutifully made a second survey with Bell and Charlewood (who was almost drowned in the raging torrent). Their highly qualified report concluded that if the *Tigris* could steam at nine or ten knots, if she steered well and if she were warped over some of the rapids, the steamer could get up to the weirs on the plain of Antioch.

Riveters, smiths and carpenters were put to work. Two weeks later the iron shell of the *Tigris* was launched by John Barker's wife with a bottle of Lebanon wine. The engines were soon installed and the steamer was loaded with some of the plates and ribs of the *Euphrates*. In Lynch's absence Cleaveland was placed in command.

The trial runs were disappointing. The vessel steered badly and the engines could not develop enough power to get beyond the second set of rapids.

A few days earlier Ibrahim Pasha's wooden-hulled steamer *Nile* had anchored in the bay. The pasha's launch approached the mouth of the river, but then turned away to land him a mile to the north. Irked at receiving no salute from the guns at Amelia Depot, Ibrahim went up to Barker's villa and from there straight on to Antioch, passing an illegal caravan carrying some of Chesney's stores. The muleteers were ordered to return to Suedia upon pain of death.

Chesney judged correctly that the impasse could not continue. In mid-April Colonel Campbell sent Mehemet Ali a copy of the Sultan's *firman*, which had been issued only to the Turkish authorities in Iraq, but could be construed as applying to all Ottoman officials, including those in Egypt and Syria.[11] The viceroy expressed his sorrow that he had offended the British government and that valuable stores had been exposed to damage. He informed the consul that he was sending two tartars to Istanbul to obtain specific orders from the Sultan and that as soon as they returned, he felt sure that all would be well. He promised that if they had not returned within twenty-five days, he would on his own responsibility instruct Ibrahim Pasha to assist Chesney in every way.

The purpose of Mehemet Ali's charade was to demonstrate his nuisance value, but he was also careful not to press too hard. A general election in Britain had returned a Whig majority to Parliament, obliging Sir Robert Peel's Tory government to resign. In April 1835 William IV reluctantly appointed Melbourne to head a Whig administration. Palmerston returned to the Foreign Office and Sir John Cam Hobhouse, a wealthy reformer who had been a friend of Byron, became President of the India Board.

As a token of goodwill Mehemet Ali gave orders for his troops to evacuate a strip of disputed territory on the right bank of the Euphrates opposite Bir, thereby transferring jurisdiction over Chesney's shipyard site to Reshid Pasha and the local Turkish appointees. On 3 June Ibrahim's deputy came to the mouth of the Orontes to inform Chesney that Mehemet Ali had authorized his master to give the expedition every possible assistance.

The following day the *Tigris*, with Lynch in command, made a last vain effort to ascend the Orontes. Returning downstream the steamer hit the river bank several times owing to unresponsive steering. In a private letter to the East India House, Lynch reported that 'she would not go up more than abt. five miles up the river, and is a failure I fear.'[12] Chesney was crestfallen; only that morning he had written to a friend in London: 'We have the *Tigris* at work, and the Pacha is now affording, in every way, all the assistance we require, so that a few days will see me arrived at Bir.'[13] With a heavy heart Chesney gave orders to unship the paddles and haul the vessel out of the water. But instead of taking her hull completely apart, he decided to break it up into eight large sections to be transported on wagons.

Cleaveland was placed in charge of transporting everything by land. Charlewood was assigned the task of organizing mule and camel caravans to carry light loads to Lynch at Bir. Fitzjames directed gangs of workmen, many of them old or feeble, who cleared rocks away from the path and constructed a zigzag road up the first steep hill, which rises 100 feet above the plain. The road from Antioch to Bir was to be improved by Lynch.

The expedition's carpenters and smiths, helped by local artisans and using lumber from the area, started work on building wagons to carry the heavier loads over the hills. The two flatboats that had brought the engines ashore were fitted with axles and wheels; it was even hoped that their motion would be aided by the addition of masts and sails, rigged to catch the prevailing west wind. Oxen had for centuries provided the power to move things overland, but many of the bullocks, procured with much difficulty, were ill adapted to team work. Horses were easier to train. The most effective means of traction proved to be a combination of human and animal power.

By the middle of June the road to Antioch was declared usable for vehicles. The first ones to test the new road were the sturdy artillery wagons brought from England and now loaded with *Euphrates* plates. One by one, the wagons were pushed, pulled and warped up Zig Zag Hill (also called the 'Hill of Difficulty') by twenty horses and over a hundred men. Carefully lowered downhill, the wagons crossed the Great Kara Chai stream and were heaved up the next hill and down again across the Little Kara Chai to reach the level country around Antioch.

Some components of the steamers were too long to negotiate the tight bends of Zig Zag Hill. The keelsons – long beams that fastened the steamer's iron hull to its wooden floor – were lashed together to form a raft and pulled up the Orontes by trackers. Where the stream was too strong the raft was unlashed and each beam was pulled separately over the rocks or overland across a bend in the river.

The first vehicles to reach Jisr Hadid were Eden's two artillery wagons, which had been pulled through the streets of Antioch by sixty townspeople, described as 'a very riotous, unruly set'.[14] To avoid such incidents the next shipments were unloaded at Guzel Burj [Güzel Burc], a point on the Orontes outside the city, and moved from there by boat to Jisr Hadid.

But Chesney now faced a far more serious hazard for the transport. On his way back from Anatolia Estcourt had observed that the lower end of the road from Bir to Jisr Hadid, certified by Lynch as fit for vehicles, crossed an extensive marsh. Estcourt advised Chesney that, in his opinion, this part of the road would not stand up to heavy wagon traffic. (Peacock should have warned the expedition that the lush pasture land through which this road passed was famed in classical times as the spongy plain of Imma, where the Romans once lured Zenobia's heavy-armed cavalry to a miry defeat that led to the fall of Palmyra.)

Today the topography and aspect of the plain of Antioch have been changed by the Orontes drainage scheme. In Chesney's time the fertile croplands that now stretch north of Antioch were a huge swamp with a lake in the middle that was fed by streams from the surrounding hills. At Murad Pasha on the north edge of the swamp the Kara Su river was bridged by an ancient stone viaduct that carried the main highway from Iskenderun to the east. The same stream emerged at the south-western corner of the swamp to draw off water into the Orontes at Guzel Burj.

Following a brief, mosquito-ridden reconnaissance by Ainsworth and Bell in a hired fishing boat, Chesney issued new instructions. Guzel Burj would now be the initial transfer point, where the wagons would unload on to boats or rafts, which would float the loads across the lake to Murad Pasha, the second transfer point, from where wagons would convey them over good roads to Bir.

Boats were hired and rafts constructed. Fitzjames, now nicknamed 'Admiral', was placed in charge of operations at Guzel Burj, which Charlewood described as 'a miserable little village, with its hovels plastered with buffalo dung, and swarming with vermin'.[15] Another camp was established near the Murad Pasha causeway, where Estcourt's task was to receive the floated material, assemble empty wagons and find draught animals to haul the loaded vehicles to Bir.

Back at Suedia, Cleaveland and Charlewood addressed themselves to moving the heavy loads – ten boilers, four engine bedplates, two flatboats, a diving bell and the eight unwieldy sections of the *Tigris* hull – up and over the hills to Guzel Burj.

Charlewood's first train of four wagons carried two boilers weighing $3\frac{1}{2}$ and 4 tons, a $2\frac{1}{2}$-ton bedplate and one of the flatboats. The combined strength of seventy oxen and eighty dragropemen barely sufficed to pull the vehicles uphill; lowering them downhill was fraught with hazard. The wagons were soundly built, but the guiding poles that moved the front axles were often damaged by running into rocks. (On one occasion, when a guiding pole was shattered beyond repair, Charlewood replaced it with the roofbeam of a peasant's house after buying the entire house from its owner and tearing off the roof to get at the beam.) This particular wagon train reached Guzel Burj on 5 August, averaging two thirds of a mile per day.

Once Chesney saw that the expedition was finally on the move, he shifted his headquarters from Suedia to the shipyard site, which he named Port William in honour of the king. Earthworks designed by Cockburn now surrounded a small quadrangular fort with three stone buildings, workshops, tents and a levelled area for assembling the steamers. Huts were being built, but Chesney countermanded Lynch's proposals to install permanent roofing as too lavish.

The shipyard stood forty feet above the Euphrates, which reminded Estcourt of 'the Thames near Westminster Bridge, but not near so fine: for tho' extremely rapid in its current, it is shallow and has an island of sand in the space'.[16] Lynch's description was more graphic: 'The broad sheet of blue water broken by its green Islets, the clear blue sky and the varied tints on the hills as the sun is getting low gives us great beauty before us, but little comfort around us.'[17] (The view is still spectacular, but Port William and its buildings have been obliterated by the western approach to the E90 highway bridge across the Euphrates.)

On 19 July, the day after he reached Port William, Chesney assured Hobhouse that he expected to make up for all the delays and that the vessels would be complete 'in about eight weeks' time'.[18] Two days later he wrote to Sir Robert Grant in Bombay, informing him that the *Euphrates* should be at Basra by 1 October, ready to take an Indian mail up the river to Syria.[19] In his letter to Hobhouse Chesney reported that 'we have as yet been spared any thing like serious illness'.

For a while things went well. The first artillery wagons reached Port William with iron plates for the *Euphrates* and soon the riveters were busily putting together the sides of her hull. By the end of July the last wagon trains were being assembled at Amelia Depot, which was shortly to be decommissioned.

One of the flatboats was already at Guzel Burj, floating heavy loads across the lake, and the second was on its way from the coast.

A letter from Estcourt conveys the mood of well-being that followed the expedition's frustrating start:

> I am entirely without care. I never was so entirely contented with my existence before. In the first place a good deal is left to my guidance and judgment: continual riding to and fro is necessary and living in the country, feeding with the Sheiks of villages sometimes, with the Agas and Begs at others and sleeping any where, as rivers and grass for the horses render convenient. I have not had such thorough good health for many years: I am entirely well. Down goes the sun, darkness soon follows, I seek out the neighbouring stream, wash from head to foot, and then lay myself down to sleep: my horses picqueted round me: and my servant, who knows nothing but Turkish and Arabic, at a little distance. The stars and a bright heaven above me. I think over all that has happened to me in my life. I fancy what you all may be doing and thank God for the happiness I now enjoy.[20]

But the summers in northern Syria are cruel. The transition from the pleasant climate of Suedia to the oppressive 100-degree heat of Bir was too much for Chesney, the oldest member of the expedition, who had scorned the comforts of the Port William buildings to live in a bell tent. At the beginning of August he came down with sunstroke.

For several weeks Chesney lay comatose or half-conscious. At times he was not expected to live. The riveters halted their work to afford him quiet, but in Chesney's words 'it was soon discovered that the stillness greatly aggravated my fever, while the sound of eight hammers hard at work gave me immediate relief'.[21]

As second in command Lynch took Chesney's place. But by the end of August Chesney was sufficiently recovered to take charge again, allowing Lynch to leave Port William on a goodwill mission to the Arab tribes on the left bank of the Euphrates.

Chapter 7
New Faces and Old Problems

Good relations with the Arabs were essential for a descent of the Euphrates. They were also the key to the maintenance of a regular service up and down the river that might give Russia second thoughts about invading Iraq.

Colonel Taylor had reported that Ali Riza Pasha, the Governor of Baghdad, would give the expedition the fullest support. But the pasha's authority ran only where he had soldiers and the Arabs generally acted as they chose. Indeed, they held the East India Company in higher regard, because its agents paid cash for their horses and their dates. Only once did Taylor have any trouble arranging for the expedition's coal to be moved from Basra to depots as far upstream as Ana.

The purpose of Lynch's journey was to reconnoitre the left bank of the upper Euphrates and the desert where the Aniza tribe of Arabs raised camels and lived off the river villagers when the pasture lands dried up. Chesney hoped to establish charcoal depots at Rakka and Deir ez-Zor if the inhabitants could be induced by gifts of Sheffield and Glasgow goods to cut the brushwood along the river banks.

The Turkish governor of Urfa provided an escort for the party, which included Robert Lynch, Andrew Staunton and a newcomer to the expedition – Chesney's old friend William Elliot, who had recently appeared at Port William looking for something to do.

The story of the Euphrates expedition is peopled with a varied cast of characters, good and bad but almost all of them recognizable as products of the early nineteenth century. William S. A. Elliot was one of a kind.[1]

He was born in Calcutta, the youngest son of John Elliot, an East India

Company official;* his mother was an Indian woman. He was brought up in England, where he received a good education, studied medicine and became an accomplished draughtsman. After a while he left England for the Orient and served as a surgeon in the Turkish navy. In the 1828–9 war with Russia he was captured at Varna. A testimonial recounts that he was taken to the headquarters of Tsar Nicholas; after 'receiving from that monarch personal Abuse' Elliot was transported to Perm in Siberia. According to one account he escaped and made his way back to Istanbul, but Estcourt relates that 'he was released to his sorrow, for it was pleasant in Siberia'.

After he returned to Turkey Elliot decided to abandon a settled existence and became a wanderer. He learned Arabic, turned Moslem and assumed the role of a dervish – the barefoot vagrant who moves from village to village preaching the word of Islam.

Elliot, now also known as Dervish Ali, was travelling through Iraq on his way to India when he first met Robert Taylor. The Resident knew at once that he had found a man he could use. Elliot was sent on his first mission in the summer of 1830, when he served as interpreter for Bowater and James Taylor and escaped to tell the story of their deaths. The following year he helped Ormsby on his survey and met Chesney at the Residency just before the plague broke out. After descending the upper Euphrates valley on foot, he took his notes and sketches to Bombay. When he started preaching there, he was put into a lunatic asylum but was let out after a while by some mistake and went back to Baghdad.

Elliot had come to Port William from Anatolia, where Taylor had sent him to survey the route by which Xenophon and his Greek army had retreated from Mesopotamia through Kurdistan to the Black Sea. Peacock would have relished the story about Elliot, told long afterwards by Ainsworth, that 'a native damsel had been given to him as a spouse, in return for his having cured her of ophthalmia; but he exchanged her for a donkey, the latter being more useful in following the footsteps of the Greeks.'

Ormsby, a kindred soul, appreciated Elliot's 'wild and roving disposition'. But Elliot's colleagues on the Euphrates expedition found him hard to handle. Ainsworth complained that 'his habits were exceedingly flighty, and he could not be depended on for a moment'. When asked to make a written report, Elliot claimed that 'he had lost all habit of writing, and was, in utter contrast to Orientals, in a perpetual fidget. At one moment the chair was too high, at another the pen was bad.' Estcourt declared that Elliot was 'as

---

* Probably John Elliot (1765–1818), who was President of the Calcutta Board of Police and Conservancy. A William Elliott (sic), son of John Elliott, was christened in Calcutta on 26 April 1807; the mother's name is not shown in the register.

wild and mad as a man can be'. But Dervish Ali was a useful member of Lynch's mission, which was accomplished despite a skirmish with the Aniza in which Lynch's groom was slightly wounded.

Lynch and his party reached Aleppo at the beginning of October 1835. During their stay there they became acquainted with an Austrian traveller, Dr Helfer, who was journeying to India with his wife and two companions. The Helfers expressed great interest in the expedition and in Lynch's mission to the Arab tribes. In her memoirs Madame Helfer recalls their pleasure in meeting Lynch, 'a clever diplomatist and expert in Oriental languages',[2] while Elliot's 'refined features and a bright dark eye gave evidence of higher culture than you would have expected from his garb'. The dervish wore 'a coarse grey robe, a broad girdle round the waist with a pair of pistols in it, a shawl of camel's hair round his head, and red leather boots', the last being somewhat out of keeping with his role. A gazelle skin, thrown over his shoulders, served him as a mantle and a couch.

The Helfers and their companions were planning to journey east by way of Bir, Mosul and Baghdad down to the Persian Gulf, where a ship would take them on to India. Lynch gallantly suggested that they might enjoy a visit to Port William to meet Colonel Chesney and the other officers of the expedition.

Romantic and impractical, Dr Helfer and his wife could have stepped straight out of the pages of one of Peacock's novels. But their stay at Port William and the subsequent adventures of these two *Wandervögel* brought some comic relief to the hard-driven members of the expedition.

Born in 1810, Johann Wilhelm Helfer was the eldest son of a prosperous Austrian family in Prague. As a child he collected plants and insects. At the local university he studied medicine, transferring to Pavia (then under Austrian rule) to receive his degree. But botany and entomology still fascinated him; and it was on a stage coach journey home from a conference of naturalists at Hamburg that he met his future wife.

Pauline des Granges is described by Estcourt as 'pretty and young but has a spirit'.[3] She was nine years older than Dr Helfer (and one year older than Estcourt). Her father's family were Huguenots, several of whom had served in the Prussian army; her mother, a Bülow, traced her ancestry to the thirteenth century. They lived in a rococo manor house at Zinnitz, a village in the Lusatian pine forests seventy miles north of Dresden where her father owned a small estate.

Following their brief stage-coach encounter, Pauline des Granges corresponded with Helfer for several years and encouraged his love of nature and his dreams of exotic travel. In 1833 Helfer inherited a sizeable fortune along with responsibilities to younger brothers and sisters. Putting aside his travel ideas, he settled down in Prague, married Pauline des Granges and applied himself to the practice of medicine.

Two years later the Helfers, who were childless, broke loose from the tedium of Prague and moved to Smyrna [Izmir], the main seaport of western Anatolia, where Helfer could collect specimens of plants and insects, while treating local patients with homoeopathic herbs.

After three months of life in Smyrna, Helfer began to feel restless again. His wanderlust was whetted by meeting two distinguished-looking travellers who told him that they were nephews of the Amir of Afghanistan, on their way home after touring Europe incognito under the names of Mr Hunter and Mr Brown and financing their journey in Oriental style by periodic sales of gems. The lure of India was too strong to resist. The Helfers sold their possessions in Smyrna and sailed to Syria with the Afghans. When Lynch met them, they had been in Aleppo for several days, planning their onward journey. The invitation to visit Colonel Chesney and his expedition was accepted with pleasure.

Thus enlarged, the Lynch mission returned to Port William on 10 October. Chesney welcomed the Helfers and supplied them with tents. He appeared in better health than when Lynch had left, but his mind had been deranged by the sunstroke and only recently had it dawned upon him that the expedition was in deep trouble.

Throughout August and September the heavy loads had lumbered along the rough road from Suedia to Guzel Burj and had been floated cautiously across the lake to Murad Pasha. The last wagon train from the coast was unloaded on 7 September at Guzel Burj. By the end of the month the transfer station there was ready to close down after sending the empty wagons around the lake to Murad Pasha to carry the loads on to Port William.

The effort required to achieve such progress could not be sustained by men exposed to the summer heats and chills. Soon casualties began to occur. Bell was taken ill in July. A few weeks later Eden caught typhoid fever. And at the end of August, when Charlewood arrived with a wagon train at Guzel Burj, he found the camp deserted. Fitzjames lay unconscious in his tent, stricken with malaria, 'his tongue black and swollen, with one large blood-red crack across it'. A doctor recommended removing him to the local hospital, but Fitzjames suddenly opened his eyes, shook his head and muttered, 'I will die here.' In true service tradition, Charlewood resumed transferring his loads from the wagons to the boats, 'and during every spare moment employed myself dropping water gently upon his poor tongue'.[4]

The expedition had three doctors on its strength and could call on local medical help. As a result none of these cases proved fatal (although two sappers and a seaman died from various causes).

Estcourt kept well by constant riding between Murad Pasha and Port William, directing the wagon trains, clearing the roads and endeavouring to hire draught animals. But animals were becoming more and more difficult to obtain. By the beginning of October Chesney was complaining that nothing had reached Port William from Murad Pasha for almost three weeks.

This new setback to the transport was distressing, because the work at the shipyard had been going well. On 26 September the *Euphrates* was launched into the great river, sliding sideways down the twenty-five-foot slope with the aid of chains attached to a capstan fixed in the ground. When one of the chains was about to part the alert Cleaveland shouted, 'Let go the other chain!'[5] and the vessel skidded into the water, splashing thousands of spectators.

Chesney had been hoping to take the *Euphrates* down the river in October before the water level sank too low, leaving the *Tigris* to be completed at Port William. This schedule depended on timely arrival of the *Euphrates* engines, boilers and heavy machinery, which – as Lynch pointed out before he left – could only be ensured if horses and bullocks were purchased to cover Estcourt's needs. But Chesney, as he soon admitted, 'made the serious mistake – though perhaps the only one – of husbanding too closely the public funds entrusted to me.'[6] No animals were bought.

Perhaps illness had sapped Chesney's will; or else he may have feared that Lynch's habit of 'following Indian rather than the English Expenditures' might entail undue cost.[7] In any case, when Lynch returned to Port William with the Helfers, the equipment was still not there. A few days earlier Chesney had ruefully advised Sir John Hobhouse in London and Sir Robert Grant in Bombay that owing to the new delays his planned dates for leaving Bir and arriving at Basra were now indefinite.[8]

Ibrahim Pasha still professed friendship and voiced regret that, owing to pressure of work, Vincent Germain could not be spared to go with the expedition. But it was common knowledge in Syria that the unhelpful attitude of the pasha's officials reflected secret orders he had given after learning that the Sultan had declined to issue a *firman* instructing Mehemet Ali to assist the expedition. This unwelcome news was confirmed by Lord Ponsonby, who told Chesney that, owing to Russian opposition and the secret intrigues of Mehemet Ali's agents, he had failed to obtain the necessary documents.[9] Instead, a letter had been sent from Istanbul to Mehemet Ali on 18 June, stating that the Sultan was troubled by the non-commercial aspects of the project and intended to discuss them further with the British government. Pending word from London, Ponsonby advised Chesney to carry on as best he could under the general authority granted by the Sultan's December 1834 *firman*.

Although Chesney corresponded regularly with Ponsonby by tartar, normal communications with London were very slow. Arrangements had been made for the Malta-Alexandria packet to deliver and collect mail at a Syrian port. But an India Board despatch dated 1 June 1835, bringing Chesney the good news that the East India Company would advance £5000 against the purchase price of the two steamers, did not reach Port William until mid-August; the acknowledgment (by Lynch) was received in London shortly before Christmas.

Communication between Port William and Bombay, by way of Aleppo, Baghdad, Basra and the Persian Gulf, was also slow. The route across the desert to Baghdad held many perils. Chesney's July letter to Grant, despatched by courier on a fast dromedary, took forty days to reach its first relay point at Baghdad. A few weeks later a European-educated Turkish officer, Seyid Ali, sent by Ali Riza Pasha from Baghdad to help Chesney with the river Arabs, arrived at Port William on foot after he and his companions had been robbed by Aniza tribesmen of everything they had.

It had been planned that the Helfer party would be guests of Colonel Chesney for a few days while they made arrangements to join an eastbound caravan from Bir. But for the sick, discouraged widower the arrival of this young, cultured couple was a breath of fresh air from another world. Within forty-eight hours Chesney invited the Helfers to join the expedition as passengers and steam down to Basra on the *Euphrates*, which was expected to be ready in December. His offer was accepted and Dr Helfer agreed to place his knowledge of medicine, natural history and geology at the service of the expedition (somewhat to the chagrin of Ainsworth, who thought those fields were adequately covered by himself).

The Helfers' two companions, 'Mr Hunter' and 'Mr Brown', presented a slight problem. Pauline Helfer recalls that 'our Affghan friends were distant with the English'.[10] Originally, Lynch had been quite dubious about them, but he later reassured her, saying: 'The appearance of these men, with my knowledge of Asiatics, at first very much surprised me, and I was in fact disposed to regard them as impostors, who are to be found here as well as in Europe; but I am now convinced that they belong to the class of honourable Asiatics, who keep their word and conscientiously follow the rules of the Koran.'[11] Chesney offered them the choice of joining the expedition as passengers, or travelling by land to Basra and meeting the

Helfers there. They chose to go on by land, accepting the Helfers' Turkish money (which would be useless beyond Basra) and giving Pauline Helfer valuable jewels in exchange.

Dr Helfer had already been sent off to Kilis, a village on the road between Murad Pasha and Bir, to attend to an emergency case. The doughty Estcourt had collapsed with typhoid fever and was under Elliot's care. Estcourt declared later that the physician 'came in time to save me from a severe system of treatment, which might have finished me'.[12] Helfer's homoeopathic remedies proved more effective, although Estcourt could not return to duty for several weeks.

Estcourt was badly missed, for the rainy season was due shortly and most of the heavy equipment was still at Murad Pasha. Some loads were moving slowly along the road to Bir as far as the Sajur river, the demarcation line where Ibrahim Pasha's jurisdiction now ended. Here, only eight hours' journey from Port William, three loaded wagons had been halted for a month because the Egyptian officials would not allow oxen to cross the river.

To replace Estcourt, Chesney put Lynch in charge of a concerted effort to bring all the material in to Port William without delay. Funds were provided to buy animals. Every fit officer, soldier, sailor or civilian was mobilized to expedite movement along the road. Seyid Ali from Baghdad was assigned the delicate task of arranging transport across the five-mile stretch of 'no-man's-land' between the Egyptian and Turkish outposts and dealing with the obstructive governor of Bir, an Ottoman official thought to be in Ibrahim Pasha's pay.

By the middle of November two of the *Euphrates* boilers had reached Port William, dragged by oxen and men. But there was now much sickness at Murad Pasha, which Ainsworth termed 'the worst of the stations' with a climate 'often replete with morbid miasma'.[13] As a scientist he noted dutifully that crickets, frogs and centipedes invaded the encampment every evening, while troops of jackals yelled and barked outside the tents at night. 'Most troublesome of all insects,' he added, 'being day visitors, were the great Amazonian or legionary ants, which penetrated everywhere and destroyed all my collections of natural history.'

The rains came on early in November and the level of the lake began to rise. The station at Murad Pasha was evacuated, leaving wagons standing in water up to their axles and the diving bell submerged, no one quite knew where. As the weather worsened and the sick list mounted, Lynch recommended to Chesney that the transport should be suspended until the spring.

By this time Estcourt was back at work as officer in charge of operations at Port William. From close contact with Chesney, now ill again, Estcourt had recognized that the colonel was an 'obstinate, unguidable and imprudent' man.[14] But on this occasion it is clear that Chesney's decision to reject Lynch's suggestion saved the expedition from a humiliating retreat. Chesney felt sure that if he could hold his men together, especially the skilled shipyard workmen whose contracts were about to expire, they could somehow complete the vessels and have them ready to go down the river when the water rose again in the spring. A belated review of the accounts showed that the expedition was badly overdrawn, but Chesney was confident that the British government would not let the project fail for lack of funds. Pending word from London, he drew down his bank balance and borrowed £2,000 from two relatives by marriage, Hampden Gledstanes and George Glas Sandeman.

The last six weeks of 1835 saw the expedition at its lowest point. Chesney's illness proved to be a bad case of malaria and once again he almost died. Lynch fell sick and was replaced by Cleaveland, the man of determination who had brought the heavy wagons over the hills from Suedia to the lake.

Cleaveland and Charlewood managed to warp the boiler wagons to dry ground 'by manual labour',[15] and on 9 December the last of the *Euphrates* boilers arrived at Port William, dragged by all the able-bodied members of the expedition, since the governor of Bir had ordered his subjects not to allow their bullocks to be used.

Recovery of the diving bell was not easy. Lynch had wanted to abandon it, but Chesney was so indignant that he got out of bed and prepared to ride to Murad Pasha in defiance of doctor's orders and salvage the bell himself. Finally the purser, Alexander Hector, who had survived the ordeals of MacGregor Laird's Niger expedition, volunteered to undertake the job.

Searchers with bamboo poles waded for several days until they located the bell in six feet of water half a mile from dry land. It weighed close to three tons and several more days were spent rolling the clumsy object under water to a point where it could be loaded on a wagon. (It stayed on the wagon for weeks due to lack of oxen and was finally brought to Port William in February 1836.)

The difficulties with the Turkish authorities at Bir were at first perplexing, since Chesney had expected that the Sultan's *firman* would be respected in his own domain. Soon, however, it became clear that Reshid Pasha, who governed eastern Anatolia, had heard exaggerated reports about the earthworks at Port William and the quantities of guns and ammunition stored there. It was even rumoured that the flatboats were designed for moving troops.

The motives of Reshid Pasha, an experienced politician, were not easy to divine. The French consul in Aleppo fancied that there might be 'un commun accord' between Reshid and Ibrahim to frustrate the entire project.[16] Chesney suspected Russian intrigues at Istanbul and reported that one of their spies had been to Reshid's camp in Anatolia.

Most probably, Reshid Pasha was concerned that the two steamers might somehow interfere with his own plans for a spring campaign, to be conducted jointly with Ali Riza Pasha of Baghdad, against a Kurdish rebel in northern Iraq. While this operation was going on, the province of Baghdad, long coveted by Mehemet Ali, would be exposed to a sudden attack from the west. Egyptian forces had already occupied the strategic town of Deir ez-Zor on the right bank of the Euphrates in September 1835, while Lynch was there. Ibrahim Pasha often masked his words, but he had been heard to say that he might accompany the British steamers on their voyage down the river with a detachment of his troops.

Reshid Pasha, no friend of foreigners, decided that it would be prudent to delay the completion of vessels that might easily be seized by the Egyptians for an invasion of Iraq. He sent a new governor to Bir with specific orders to forbid anyone to help the expedition. In response to Chesney's complaints, Lord Ponsonby promised to ask the Sultan to clear up the misunderstanding with a strong *firman*.

The beleaguered occupants at Port William were now exposed to the winter rain and snow. The leaky buildings were converted to a hospital, except for a portion used by the officers for a mess room. Pauline Helfer, suffering from typhus, was dimly aware that in the evenings, after the officers had left, her husband would carry her, wrapped up in rugs, from their snow-covered tent to the mess room and watch over her all night, carrying her back again before breakfast.

By mid-December the interior of the *Euphrates* was far enough along to permit Chesney, the Helfers and some others to move into quarters on the vessel. Cockburn, who had been ill for some time, was invalided home (though he reappeared a few weeks later, after his mother – described as 'a lady of superior mind' – urged him to return[17]). The remainder carried on as best they could ashore. One of Estcourt's letters paints a sorry picture:

> Last night was again a deluge of rain: the whole hospital were obliged to decamp in the middle of the night, and seek shelter from the receptacle of the destitute, a large flat bottomed boat. This boat of unusually large dimensions was fortunately built some time since in order to transport coals down the river: it has never been launched but capsized on shore has been occupied as a lodging, and was, except the *Euphrates*, the only dry lodging to be found. Under it have crept boiler makers,

soldiers and sailors: every one in deed, who was driven in
succession from his summer habitation by either cold or rain.
Now it has become, I believe, tolerably comfortable inside, tho'
I never saw the interior: I only see people coming in and out
on their bellies: but I conclude there must be some comfort
within, for a funnel has shewn itself thro' the bottom, i.e. the
present top, from which occasionally issues smoke.[18]

The advent of cold, dry weather improved the expedition's health and
spirits. One by one, the *Tigris* boilers reached Port William despite Reshid
Pasha's ban on local assistance, which stayed in force. The vessel was being
modified to correct the defects noted on her abortive Orontes trip. All
thought of a December voyage by the *Euphrates* had been given up, because
there were not enough fit seamen to man the boat.

By now the Helfers had become accepted members of the expedition,
although one Lancashire boilermaker, described by Estcourt as 'a funny
fellow', remarked on Pauline Helfer's sensible custom of wearing her hair
short and dressing as a man: 'Them two, Sir, puts my pipe out. I never
knows which is the man and which is the woman.'[19] Opinions among the
officers were mixed. Estcourt, a grateful patient, found Dr Helfer 'a famous
fellow: clever and enterprising: speaks English: and is ready for any thing',
whereas Ainsworth noted sourly that 'the learned doctor had many of the
characteristics of his countrymen. He was at once secretive and stubborn.'[20]
Pauline Helfer irritated Estcourt by her requests for special favours and he
wrote his sister that 'Ladies have no business on such parties'.[21] Charlewood
recalls that she was 'a kind-hearted, amiable woman, rather romantic',
adding that he 'never was very attentive to her, but she had plenty of
attention from others'.[22] Chesney gladly assigned them the stern cabin on
the *Euphrates*, which had been intended for himself. It became his habit to
accompany Pauline Helfer on her daily walk to the only two trees at Port
William, although she could sometimes see him shivering with fever as they
conversed politely in French.

Recognizing finally that his health would never improve as long as he
stayed at Port William, Chesney decided to go to Iskenderun in January
1836 to arrange with the British Consul for the artisans' passage home and
then to tour Cilicia, a mountainous province with a brisk climate, where it
was thought that coal might be found.

The exploring party was made up of the surveying team: Murphy,
described by Pauline Helfer as 'an amiable and scientific man, but never
ready, and therefore called "Mr Tardy" ';[23] his assistant William Thomson;
Andrew Staunton; Ainsworth, who was nicknamed 'Tertius' because, next

to Estcourt, Chesney seemed to rely on him most; and Yusuf Sadr, an interpreter from the British consulate in Aleppo. Dr Helfer was prevailed upon to join the party despite his protests that he could not find interesting plants or insects when the ground was covered with twelve inches of snow.

On the day set for their departure Chesney fainted as he climbed up from his cabin to the deck. But the next day he resolutely got up, went ashore and was helped to mount his horse. Murphy and Ainsworth had both been ill and the horses were lame. As the party filed off, led by Chesney in his cloak, Pauline Helfer was reminded of the image of Don Quixote and his horse Rosinante.

Ainsworth noted gleefully that at Aintab [Gaziantep], the first town on the journey, Dr Helfer was thrown by his horse into a snowbank. The next morning he announced that he was going back to Port William. (Actually he had located a friendly compatriot in Aintab, and his motive was to fetch his wife and spend some pleasant weeks there before they moved back to the comfort of Aleppo.)

Chesney and his other companions regained their health exploring the Cilician hills. No coal was found, but they did locate a rich deposit of plumbago (the lead used in pencils).

Chesney returned to Port William in time to witness the arrival, on 27 February 1836, of the last boiler for the *Tigris*, which had been launched the previous week. The wagon was drawn by 104 oxen, urged on by 52 local drivers. This memorable event, celebrated by a discharge of guns and rockets, took place 329 days after the expedition had first landed at the mouth of the Orontes. In his testimony before the select committee of the House of Commons Chesney had allowed thirteen days for the whole transport from Suedia to Bir.[24]

The expedition was now back to strength. The *Columbine* had come to Iskenderun, bringing four sappers (two of whom had been originally put on the *Alban* steamer and then sent back to England) and contributing six volunteer seamen from her crew. But eight men had been lost from sickness, not counting the local workmen, whose casualties are not recorded.

Spring was approaching, the water was rising in the river, and the local authorities had changed their tune. At the last moment Reshid Pasha had received the Sultan's *firman*, while Ibrahim Pasha provided all kinds of help, following a stern warning Mehemet Ali had received from Palmerston in December 1835. The viceroy had been told bluntly that 'His Majesty's government are determined that the undertaking which they have commenced, and which so far from being dangerous to the Sultan, must be advantageous to Turkey, shall not fail in consequence of the obstacles which bad faith in any quarter may oppose to it.'[25]

This was an opportune time for Estcourt's clergyman brother to pay a visit to Port William, where he recorded that 'many a wan and haggard countenance which has scarce known a smile for months, now brightens up at the idea of quitting the glaring white cliffs of Bir'.[26] In fact, things moved faster than expected. A despatch from Lord Ponsonby warned Chesney that a Russian move into Anatolia was once again a serious threat and that if war broke out Ibrahim Pasha might be tempted to seize the two British steamers for an invasion of Iraq.[27] The ambassador urged Chesney to get the vessels down the river as quickly as he could.

Following Ponsonby's advice, Chesney quietly made preparations for the *Euphrates* to drop down from Port William to a new anchorage at Beles, a remote spot frequented by Arab tribes where there were no Egyptian troops. As a decoy, he sent Lynch north with a party to survey the mountain gorges of the Euphrates and call on the local provincial governors. The *Tigris*, now almost ready, would take the rest of the expedition down the river as soon as Lynch returned.

The principal duty assignments had already been set before the expedition left England. Cleaveland would command the *Euphrates* with thirty-four persons aboard in addition to Chesney, who planned to divide his time between the two steamers. Besides the Helfers, this vessel would carry Estcourt, Murphy, Charlewood, Fitzjames, Ainsworth, the two interpreters Seyid Ali and Rassam and an engineer from the Laird shipyard. The crew would number thirteen, including a resourceful Maltese steward and an American negro cook who is described by the discriminating Dr Helfer as 'unfortunately not skilled in his art'.[28]

The *Tigris*, under Lynch's command, would carry thirty-one persons, including Lynch's brother, Eden, Cockburn, the two Stauntons, Thomson, Hector, Elliot and Yusuf Sadr (the two interpreters) and a Laird engineer. The crew numbered twelve, including two Maltese cooks.

Dr Helfer and his wife were summoned from Aleppo. Pauline Helfer occupied herself during the few days before the *Euphrates* was to leave Port William by arranging the books in the ship's library. Peacock would have appreciated Dr Helfer's pleasure that, in addition to technical works, it included 'Addison, Johnson, Shakspeare, Gibbon and a few humourists, which she has placed upon the drawing room table, that they may be always at hand'.[29]

Chapter 8
Steaming down the Great River

Shortly after Chesney returned from Cilicia, a despatch arrived from Sir John Hobhouse, the new President of the Board of Control, dated 2 November 1835 and received at Port William on 29 February 1836. Hobhouse had just learned about Chesney's sunstroke in August and urged him to be more careful of his health. He recognized that the delay caused by Mehemet Ali had entailed unforeseen expense and promised to seek additional funding. Chesney and his officers were cheered by this news and by Hobhouse's assurances that:

> due allowance is made for all these obstacles, and full credit
> given for the spirit, energy and perseverance which have
> distinguished your own conduct, and that of the officers under
> your command. You may depend upon receiving every support
> from the home authorities.[1]

The minister had himself experienced the delays and frustrations of Oriental travel. In his twenties Hobhouse had accompanied Byron to Albania, Greece and western Anatolia and had written a two-volume account of their journey. As a friend of Byron, and later his executor, Hobhouse had supported the Greek independence movement, although he had never been back to the Near East.

Hobhouse had entered politics as a radical Whig and had once been jailed for libellous contempt of the House of Commons. He entered parliament in 1820 and held various posts in the Whig ministries between February 1832 and April 1833 and from June to November 1834. When Melbourne became premier again in April 1835, Hobhouse was made President of the India

74

Board, while his predecessor Charles Grant was appointed Colonial Secretary and created Lord Glenelg. In his new position Hobhouse combined the enthusiasm of his youth with the gravity that comes with public office and inherited wealth. In some ways his character developed along the same lines as Peacock's, although they came from different worlds and in the 1830s were not acquainted with one another. In old age, however, they became neighbours and close friends.

One of Hobhouse's first achievements was to persuade the East India Company directors in August 1835 that they should place orders for two large steamers capable of maintaining a service between Bombay and Suez for eight months out of the year in conjunction with the Admiralty packet to Alexandria. (The enterprising Thomas Waghorn had already organized a firm to transfer mail between Alexandria and Suez.) The new vessels, costing £29,000 apiece, would steam from England around the Cape to Bombay. Pending agreement on the sharing of expenses between the British government and the East India Company, the canny directors reserved the right to assign them to the Persian Gulf squadron of the Indian Navy.

Hobhouse's attitude towards the Euphrates expedition was dispassionate. He had been out of Parliament between April 1833 and July 1834 and had not participated in the cabinet decision to endorse the project. On the other hand, like many Whigs, he had put aside his Greek inclinations to support Palmerston's policy of backing Turkey against the Russian threat. Now, as head of the department in charge of the expedition, it was his duty to ensure that it should not fail. But in seeking additional funds from parliament and the East India Company, Hobhouse was determined that the object of the expedition should be more narrowly defined. Relations with Russia had improved during 1835 and there was less fear of a Russian advance into Iraq; in consequence, the concept of the Euphrates as a barrier patrolled by armed steamboats began to lose appeal. Hobhouse saw clearly that, in order to get money for the expedition, he must stress its limited purpose as an experimental survey of the river that would be terminated when its work was done.

Chesney's October letter announcing an indefinite delay did not arrive in London until the end of December. By that time officials at the India Board had calculated that £16,000 would keep the expedition going until the end of July 1836, when Chesney should have completed the survey of the Euphrates river. The East India Company was invited to contribute one half of this amount. A six-page 'Memorandum respecting the Euphrates Expedition and the Designs of Russia',[2] prepared by Peacock, failed to sway the directors. Hobhouse's request was turned down and a deadlock continued until the end of March 1836, when the Company agreed to make the contribution after it obtained satisfactory assurances for sharing the costs of the proposed Red Sea service. It was not until 10 August 1836 that Parliament voted £8,000 for the expedition after the East India Company had committed an equal amount, to be paid when Chesney had completed the return voyage. Hobhouse, wise in the ways of public finance, had already secured from the Treasury an advance of £5,000 against the India Board vote.

Wednesday 16 March 1836, Chesney's forty-seventh birthday, was chosen to be the date of the first trial trip for the *Euphrates*. After the customary morning service the king's commission was read out, reciting the purpose of the expedition and praising 'his dear and powerful ally', the Sultan.[3] (The governor of Bir and many other notables were on board for the occasion.) Rules of conduct were set forth: breakfast at daybreak, dinner at 5.30 p.m., lights out at 9.30 p.m. and, to Dr Helfer's regret, no smoking allowed below deck.

Steam was already up and the smoke had attracted a huge crowd to the scene. Around noon the gangway was removed and the lines cast off. Helfer's diary records that 'even the rigid muscles of the Colonel's face betrayed his emotion by a slight quiver when the inevitable "Hip, hip, hurrah!" of the sailors was heard, and the steamer was for the first time in motion.'

The course was set upstream for Bir. As the heavily laden vessel struggled up a narrow channel between an island and the bank of the river, the engines could not prevail against the strong current and a contrary wind. An anchor was cast but the chain cable broke and the *Euphrates* went aground, freed herself and grounded once again. Helfer was told that the main cabin was full of water and that the plants he had put under the table were soaked. While putting them into fresh blotting paper, he heard the vessel grating on the pebbles in the river bed, hold fast for a moment and then suddenly turn around to head downstream.

The steamer was brought under control and anchored below Port William. There was no damage to the ship but the quartermaster had been injured. Estcourt reported that he 'was engaged in steering, when the vessel tailing into shoal water, the rudder was forced out of its position with considerable violence; his thumb became jambed with one of the tiller ropes, and was entirely torn out of the socket.'[4]

The next morning, after the best hard coal had been used to get up steam and all unneeded objects had been taken ashore, the *Euphrates* steamed briskly up to Port William. Mindful of British prestige, Chesney gave orders to repeat the ascent to Bir by a deeper channel. This time he was pleased to see her go up the rapid 'in the finest style'[5] and a 21-gun salute was fired in honour of the Sultan. The vessel turned around above Bir and returned to Port William. The inhabitants of Bir believed that they had seen a miracle and Fitzjames thanked St Patrick for a successful day.

Chesney's letter to Sir Robert Grant in Bombay was proudly headed '*Euphrates* Steamer descending, March 17/36'. After reviewing the state of the expedition, Chesney advised the governor that he expected to be 'at Bussora, or rather Korna, ready to ascend the River between the middle and the end of May'. He attached a list of stores that would be needed for the return voyage and suggested that, to be on the safe side, 9 July should be the return date. If Grant could send off a mail by steamer from Bombay to reach Korna by the first week of July, Chesney would get it to Iskenderun in time to put it on an Admiralty packet expected there on 28 July. The packet would bring the 1 July mail from England, which Chesney would immediately take down the river so that it might get to Bombay by 18 or 20 August.[6] A copy of this letter was sent to Sir John Hobhouse in London with an urgent request for the Admiralty packet to be arranged.[7] To expedite matters, Chesney also wrote directly to Admiral Sir Josias Rowley, commander-in-chief of the Mediterranean fleet.[8]

Chesney's immediate task was to move the two steamers 101 miles downstream to the relative safety of Beles. He decided that the *Euphrates* should leave immediately after reloading the articles that had been put on shore. Lynch, who returned to Port William on 18 March, would follow with the *Tigris* in a few days. The *Euphrates* would conduct a survey of this uncharted stretch of river and would pass the information back to Lynch.

The survey was carefully planned. Estcourt and his brother, who had nervously agreed to join the expedition as far as Beles, mapped the right bank of the river on foot, spending the nights among puzzled but friendly Arabs. Their data was correlated with astronomical observations carried out by Murphy from a boat. Two other boats, commanded by Cleaveland and Charlewood, would take turns floating down the river once the *Euphrates* was anchored; they would take soundings for the next twenty miles, leave their boat with the Arabs or hide it in the grass, and return on foot to the steamer, to act as pilots for the stretch they had covered.

The *Euphrates* was accompanied by an ungainly craft derided by everyone save Chesney, who had ordered that the flatboat (the former dormitory) should be used to convey coal and other bulky supplies down the river, thereby lightening the steamer's draught. Fitzjames, who had poled this rudderless boat across the Lake of Antioch, was placed in charge.

On 20 March the *Euphrates* commenced her voyage, piloted by Cleaveland, who had been down the river the day before. Ainsworth, looking at the paddle wheels' double wake, mused that 'The scream of the startled pelican or the gurgle of some large siluroid wallowing in the waters, was no longer necessary to break the silent ripple.'[9]

Fifteen minutes later they heard a noise like thunder. The vessel grounded on a sandbank and despite every effort remained stuck fast for two days.

Freed by a rise in the water, they steamed safely through a rocky gorge where Estcourt was standing at the top of a cliff, waving his hat to warn them of a dangerous whirlpool. But more groundings and releases occurred as they descended the winding river. Finally, on 31 March as the vessel rounded a bend north of Kara Bambuj, only thirty miles short of Beles, Cleaveland's eyes were momentarily blinded by the sun and he steered the *Euphrates* on to a bank of pebbles where she remained for eighteen days.

While stranded here, Chesney and his companions had their first taste of Arab tribal feuds. Sheikh Hasan of the Beni Said tribe, who lived along the river and had been kind to the British surveyors, was invited aboard the *Euphrates* and presented with a shotgun. One of the ship's boats was taking the sheikh ashore when they were fired on by a hostile tribe. A single blank cartridge discharge from the steamer's gun scattered the assailants. One of them had been winged by a shot from the sheikh's new present, but philosophically remarked: 'Inshallah! I shall get well and have my turn.'[10]

Swallows were starting nests in the *Euphrates* paddle boxes when a rise in the water freed the steamer. As Chesney was preparing to move off, Fitzjames arrived on foot to report that the flatboat, which had been sent on ahead, had been carried away by the current and was shattered on some rocks. The crew were all safe but fifteen tons of coal, along with provisions, chains and all of Fitzjames's effects lay in water seven fathoms deep. The *Tigris*, which arrived at that moment after having been thirteen days aground further up the river, was ordered to gather up whatever could be saved. Next morning (19 April), in Estcourt's words, '[the *Euphrates*] sailed down the river from Carrabambouge in gallant style'[11] (eleven and a half knots according to Helfer) and anchored in a narrow, deep creek near Beles between the right bank and an island covered with shrubs. The *Tigris* arrived soon afterwards.

The Euphrates valley broadens as the stream approaches its great turn towards Iraq. In Roman times the river flowed close to the western escarpment, where the ancient city of Beles dominated the river bend and was known as 'the port of the Syrians'. But over the centuries the river changed its course and in April 1836, when Chesney's two steamers cast anchor, rich meadows lush with spring flowers and knee-high grass stretched on either side as far as the eye could see. The ruins of Beles were barely visible three miles off to the west. (The construction of the Assad dam opposite Kalat Jaber has created a vast lake that extends fifty miles upstream, so that water laps once again against the Beles cliffs.)

Ainsworth, a keen antiquarian, declared that this verdant pasture land had once been a 'paradise', or boar-hunting preserve, for Persian satraps.[12] Helfer was also enthralled, for he had discovered that the *Euphrates* was anchored in a fetid backwater where decaying vegetable matter bred swarms of insects, including the rare *Megacephale euphratica oliv.*, which he had long desired to net.[13] Both doctors, however, noted recurrences of malaria in this hot, unhealthy place. In a letter to his friend Cabell at the India Board, Chesney wrote glumly: 'The ague only spares me alternate days at most, but I have had more here owing to many causes.'[14]

The published accounts of the Euphrates expedition gloss over a strange incident at the Beles anchorage that vexed Chesney for a fortnight and reveals some of the tension that had been built up by months of frustration and delay. In a letter to Cabell dated 2 May, Chesney alluded to some disciplinary problems on the *Tigris*, now resolved, that had prolonged his stay at Beles.[15] In a subsequent letter to Hobhouse, Chesney stated the facts as follows:

> The dispute arose about reading aloud after dinner, between Lt. R. Lynch of the Indian army and Dr. Staunton and Mr. Cockburn; Lt. [Henry] Lynch ultimately took the part of his brother, although only a passenger; and he placed the other two gentlemen in arrest, in which state they remained 18 days until I released them on the grounds that the proceeding was illegal, because charges were sent of which they did not receive the copies enjoined by the Articles of War.
>
> This step of mine was followed by a severe order; calling for mutual apologies beginning with Mr. Lynch, and making known my determination to suspend all from duty, and leave them at Aleppo pending the orders of Govt. The concessions were immediately agreed to by all the parties except Lt. Lynch, who expected that I would have supported him unhesitatingly; it required therefore more time to make him see reason; and preparations were already made to supersede him, when he made the desired concession, and, as all promised it should be a real and cordial reconciliation, I promised to bury the matter in oblivion.[16]

Concerned that Lynch might be too much under his elder brother's influence, Chesney decided to move his quarters permanently to the *Tigris* instead of keeping his papers and belongings on the *Euphrates* and spending part of his time on each vessel.

Chesney had never felt warmly towards Lynch, the second in command eighteen years his junior who had been wished upon him by the India Board. Although both of them were Irish, their temperaments and traditions were worlds apart. Their relationship had started badly when Lynch's survey of the Orontes and his failed ascent with the *Tigris* had shown up Chesney's own poor planning. Lynch had been at fault in failing to detect the Imma swamp. But his proposal to postpone the transport always rankled Chesney, who wrote months afterwards when reviewing what the expedition had achieved: 'I never heard of a feeling of doubt, save for a time with Lynch.'[17]

At least one of Chesney's colleagues was shocked by the harsh way in which he had handled this affair. After the expedition was over, Estcourt, whose brother had served as Chesney's secretary during the Beles stay, wrote home: 'I should desire to take breath before I engaged under his guidance again. Willy will best understand, why I should hesitate in taking on again.[18]

When the surveying boats first reached the Beles anchorage, the river banks were deserted. But when the steamers arrived, the plain on the left shore was covered with Arab tents; men, women and children lined the bank, while herds of camels, water buffaloes and horses and flocks of sheep were grazing in the fields. A similar encampment, belonging to a part of the Aniza tribe, was pitched on the right bank where the Arabs could overlook the vessels and command the road that led west to Aleppo.

The first skirmish occurred when some of the Aniza pounced on Corporal Greenhill, one of Murphy's surveying team, and cut off his brass buttons, thinking they were gold. A detachment led by Estcourt, Cleaveland and Fitzjames went after them, but encountered a larger force of cavalry which tried to cut the British off. Cleaveland fired at them and as he raised his naval telescope to see them better they shied off. Meanwhile Estcourt quickly led the group to higher ground where he could signal to the steamers. It started to rain and, after several feint attacks, the Arabs moved away. Estcourt's force marched back to their vessels; however, in sliding down the hill Fitzjames broke his ankle bone.

Anxious to avoid a real conflict, Chesney sent Elliot, dressed in his dervish robe, to the main camp of the Aniza with a message inviting their chiefs to visit the steamers. A few days later Elliot returned on horseback with three young sheikhs and an escort of dromedary-mounted lancers. After Chesney had welcomed them to the *Euphrates*, Elliot and Rassam, another interpreter, conducted them to their tents, where they watched a display of Congreve rockets as they ate.

The next day Chesney showed them over the ship and fired off a few of her guns. In the course of their visit they saw Fitzjames stretched out on his couch and recommended eating lamb as the best means of curing a broken bone. Serious discussions followed and the sheikhs proposed that there should be a treaty of eternal peace and friendship between the Aniza tribe and the government of King William IV. Chesney was unsure of his authority in this field, but Rassam drew up documents in English and Arabic that were duly signed. There was also talk of bartering Arab wool for British manufactures, although Ainsworth noted that aphrodisiacs were the products the sheikhs most desired.

Chesney hoped to build on this foundation by arranging a peace treaty between the Aniza and their traditional enemies, the Shammar tribe who lived farther east. But the sheikhs demurred strongly and Chesney's subsequent claim that he had convinced them with a quotation from the Koran is difficult to accept.[19]

One important task, delayed by these side issues, remained to be done: the trials of the two vessels under controlled conditions with and against the current. They were made at the beginning of May in the presence of John Caldow and John Struthers, two new Laird engineers who had come out to relieve the original team.

Despite the changes made at Port William, the *Tigris* trials were disappointing. The engines worked well and the steering was much improved, but she could not stem the six-knot current and had to make her way upstream by keeping out of the main stream. The blunt formation of the bow caused a wave to build up ahead of the vessel, while the rounded stern retarded her movement through the water. Chesney admitted that he had insisted on these features of the original design to ease the passage through the twisting stretch of river in the Lemlum swamps, so that Laird was not in any way to blame.

The *Euphrates* trials were entirely satisfactory and the vessels made ready to proceed. The *Tigris* departed on 4 May, followed by the *Euphrates* on 8 May, and William Estcourt went back to Aleppo on his journey home. The interpreter John Bell stayed behind with the expedition's horses, which were tended at pasture by the Arabs until they should be needed to carry the Indian mail to the Mediterranean coast.

A letter from the India Board, brought by the Laird engineers, warned

Chesney that the new funding would only carry him through 31 July.[20] In his reply to Cabell, Chesney assured him that 'in my view the main objects are accomplished and I support the Govt. decision. In any case', he added, 'war may end the matter another way.'

1 Thomas Love Peacock as a young man, Roger Jean, *c.*1805

2 Francis Rawdon Chesney, sketch made in 1841, C. Grey

3 Chesney descending the Euphrates on a kelek in 1831 (note well section left foreground)

4 View of Ana on the Euphrates, drawn by Fitzjames, 1836

5 View of Baghdad and the Tigris Bridge, drawn by Fitzjames, 1836

6 Lord Ellenborough, President, India Board 1828-30, 1834-5, 1814, F. R. Say, *c.*1845

8 Sir Robert Grant, Governor of Bombay 1835-8. F. C. Lewis after J. Slater, Grillion's Club portrait, c.1813

7 Charles Grant, President, India Board 1830-4, F. C. Lewis after J. Slater, Grillion's Club portrait, 1812

10 Viscount Palmerston, Foreign Secretary 1830-40, 1835-41, John Partridge, c.1844-5

9 Sir John Cam Hobhouse, President, India Board 1835-41, C. Turner after J. Lonsdale, 1826

12 Ibrahim Pasha, drawn by Estcourt, 1835

13 Major-General James Estcourt, Roger Fenton, 1855

14 Commander James Fitzjames in 1845

15 The boiler passing the bar of the Orontes, drawing by Fitzjames, 1835

16 The first caravan preparing to leave Amelia Depot, drawing by Estcourt and A. Staunton, 1835

17 The first boiler fording the Kara Chai, drawing by Fitzjames, 1835

18a Buyuk Kara Chai, facing north, May 1988, J. S. Guest

18b Kuchuk Kara Chai, facing north, May 1988, J. S. Guest

19 Jisr Hadid (the Iron Bridge): (a) view facing west, (b) view facing east, 1988, J. S. Guest

20 Guzel Burj, modern irrigation ditch: (a) view facing south, (b) view facing north, 1988, J. S. Guest

21 Murad Pasha in 1835, drawn by Fitzjames

22 Murad Pasha in 1988: (a) view facing east, (b) view facing west, J. S. Guest

23 The *Euphrates* on the stocks at Port William (town of Bir in the background), drawn by Vincent Germain, 1835

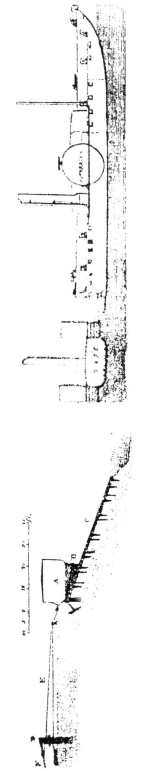

24 The *Euphrates*: (a) being launched 1836, (b) profiles, 1836

25 The *Tigris*: (a) on the stocks, drawn by Estcourt, 1836, (b), profiles, 1836

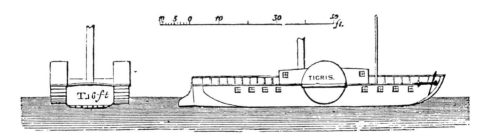

26 The last boiler entering Port William, drawing by Pauline Helfer, 1836

27 Bald ibis at Birecik bird sanctuary, 1988, J. S. Guest

28 Birecik, 1988: (a) cliffs, (b) citadel, J. S. Guest

29 View of Euphrates below modern bridge south of Birecik, 1988, J. S. Guest

30 Rumkale: (a) in 1836, drawn by Eden, (b) in 1990, J. S. Guest

31 Arabs attacking Lt Lynch and party near Deir ez-Zor, drawn by Estcourt, 1835

32 Arabs attacking Sheikh Hasan (note families crossing the river on inflated skins), drawn by Estcourt, 183

33 The anchorage at Beles, drawn by Cockburn, 1836

34 Kalat Jaber in 1836, drawn by Cockburn

35 Kalat Jaber in 1988, facing north, A. Shahinian

36 The steamers passing Thapsacus (Funsa), drawing by Fitzjames, 1836

37 The ruins of Rakka, drawn by Estcourt, 1836

38 Halebiye, north wall, 1988, J. S. Guest

39 View of Euphrates facing north from Halebiye, 1988, J. S. Guest

40 Deir ez-Zor, drawn by Estcourt, 1836

41 View of Euphrates above Deir ez-Zor facing south (note modern bridge in background), 1988, J. S. Guest

42 Ruined castle at Rehabah, west of Meyadin, 1988, J. S. Guest

43 Dura Europos (Salihye), West Gate, 1988, J. S. Guest

44 View of Euphrates below Dura Europos, 1988, J. S. Guest

45 The loss of the *Tigris*. Note Charlewood's party securing *Euphrates*. Drawn by Estcourt, 1836

46 View of Euphrates below Is Geria, 1989, Robert A. Mitchell

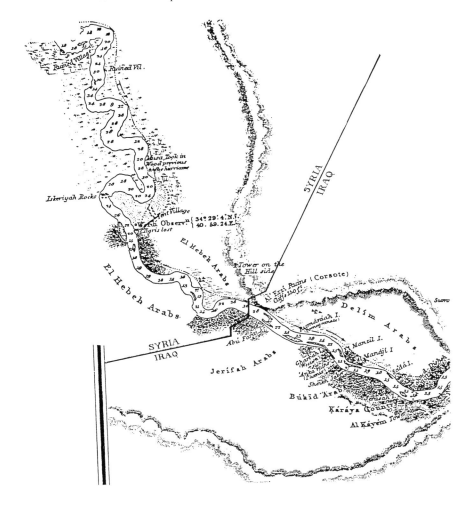

47 Location of *Tigris* wreck, from Chesney's map, 1836, enlarged to scale approx. ½ inch to a mile

48 View of Hit, drawn by Fitzjames, 1836

49 Korna, junction point of the Tigris and Euphrates, drawn by Estcourt, 1836

50 Salute at Basra, drawn by Estcourt, 1836

52 William Francis Ainsworth in his old age

51 Melek Ga... F.R.Ch... m in 1863, artist unknown

Chapter 9

The Wreck of the *Tigris*

'The most perfect harmony has now been restored,' wrote Chesney two weeks after the expedition left Beles.[1] Indeed, the descent of the uncharted 211 miles from Beles to Deir ez-Zor, the first fuel depot, was accomplished smoothly. The river was still rising, which made navigation easier although detailed survey work was no longer possible. The *Euphrates* now followed the lighter-draught *Tigris*, which was usually preceded by four small flat-boats. These flatboats had been built at Bir to take depth soundings of the water, to locate the navigable channels and to carry the diving bell for possible blasting operations.

After passing the ruined castle of Kalat Jaber on the left bank and the narrows where the Assad dam now stands, the vessels entered a wide stretch of river with several channels that had united in the high water season to form a vast lake with many treacherous pebbly shoals. The banks were covered with tamarisk bushes that sheltered flocks of songbirds and provided good fuel to replace the coal lost on Fitzjames's flatboat. Barren plains stretched on either side toward distant hills.

The Arabs in this region were primitive and poor. Elliot's account of his Euphrates journey in 1831 calls them 'worse than Russian boors, Bashkirs, or Calmucks'.[2] However Rassam, a shrewd interpreter, soon persuaded them to barter milk, butter and sheep for yellow handkerchiefs. Charlewood recalled that on such occasions Pauline Helfer and Rassam, who both enjoyed good food, 'managed to get the liver, and have a good tuck out together'.[3]

Progress was leisurely, with stops for wood cutting and historical research. Sunday was observed as a day of rest. Chesney and Ainsworth inspected the old bridge piers at Thapsacus [Funsa], where Alexander the Great had crossed the river, and the nearby remains of the caliphs' place at Rakka. Chesney also noticed that at each stopping place a horseman – always the same one – would watch them for a while and ride away.

Below Rakka the Euphrates flows broad and deep until it approaches the Jebel Bishri mountain range. Here the river turns sharply to the south and enters a dark cleft hemmed in by black basalt cliffs described by one of Peacock's sixteenth-century sources as 'mountainous beetle-browed over-lookers'.[4] The steamers passed safely through this gorge and tied up on the right bank beneath the white walls of Halebiye, a ruined town that was once called Zenobia.

The next morning (15 May) Chesney and his companions explored this remote fortress, which had been built by Queen Zenobia in the third century AD to guard the trade route between Palmyra and the east. Viewed from the river, the ramparts, built of sparkling gypsum rock, stretch up the mountain slope to a citadel; from here the garrison could watch the approaches and signal to Zelebiye, a sister castle that looks down the Euphrates from a commanding ridge across the river on its eastern bank. In his youth Peacock would have been inspired by this magic place, where Chesney and Ainsworth believed they had found the summer residence of the queen. The ruined building thought to have been her palace is of later date, but certainly it was here that the Romans captured Queen Zenobia as she was crossing the Euphrates to seek refuge in the castle that still bears her name.

As Chesney and Ainsworth mused over the fall of empires, a tartar arrived from the Aleppo consulate bringing a despatch from Sir John Hobhouse dated 31 March.[5] The tone of the letter was cool. At the time of writing the India Board had received no current progress reports from Chesney or Lynch for several weeks; as a result, Hobhouse had not known if or when the expedition would set off. For some reason Lynch had sent his February report with the boilermakers, whose sailing vessel did not reach Liverpool until May.[6] However, some private letters, sent from Port William in mid-February, had reached London in March because the *Columbine*, which left Iskenderun toward the end of February, had forwarded them on the Malta steam packet. Among them was a gloomy letter written by Fitzjames from his sickbed to a friend, predicting that the expedition would not leave Fort William before May.[7] Hobhouse was annoyed that the friend (perhaps Barrow at the Admiralty) had sent a copy of Fiztjames's letter to the king.

Hobhouse's despatch confirmed Cabell's earlier warning that Parliament and the East India Company would only provide more money for the expedition if the India Board set 31 July 1836 as its termination date. Assuming that the vessels would be on their way by the time his despatch reached Chesney, Hobhouse urged him to attempt a return voyage upstream and a final descent to the Persian Gulf if possible before the end of July. If not, Chesney should break up the expedition at Basra and prepare to turn over the vessels to the East India Company. The letter closed with a request for a complete accounting of the expedition expenses incurred to date and estimated for the remaining period.

Chesney's reminiscences suggest that Hobhouse's despatch was a crippling blow to the project.[8] In fact, it came as no surprise to Chesney, who carried on with his plans to reach Basra around the middle of June and leave again on the upstream voyage on 9 July, which should make it possible to be back in Basra by the date of termination. Nevertheless, Chesney kept these orders to himself for fear of damaging morale.

The steamers pressed on, stopping briefly at Deir ez-Zor to refuel. The Euphrates valley below this point is a fertile strip of alluvial soil; on the left bank the fields stretch off into arid land, while on the right bank the limit of cultivation is set by a sheer escarpment that marks the edge of the Syrian desert. At Buseyra, where the Khabur river flows in from the north, the *Tigris* steamed up the tributary for eighteen miles until the channel became too shallow for passage. Finally, on 19 May the two steamers reached Meyadin, the first town belonging to the province of Baghdad. The steamers hoisted the British and Turkish ensigns, while Chesney led a party to inspect an imposing but ruined castle nearby. Henceforth the mysterious rider was seen no more and Chesney breathed more freely now that the vessels were no longer being watched by Ibrahim Pasha's covetous eyes.

The next day's run brought them to Salihye, forty-four miles below Meyadin, where they stopped to purchase wood. The river here runs right against the escarpment; the high ground beyond is covered by the ruins of a vast walled city. Its identity was unknown; Ainsworth speculated that it was a fortress of Saladin, the medieval Saracen hero of the Crusades. (Excavations in 1921 proved that it was the long-lost city of Dura Europos, founded by Macedonians who had served with Alexander and destroyed by the Persians in the middle of the third century AD.)

Ana, the next refuelling depot, was 130 miles below Salihye, with two danger spots – the Is Geria reef and the Karabla rapids – lying between. Since Chesney was anxious to make up time, he gave orders for an early start.

On Saturday 21 May the expedition left Salihye around 6 a.m. The flatboats, under Hector's command, had already gone ahead. Lynch moved off first with the *Tigris*. This was now Chesney's flagship and he had invited the Helfers to join him for lunch and spend the afternoon on board. Cleaveland followed with the *Euphrates* in the rear. Chesney recalled later that the weather that morning was 'very fine and promising'.[9]

After five hours of uneventful steaming down the broad, deep river Cleaveland reported that the *Euphrates* wood supply was almost exhausted and that he would have to switch to coal. Fortunately, a pile of wooden poles was noticed outside a village; the two steamers came to alongside the left bank, where the officers arranged for the purchase and loading of the wood while the crews enjoyed their midday meal. The Helfers went ashore and noted that the sky was unusually clear, but the air very sultry, although the temperature was only 84 degrees F. Owing to some misunderstanding their boat took them back to the *Euphrates* and they missed their appointment with Chesney.

When the steamers moved off again around 1.30 p.m. a gentle south-east breeze was rippling the surface of the water. But a few minutes later black clouds in the western sky warned that a storm was approaching. The breeze died down; Ainsworth observed a 'portentous' fall of the barometer,[10] while Andrew Staunton noted that 'the atmosphere then felt as if loaded with sulphur'.[11] The vessels furled their deck awnings but the cabin windows on the *Tigris* were left open for ventilation.

Eyewitness accounts recall the contrast between the low hills to the south, still bathed in sunshine, and the western horizon that was blotted out by a dense arch of blue-black clouds with a brick-red lining, beneath which floating columns of orange, red and yellow sand whirled around. (Immune to the lure of romantic prose, Fitzjames described the storm as 'looking like a large cloud of black mud'.[12]) At first the rapidly advancing squall seemed likely to miss the steamers, but all too soon it was realized that they were directly in its path.

The expedition had survived other sandstorms by trying up the steamers to the bank and waiting until the sky was clear. Unfortunately, at this crucial moment such a manoeuvre was impossible. In Chesney's words: 'We were arriving at the rocky pass of Is-Geria. Indeed, we were already so close to it that there was not sufficient space to round to and bring up; consequently, it became most prudent to steam onwards.'[13]

Once past the rocks, Chesney ordered Lynch to bring up the *Tigris* to the left bank of the river and signalled the *Euphrates* 'to choose a berth and make fast' further down.[14] The *Tigris* did not respond well to the command; Chesney recalls that on the first attempt 'our vessel was caught by the hurricane and refused to answer the helm by coming round'.[15] Lynch tried again lower down and, as the *Tigris* neared the bank, two seamen were standing at the bow, ready to leap ashore with hawsers and anchors to make her fast.

Meanwhile Cleaveland had put the *Euphrates* helm to starboard and the vessel was rounding up towards her intended berth on the left bank below the *Tigris* when he saw that the other vessel was having trouble coming around and that there was a risk they might collide. 'We had to reverse engines,' his report reads, 'so as not to embarrass the *Tigris* in securing to the bank.'[16] The paddle wheels backed the *Euphrates* downstream with the current – a daring manoeuvre, since if the vessel lost way she would be at the mercy of the storm.

'At this moment', Ainsworth recalled years later, 'the hurricane came on us – a warm dry wind, laden with the fragrance of the aromatic plants of the wilderness, followed in a few instants by a tremendous blast of wind, with some rain in large drops.'[17]

The first gust blew the stern of the *Tigris* violently against the bank, forcing her head outwards toward the stream. One of the men at the bow had managed to leap ashore, but an instant later Chesney felt 'a lurch in the wind'[18] that snapped the anchor cable and drove the vessel further from the bank so that she lay broadside to the storm.

Andrew Staunton had been sitting in the forward cabin of the *Tigris*, helping Cockburn with his maps, 'when the vessel suddenly began to roll, and a swelling sea washed in at the windows of the cabin'.[19] It proved impossible to put back the window frames and the cabin began to fill with water. (Cockburn had planned to spend that day on the *Euphrates*, but had not put in for leave in time.)

The impact of the wind hurled the *Euphrates* against the shore and in Charlewood's words 'nearly laid us on our broadside'.[20] She righted herself and Cleaveland turned the paddles ahead again, brought up her head and set the engines at full speed. As the vessel gathered way against the wind and the current, Fitzjames and others on deck saw the *Tigris* 'drift past us at a fearful rate, broadside to the wind, and heeling over considerably'[21] before she disappeared in a cloud of sand. A moment later the *Euphrates* drove against the bank.

It was now as dark as midnight, but in an instant Charlewood and five others leaped to the shore with a hawser and a light anchor which they sank into the earth. Unable to stand up against the sandstorm, they lay on the ground, holding on to the hawser and watching the anchor being dragged to within five yards of the river edge. However, their exertions had given the crew time to get the two bower anchors and their chain cables ashore.

Cleaveland worked the engines at full speed to keep the vessel to the bank. Waves ten feet high broke over the deck and forced open the forward cabin windows, but carpenters quickly closed them up again. At one moment

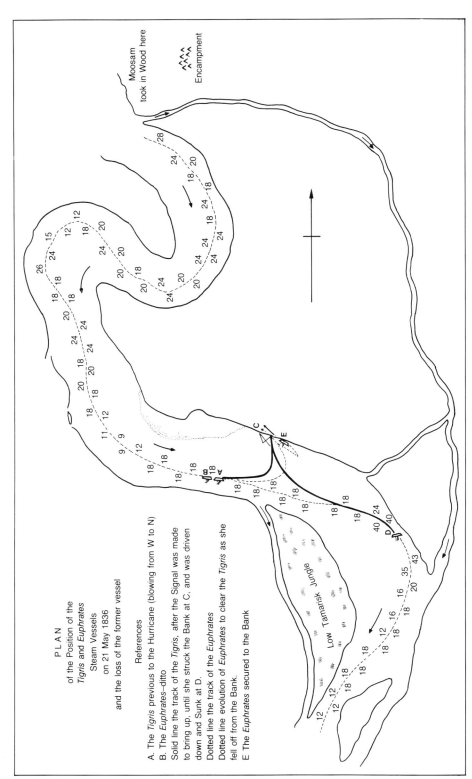

PLAN
of the Position of the
Tigris and *Euphrates*
Steam Vessels
on 21 May 1836
and the loss of the former vessel

References

A. The *Tigris* previous to the Hurricane (blowing from W to N)
B. The *Euphrates*–ditto
Solid line the track of the *Tigris*, after the Signal was made
to bring up, until she struck the Bank at C, and was driven
down and Sunk at D.
Dotted line the track of the *Euphrates*
Dotted line evolution of *Euphrates* to clear the *Tigris* as she
fell off from the Bank.
E The *Euphrates* secured to the Bank

Moosam
took in Wood here

Encampment

Low Tamarisk Jungle

The wreck of the *Tigris* (plan taken from Chesney's *Narrative of the Euphrates Expedition*)

Dr Helfer heard that the stern cabin was flooding. 'I rushed down stairs [*sic*]', he recorded, 'and saw the water streaming in at a window shutter, which had been driven in; I contrived to close it by leaning my back against it and putting my foot against the wall opposite, until a carpenter made it fast.'[22] He rejoined his wife on deck, in time for them to see a shaft of light illuminate the *Tigris* in the distance, 'apparently standing still, but with her funnel bent on one side'. Fitzjames could see that her bows were under water and Charlewood, holding on to his hawser, thought he saw her go down, but fresh clouds of sand and rain obscured their vision and the *Euphrates* engines began to choke with sand.

Suddenly, after twelve minutes of fury the storm abated and the sun came out again. The *Tigris* was nowhere to be seen.

Lynch was an experienced naval officer who had taken the *Enterprize* steamer back to Calcutta from Bombay. He knew at once that the *Tigris*, broadside to the gale, must quickly get her head to wind. The larboard (port) anchor was let go, but the vessel's heel prevented the crew from getting out the starboard anchor, essential to bring her round.

In pitch darkness, almost on her beam ends, the *Tigris* drifted down the river with water pouring through the windows, which nobody could close. Lynch made one last vain attempt to bring her round before the boiler fires were extinguished. At that point the water-logged vessel began to right herself and started sinking at the bows. The engineer remained at his post and two other men struggled vainly with the windows, while the rest of the ship's company gathered in silence on the after deck.

The vessel began to settle and with Chesney's permission Lynch gave the order to abandon ship. At that moment a break in the clouds showed that they were drifting close to the left bank of the river. Hoping that the stern might run aground, Lynch ordered 'Stand fast'.[23] But the channel at this point was deep and most of those huddled together on the deck were unprepared when the *Tigris* suddenly went down in thirty feet of water.

Except for Cockburn – last seen holding on to a carronade gun[24] – and some of the Arab workers, everyone on board the *Tigris* could swim. Andrew Staunton recalled 'being balanced on the awning ropes, with a native holding my feet and screaming piteously'.[25] Chesney and Lynch dived overboard when the water on the deck was up to their waists. Chesney was hurled ashore by the waves and landed in a corn field. Henry Lynch's escape was more traumatic; a newspaper report of his letter home described how he and his brother went down together, 'but in their struggles for life while in the water he shook his brother off and was saved.'[26]

Twenty of the thirty-seven persons on board were drowned – Robert

89

Cockburn; Robert Lynch; John Struthers, the engineer from Lairds who had joined the expedition two weeks earlier at Beles; Yusuf Sadr, the interpreter from Aleppo; all five gunners; a sapper; five seamen; and five Arab workers.

(Yusuf Sadr had served as a courier between the expedition and its diplomatic and financial correspondents in Aleppo. On his last trip back from Aleppo he had reached Beles empty-handed, claiming that Arab robbers had taken the funds that were in his care. Ainsworth's comment on this episode, written fifty years later, provides a sorry epitaph for Yusuf Sadr: 'I fear he was not an honest man.'[27])

Besides Chesney and Henry Lynch, the survivors included Eden, the two Stauntons and Thomson (the assistant surveyor), together with a sapper, four seamen (two volunteers from the *Columbine* and both of the Maltese cooks) and six Arabs.

The second interpreter assigned to the *Tigris*, William Elliot, was not on board the vessel when she sank. The dervish with nine lives was on one of Hector's flatboats ten miles downstream, where according to Chesney 'they experienced nothing more than a moderate gale'.[28]

As the weather cleared and the sun came out, the few who had survived the wreck looked back toward the river and saw their *Tigris* for the last time, her keel upended, foundering beneath the waves. Chesney, the strongest of the group, helped some of the others to their feet and started to lead them towards the shore, but Lynch and Eden were so weak that they could only crawl, while Dr Staunton lay unconscious on the ground.

A few minutes later Charlewood appeared, exclaiming: 'Oh! Colonel Chesney, I am so delighted to find you saved! Let me help you to the boat.'[29] His words made no sense to them. They did not know that the *Euphrates* had been made fast to the bank and that Charlewood had been sent down the river to search for survivors of the *Tigris*.

Chesney answered glumly: 'Is that you, Charlewood? Well, I am glad indeed to see you saved, too. Are you the only one saved from the *Euphrates*?'

Charlewood pointed to the steamer's funnel, visible across the bank. Chesney's face lit up as he started to make new plans.

Meanwhile Murphy and Ainsworth arrived, followed by the Helfers. Chesney was still suffering from euphoria when he greeted Pauline Helfer with the words of a popular song:

> Si vous voulez danser,
> je vous prie de le faire commencer.'[30]

Ainsworth did not record this pleasantry, but he poignantly described the sad procession to the boat. 'Except Lynch, who had to be supported, and Chesney, who struggled away in advance, most of the others fell mechanically into pairs, and walked holding each other by the hand.'[31]

For three days they searched in vain for more survivors and tried to locate the sunken vessel. At first they went about well armed, for fear of Arab looters, but the tribesmen were sympathetic and helped to gather pieces of wreckage, including Chesney's Bible.* But the *Tigris* lay hidden deep beneath the water with its cargo of provisions, spare parts and personal baggage, as well as all the expedition's records, accounts and cash.

On 24 May Chesney called a meeting of the members of the expedition to consider their future plans. He reviewed what had happened, commended Cleaveland and Charlewood for saving the *Euphrates* and announced that an *ad hoc* court of inquiry had praised Lynch and Eden for their efforts in trying to save the *Tigris*.

It was now, Chesney said, his duty to reveal that he had received orders to disband the expedition by the end of July. However, he believed that the wreck of the *Tigris* had changed everything and he felt sure that the government would not want to lose prestige by abandoning an important British project after one vessel had been accidentally lost. Pending further instructions from London, Chesney was determined, if his colleagues all agreed, to continue the descent of the river with the *Euphrates* and bring back the Indian mail. Meanwhile, to comply with the India Board's directions, the expedition would reduce expenses by sending the *Tigris* survivors home to England, except for Hector and a small party, who would remain to find and salvage the sunken vessel.

The annals of the British empire and the chronicles of Greece and Rome contain many scenes where a resolute leader, saved from the jaws of death, rallied his discouraged followers after some calamity in a foreign country far from home. Indeed Chesney's speech at Is Geria unconsciously echoed similar harangues by Xenophon and Julian in their Mesopotamian campaigns.†

Predictably, Chesney's appeal was effective. 'One and all,' he records, 'officers and men, at once expressed themselves not only ready, but anxious

---

* Chesney's Bible, which had already been soaked by the Euphrates waters in 1831 when Major Taylor's schooner capsized, is now in the possession of a private collector.

† Estcourt and others noted the coincidence that a hurricane struck Julian's fleet at Ana, eighty miles below Is Geria.

to second me in every way, and volunteered to forego their Expedition pay, in order to lessen our expenses as much as possible.'[32]

After burying the few bodies that came to the surface of the river, the expedition left Is Geria on 25 May. The *Euphrates* had not suffered any serious damage and the voyage to Ana was uneventful. As they passed El Kaim, where Chesney had first laid eyes on the river, the scenery began to change. Ancient stone dams jutted out into the stream, diverting the river water towards the banks, where creaking wooden water wheels raised it in buckets up to the conduits of graceful aqueducts that led to irrigated groves of fruit trees and date palms. At one village Chesney was gladdened by the sight of 'Getgood', the pilot who had accompanied him five years earlier on his initial survey of the river. Chesney's old friend, who had been reported to have died, now guided the *Euphrates* past the irrigation works, where the stream sometimes raced between dams on either side, and through the Karabla rapids, where limestone rocks come down to the water on the left bank and form a ledge across the river.

The expedition spent several days at Ana, repairing and refuelling the *Euphrates*, writing up reports on the *Tigris* disaster and making arrangements for the survivors to get home. Lynch and Eden struck north across the desert with an Arab escort, bound for Mosul and Trebizond [Trabzon] on the Black Sea. Thomson went back to Aleppo; his survey notes had gone down with the *Tigris* and some of his work needed to be done again. The Stauntons remained with the *Euphrates*; they were planning to spend some time in Baghdad.

Alexander Hector stayed behind at Ana with the diving bell, which might be needed for rock blasting at Karabla and Is Geria when the water level went down. His immediate assignment was to locate the *Tigris* and prevent the Arabs from removing the guns, instruments and other valuable property from the wreck. Chesney suggested that Elliot should work with Hector, but the dervish preferred to go back to Syria with Thomson and resume his roving life.

As purser to the expedition, Hector had good reasons for taking on the task of salvage, since he had invested several hundred pounds in buying provisions and other supplies. He hoped that some of these stores might be salvaged and that he would be compensated for the rest. He also hoped that if he could raise the vessel and recover its contents he might receive a substantial reward.

In the ensuing weeks the river level began to fall and the steamer's hull could be seen, bottom up, a hundred feet from the bank. Hector cut a hole in her side and found that she was half filled with mud. Divers recovered the deck guns, some instruments and miscellaneous objects such as Lynch's flute. During the low season Hector tried to raise the vessel by means of capstans, chains and hawsers, but his report states that they gave way under the strain without moving the *Tigris* in the least.

Over the years the river has changed its course and the position of the wreck, close to the modern town of Abu Kemal on the border between Syria and Iraq, is difficult to locate. However, a new bridge now spans the Euphrates at Is Geria and travellers can look down the broad river in the knowledge that they are near the place where the *Tigris* went down.

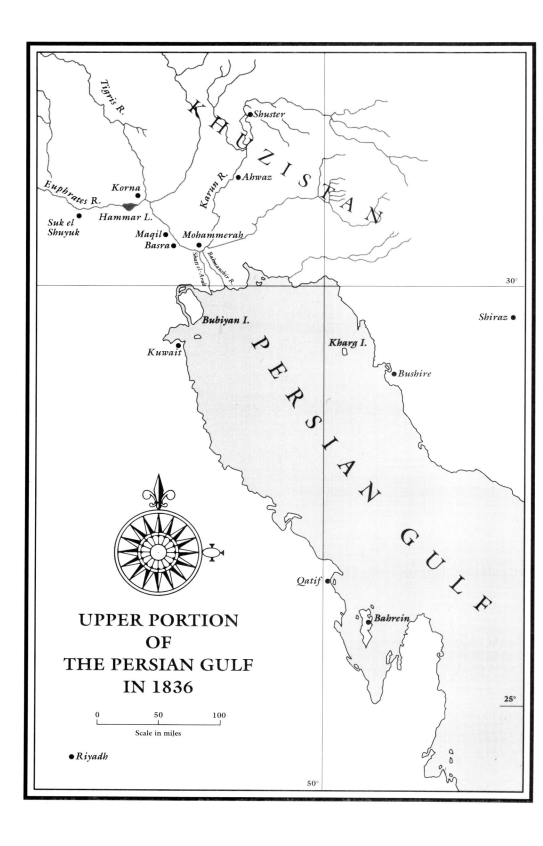

KHUZISTAN

Tigris R.

●Shuster

Karun R.

●Ahwaz

Euphrates R. Korna ●

Suk el ● Hammar L.
Shuyuk

Maqil ● Mohammerah
Basra ●   ●

Shatt-l-Arab

Bahmanshir R.

30°

Bubiyan I.

Kharg I.

Shiraz ●

Kuwait ●

●Bushire

PERSIAN

GULF

Qatif ●

Bahrein

UPPER PORTION
OF
THE PERSIAN GULF
IN 1836

0	50	100

Scale in miles

25°

●Riyadh

50°

Chapter 10

Down to the Persian Gulf

The tragedy at Is Geria was followed by several episodes of comic melo-drama. The first of these occurred on 31 May 1836, the day the *Euphrates* steamer left Ana.

Summer was now approaching and malaria victims once again endured its enervating sequence of fevers and chills. Chesney's attacks, which occurred every other day, had one peculiar symptom – a total loss of memory. 'While these attacks were upon me', he recalled in his memoirs, 'I could not remember my own name, nor the termination of any word that I was in the act of writing when the fit came on.'[1]

After leaving Ana, the *Euphrates* made a brief stop by the left bank of the river a few miles downstream near the ruins of Anatho, the old site of Ana, to take on stores. Chesney went ashore to supervise this work, while Ainsworth planned to examine the geology of some nearby cliffs. At that moment Ainsworth observed from Chesney's appearance that an attack of malaria might be coming on and advised him to return to his cabin. The colonel went back on board to rest, while Ainsworth proceeded on his fossil hunt.

When the stores had all been loaded, Chesney gave orders to move off and the *Euphrates* steamed past sixty-six miles of picturesque scenery to Haditha, an island settlement that is now the site of one of Iraq's largest dams. 'Here', Chesney relates, 'we brought up. Dinner followed, as usual, when our day's work was over, and in passing by Ainsworth's cabin-door, I tapped, as was my custom, to let him know that it was ready – when, for

Upper portion of the Persian Gulf in 1836

the first time, I recollected that I left him absorbed in the round tower and other ruins of Anatho!'[2]

The river makes big bends between Ana and Haditha; consequently, there was a risk that, if the *Euphrates* went back upstream, Ainsworth might be somewhere out of sight. Chesney decided to send off a messenger to search for him, while the steamer stayed at Haditha.

Ainsworth had been absorbed in digging out fossils from the cliff that proved the alluvial origin of the Mesopotamian valley. After a while he turned around and saw the stern of the *Euphrates* on its way downstream. He realized that his absence had not been noticed because his customary place on the steamer, when she was in motion, was a sheltered spot in front of a paddle box.

The obvious course was to go back to Ana, where Hector could somehow get him back to his ship. But Ainsworth reasoned, perhaps too quickly, that he would never find a boat to take him across the river to the right bank, where Hector's quarters were located. He was twenty-eight years old and had survived the swamps of Iskenderun, the miasmas of Murad Pasha and the snowdrifts of Cilicia. Unarmed but blessed with four gold ghazis, each worth four shillings, in his pocket, he decided to make his way overland to wherever the *Euphrates* might be waiting for her errant scientist to return.[3]

Against payment of a ghazi, an Arab villager guided Ainsworth for two hours to a point where a bridge crossed a little ditch. When the guide attempted to turn his client over to another Arab, Ainsworth decided to go on alone. He kept the river always in sight to direct him, but as night drew on he noticed that there were no more villages, while in the gathering darkness he could see foxes, hyenas and wolves crossing his path. 'The latter', he recalled, 'also would sometimes turn sulkily round, snarling defiance, as if questioning my right to be there.' Jackals dashed up close to him, 'yelling or gnashing their teeth, and bristling up their backs like so many angry cats.'

Finally, Ainsworth discovered an old man and a boy sitting by a fire beneath an aqueduct. After giving him bread and water, they told him that the steamer had gone by; however, the old man agreed to guide him for a ghazi once the moon had risen. Ainsworth was settling down to sleep when another Arab appeared and began talking to the old man. From the fierce tone of their conversation Ainsworth sensed that he had fallen among robbers and that they were arguing over their prey. But he was too tired to worry. 'In the meantime', Ainsworth relates, 'passing events did not affect me much, for I fell into a profound sleep.'

He was awakened by someone pinching his big toe. The bright moonlight showed the old man's face peering down at him. The other Arab and the boy had left. As they started on their way Ainsworth could see that his guide was armed with 'a big round ball fixed to the end of a short stick or handle'. After following the river for a while, they started climbing a hill when the old man made signs for Ainsworth to sit down while he looked around. When he returned, Ainsworth records that:

> he sat down by my side, in closer proximity than was desirable, and began to examine the steel buckles of my braces, which shone like silver in the moonlight, as also to feel for the girdle which generally serves as a purse with Orientals. In doing this his hand trembled, betraying his intentions.

Ainsworth drew back and grabbed a large stone that lay nearby. The old man raised his club, holding out his other hand and rubbing his forefinger and thumb together.

For a long, tense moment Ainsworth faced the old man, noting that 'his forehead was "villainously low", his nose long, and his eyelids red and purulent'. Finally they resumed the climb, with the guide still demanding money while Ainsworth held on to his stone and carefully kept his distance from the old man's club. Thus, Ainsworth relates, 'we argued the matter over as we progressed in a pleasing and edifying manner.'

Finally, a truce was arranged whereby Ainsworth gave a kerchief to the old man. They trudged on until daybreak, when they reached the crest of the last hill and Ainsworth could see a broad plain with the river in the distance and the *Euphrates* anchored beside an island in midstream. The old man would go no further and Ainsworth made his way to the vessel after having walked more than fifty miles.

The river was now at its highest level. Two days after leaving Ana, the *Euphrates* steamed swiftly between two dams and brought up at Hit. After inspecting the tar springs that covered the town with a dense cloud of smoke and steam, Chesney discovered that a mixture of bitumen and earth provided good boiler fuel for the steamer. He also sent off a messenger to Colonel Taylor in Baghdad with a request that the Resident should send a supply of Turkish money to meet the steamer upon arrival at Hilla, 190 miles downstream.

The next day they passed the old Saklawiya canal (the link between the Euphrates and the Tigris that James Taylor's project had planned to use) and arrived at Felluja. The flat countryside was flooded, but a number of people from the steamer were planning to make the forty-mile overland journey to Baghdad. Estcourt and Murphy had been detailed by Chesney to carry despatches to the Residency and bring down the money to Hilla; Charlewood, Fitzjames and Ainsworth also went along, as did the Helfers, who wished to see the city. The interpreter Seyid Ali and several servants accompanied the group.

With much difficulty horses were obtained for this large party. Some had saddles but no stirrups, others had no saddles at all. Since it was too hot to travel by day, the group left Felluja at sunset, hoping to reach Baghdad the next morning.

Pauline Helfer, who had insisted on joining the Baghdad trip, describes her feeling of enchantment as they rode through the moonlit night, recounting stories and legends of the east. She also describes her horror when, instead of mosques and minarets, the rising sun lit up a vast marsh with only a line of hillocks to mark the way. The Tigris had also overflowed; its receding waters had left a muddy bog, too soft for horses to cross.

For six hours they walked, slipped and jumped from hillock to hillock under a broiling sun. Charlewood recalls that it was a hard trial for Pauline Helfer, who 'constantly had to tuck up her Turkish nether garments above the knee'.[4] However, she had been shrewd enough to bring her own supply of food, which she shared with the others, who had expected to breakfast in Baghdad.

At last they reached a mound from which they could see the city, the Tigris and a ferry boat that was just pushing off from the western bank. They fired pistols as a signal, but the boatmen took fright and refused to turn back. When Colonel Taylor finally learned that some Europeans were stranded across the river, the city gates were about to close and there was nothing he could do.

The weary travellers lay down on a sandhill, the driest spot they could find, and spent a sleepless night tormented first by mosquitoes and later by a chilling wind. No one had eaten since the morning and Pauline Helfer was heard to exclaim: 'I could go through any fatigue if I had something to eat every two hours.'[5]

The next morning the ferry boat still did not come and the group spent the day, in Estcourt's words, 'partly famished, partly fried; no body near, and no shelter from the sun'.[6] Late in the afternoon a boat came to take then to Baghdad, where Pauline Helfer's spirits revived. 'At the gates', she wrote, 'we mounted splendid horses, ready saddled from the consular stables, and with a numerous escort, headed by a kawass [guard] with the silver staff, we made our solemn entry into the Residency.'[7]

Her joy was short-lived, for the next day her husband brought some distressing news about 'Mr Hunter' and 'Mr Brown', the Afghan princes who had travelled with the Helfers from Smyrna to Bir and had agreed to rejoin them when the steamer reached Basra. Colonel Taylor had met them as they passed through Baghdad and with some misgivings had advanced them travel money. Now the Resident had found out that when they were in Mosul they had borrowed from a local banker by issuing drafts on Colonel Taylor without his knowledge. The doctor was starting to make excuses for his friends, when he remembered that he and his wife were holding some jewels as security for Turkish money loaned to the Afghans when they left Bir. He had brought a few of these jewels to be sold in Baghdad, where the Helfers were planning to buy some clothes to replace items they had lost when the *Tigris* went down. When Dr Helfer showed the stones to Colonel Taylor, the Resident recommended calling in a reliable jeweller. After exmining them carefully, this expert pronounced them 'a clever imitation, by which even connoisseurs might have been deceived'.[8]

As the wool finally fell from their eyes, the Helfers realized that they had been tricked. The doctor was broken-hearted, for he had liked the two Orientals and had trusted them to lead him and his wife to a new, better existence in the highlands of Central Asia. Now, with their companions exposed as rogues, the Helfers had to reconsider all their plans. The financial loss was tiresome but not crippling; Colonel Taylor readily advanced them a hundred pounds to cover their needs. The real decision to be made was whether they should go forward with their plans to start a new life in the Orient, or give up their dreams and go back home.

Neither of the Helfers wanted to turn back. In Pauline Helfer's words, 'our courage and confidence had been so much strengthened by the good and evil fortune that had befallen us, that we resolved to go on.' The *Euphrates* would take them down to Basra, but they could not decide where their next destination should be. Dr Helfer was intrigued by Persia, as the shortest route to Central Asia. Colonel Taylor, who had met his wife in Persia, remarked that the country 'might serve as a temporary station, but would never do as a residence for a European doctor, as, though the Persians were ready enough to avail themselves of his advice, they were not in the habit of paying for it.' He suggested that the Helfers should go on by boat from Basra to Bushire, where Captain Samuel Hennell, the East India Company's Resident, would be able to give them good advice.

In comparison with the palmy days of Daud Pasha, Baghdad in 1835 offered little to a visitor. The Residency still maintained its comfortable way of life, but outside its walls empty houses and shops revealed the impact of the recent plague. The Plymouth Brethren missionaries, discouraged by their lack of progress, had left Baghdad to spread the word in India. Ali Riza Pasha, the new governor, was encamped outside the city preparing to advance against the Kurds. Ainsworth, who accompanied Colonel Taylor and Major Estcourt* on an official visit to Ali Riza, describes him as 'a fine old man, very fat, but his eye intelligent and animated, his forehead good, his aspect benevolent, and his manner courteous'.[9] Meanwhile Mrs Taylor took Pauline Helfer to the Pasha's harem and introduced her to his two lawful wives and their many ladies in waiting.

The group departed from Baghdad in Colonel Taylor's barge, accompanied by Dr Ross, the Residency surgeon, who was famed for his travels through the desert and his love of animals; at one time a lion, a leopard, a monkey and a bulldog lived happily in his house. Horses and donkeys (one of the latter laden with sacks of Turkish coins for Chesney) met them a few miles downstream to take them to Hilla, where they crossed a bridge of boats over the Euphrates and re-boarded their steamer, which was moored above the bridge.

All was now ready for the vessel's departure on the final segment from Hilla to the Persian Gulf. Arrangements had been made for Dr Ross to take the Staunton brothers back to Baghdad, together with despatches and private letters home. Compliments had been exchanged with the Turkish governor of Hilla, who had visited the *Euphrates*. Steam was up and the only remaining task was to disembark 'Getgood', the pilot from Ana, who had been kept on board the vessel while she was at Hilla because he feared for his safety ashore. (Estcourt's version of the story implies that Getgood refused to leave until his 'avaricious' demands for money had been met.)[10]

The accounts of what followed are conflicting. It appears that a group of Getgood's fellow-tribesmen thought he was being held prisoner and threatened to storm the ship. All at once the crowds on the river bank melted away; gun barrels appeared on rooftops and men were seen creeping among the huts. Using his hands as a trumpet, Dr Ross whispered hoarsely from the shore that an attack was imminent. All hands were called to quarters and the steamer promptly cast off. A boat took Getgood to the shore, where he was set upon and wounded by robbers.

Fortunately, the governor had already ordered the floating bridge to be opened for the scheduled departure of the *Euphrates*. As the vessel gathered way and sped downstream, the crowds gathered again on the banks and, in Ainsworth's words, 'their triumphant shouts of defiance rang through the date groves, and from side to side of Euphrates.'[11]

Chesney was furious. Orders were given to bring the steamer about and turn her head to the stream. When Ainsworth saw the crew of the nine-pounder gun taking up their position in the bows, he remarked to Chesney

* Estcourt had learned of his major's commission in mid-May.

that they were outnumbered by the masses of armed men along the banks. Chesney answered savagely (and out of character, since he always wanted to be friends with the Arabs): 'The more we shall have to kill.'

The crowds on the banks fell silent as, for the first time in their lives, they saw a vessel move by its own power against the stream. The *Euphrates* passed the still-open bridge and rested in mid-channel, with her paddle wheels turning just enough to stem the current and her guns trained on the centre of the town. Not a shot was fired on either side. After a while the steamer moved further upstream to draw level with the governor's castle and waited there, while Estcourt and Rassam went ashore and obtained a formal apology and a promise of compensation for Getgood. Thereupon the *Euphrates* proceeded calmly on her way.

It is not clear what caused the trouble. Chesney should have known that the expedition was now entering the part of Iraq where the Turkish rulers had little control over the Arab population, which was largely Shiite and hostile to foreigners. One account states that Getgood was attacked because he had piloted the 'Satanic' vessel down the stream. Hilla was a dangerous spot because it was an important stopping place for Shia pilgrims who came down from Persia, many of them bringing their parents' bodies in their coffins, and crossed the bridge of boats on their way to the shrines of Caliph Ali and his martyred son Hussein. In such an environment, where the slightest incident can set off a riot, Chesney's firmness and restraint probably averted a serious conflict. He hoped that the steamer would be treated with more respect on her return voyage upstream.

The *Euphrates* was now approaching the Lemlum marshes, one hundred miles below Hilla. After their arduous trip to Baghdad and the dramatic departure from Hilla, many members of the expedition were glad to be once again steaming down the broad river and gazing at the dense groves of date-palms that lined the banks.

The first stop was at Diwaniya, a fortified town two-thirds of the way to Lemlum. This was the last outpost of Turkish authority, manned by a garrison constantly at war with the unruly Khezail tribesmen to the south. The weather was so hot here that the Helfers and some others slept on deck, untroubled by the sound of lions roaring throughout the night. Tamarisk had now begun to replace date palms on the river bank and wood-cutting parties reported seeing lion tracks on the ground.

Entering the marsh country, the current quickened and the flow of water was constricted by man-made embankments raised above the surrounding swamps barely six inches higher than the surface of the river. The main channel, described by Ainsworth as 'calm, glassy, and diversified by flower-

101

ing plants',[12] was at the most only 200 feet broad, narrowing in places to 35 feet, with sharp turnings every hundred yards and small canals branching off on either side. (This was in fact an intricate system of water management, established by the Babylonians, poorly maintained but still used by the Khezail tribe for cultivating rice.) The *Euphrates*, which was 105 feet long and 32 feet broad with her paddle boxes attached, steamed cautiously but successfully through this fragile maze.

Those not engaged in navigation could watch pelicans soaring over the vast flooded expanse of reeds, bulrushes and bamboo; the shining lily-covered pools; and the hillocks where water buffalo grazed. Sunset turned the whole landscape red and gold; marsh birds flew off to their roosts, while Khezail tribesmen paddled their canoes back to their reed huts. Pauline Helfer was reminded of the Spreewald near her home, while Ainsworth recalled that Alexander the Great had lost his tiara in the swamps when a gust of wind had blown it off his head.

The Khezail were at that time the strongest and the richest tribe on the middle Euphrates with a long tradition of defending their freedom and their Shia faith against the Turks. Their wealth was derived from rice cultivation and from tolls levied on river shipping. Chesney, descending the river in 1831, had stopped at New Lemlum, a toll station established to replace a previous one that had been washed away. The Khezail tribesmen there had stripped him of all his possessions except his charts.

The *Euphrates* reached New Lemlum on the afternoon of 13 June. The main channel here was about 125 feet across and the steamer was obliged to anchor close to the town. Soon the vessel was surrounded by half-naked Khezail boatmen bartering, begging and examining every detail of her construction. Watching the crowd of curious onlookers gathered on the bank, Ainsworth observed 'the unusual sinewy length and thinness of their limbs, a peculiarity of development which, as seen on a smaller scale in the shrimp girls of Boulogne, we could not but attribute to their living in a marsh.'[13] Some of them were frowning 'with an expression of infinite malignancy', while others laughed and jeered at the strangers, singling out Pauline Helfer with 'looks and actions which admitted of no misinterpretation'.[14]

The night was hot and humid, with swarms of mosquitos. Fully clothed and wrapped up from head to foot in linen sheets for protection, the Helfers slept on deck with several of the ship's company. Chesney, Murphy and Ainsworth stayed in their cabins, while Estcourt and a guard camped on shore. Sentries patrolled the vessel and the river bank.

Some time during the night Estcourt felt a tug at his bedding and discovered that his silk coverlet was gone. As he drowsed off again, he was awakened by a second tug, this time at his pillow, under which he kept his pistol. He seized his pistol and looked around for the robber, but the moon had gone down and he could not see anyone. By now quite awake, he decided to go back to his cabin on the steamer. As he approached the vessel, Estcourt glimpsed on the aft deck the shadowy figure of an Arab threading his way among the shrouded sleepers, one of which he appeared to clutch at as he made for the stern.

Pauline Helfer had been dreaming of lions and imagined that a lion had pounced on her and was dragging her away. Unable to disentangle herself from the folds of the sheet, she shrieked: 'A lion, a lion!'[15] Her cry awoke her husband, similarly swathed, who at first could not make out what was going on. A moment later he grasped her arm and, as the Arab dragged her further towards the edge of the deck, he held on to her legs, while someone else held on to the doctor's legs. In Charlewood's words:

> The Arab must have been a strong fellow, for he dragged all
> three to the stern, and then leaped over, still holding and
> dragging poor Mrs. Helfer. At last Estcourt came to the rescue,
> ran to the stern, and fired his pistol at the man, who at once
> let go his hold, and dropped silently into the water. We did
> not discover whether he was wounded. Of course, when the
> affair was all over, Dr. Helfer gave it out that the Arab wanted
> to steal his wife's cloak, and it was tacitly agreed that such
> was the fact; but some of us wicked youngsters could not help
> remembering the leering looks with which a number of the
> Arabs treated Mrs. Helfer during the evening, and we came to
> the conclusion amongst ourselves that it was Mrs. Helfer
> herself, and not her cloak, that the Arab was trying to walk off
> with.[16]

It was later established that the Arab had swum around the vessel's stern and had crawled through a porthole into the main cabin, where he had tried in vain to remove the chronometer but had taken Fitzjames's watch, one of that officer's few remaining possessions, which had been hung along-side the chronometer to verify its time. The intruder had then crept along the passage between the cabins and climbed up the companion-way to the deck.

The rest of the night was enlivened by noisy celebrations ashore, but there were no more incidents. In the morning the watch was recovered and the *Euphrates* left New Lemlum. Unfortunately the Khezail tribesmen misdirected the vessel down the wrong channel, causing her to get stuck in the mud. After a sleepless night at a spot long remembered as 'Mosquito Station', the steamer was freed by warping and backing the paddles. With some trouble the expedition found its way out of the marshes into the clear, broad channel of the lower Euphrates and anchored beside a thick grove of poplars above El Khidr, a village of the Beni Hucheyim tribe.

The Beni Hucheyim, a Shia tribe, were at that time a loose confederation that owed allegiance to the powerful Montefik tribe further down the river. At first they welcomed the expedition and agreed to provide firewood for the steamer. But the next morning there was a change of mood. Ainsworth and Dr Helfer,* who had been walking through the wood in search of wolves and other game, heard 'a great hubbub' in the village and saw women, children and animals running into the bush.[17] Then they heard musket shots and the whiz of a Congreve rocket.

The way back to the steamer led past the village and beneath the walls of a fort where Murphy and Corporal Greenhill had been making astronomical observations. It was too risky to attempt a detour through the bush, so Ainsworth and his companion walked 'not fast, but quite composedly' towards the fort, passing a group of armed Arabs who watched them but made no move to block their path.

Murphy and his assistant were still at the fort, busily setting up a rocket tube where it could command the village. They reported that a party of wood-cutters from the *Euphrates* had been fired upon by the Arabs and that several of the men had been wounded. (It turned out later that this portion of the wood was a sacred grove.) The rocket tube had been brought from the steamer to cover the wood-cutters' retreat and help Ainsworth and Helfer to get back.

In a short time everyone was safely on board, except for the two-man garrison of 'Murphy's Fort'. After the boiler fires had been lighted to get up steam, they all spent an anxious half hour watching the Arabs conduct a war dance and fire random shots at the vessel. Before getting under way, Chesney sent the interpreter Seyid Ali ashore to propose mutual apologies and a truce, but the Arabs replied with insults and ordered the steamer to go away.

The dancers now dispersed to take up positions in the wood. Once Murphy and his assistant had come back on board, the vessel moved off upstream (to the amazement of the Arabs) to a position opposite the wood, where she met heavy fire from the shore. No one on board was hit, although

* The accounts by Chesney and Ainsworth do not mention Helfer, but his wife's memoirs state that he was also there.

Ainsworth records that while he was helping one of the swivel gun crews, 'a ball passed between the heads of a young seaman and myself, just as we were stooping over the gun. He looked up at me, as if in intimation of the fact, and I smiled, but it was a narrow escape for one of us.'[18]

Finally, Chesney ordered the nine-pounder gun to fire a broadside of grape and canister shot into the wood. Several discharges killed three Arabs and wounded some others; soon there was no more fire from the wood. A fort on the opposite side of the river continued firing, but was silenced by a Congreve rocket and some Coehorn mortar shells. All was quiet as the *Euphrates* turned around and resumed the descent of the river.

This was the expedition's only fatal encounter with the Arabs. Chesney regretted that it had occurred, but considered it his duty not to allow an attack on his wood-cutting party to go unpunished. The following day, when visiting the Sheikh of the Montefik at his encampment beside the river, Chesney explained that he appreciated the feelings of the tribesmen and that the trouble had arisen because they had fired at the wood-cutters without first requesting them to desist. Ainsworth recalls that 'the chieftain only laughed at the matter, and said that he did not know before that the Beni Hikayim had been so warlike'.[19]

The Montefik tribe live on both banks of the Euphrates in the province that bears their name. But in those days they spent much of the year in the desert, where they raised Arab stallions for export to India. Colonel Taylor was a valued friend of the tribe because the East India Company was their best customer. In addition, he had once persuaded Daud Pasha to spare the life of a rebellious Montefik sheikh. Ormsby and other English travellers had been lavishly entertained. Chesney and his companions were ceremonially received by the Montefik sheikh Isa ben Mohammed, but their host showed some embarrassment when Chesney complained that the coal boats which Colonel Taylor had ordered up the river from Basra to the expedition depot stations had encountered date-palm trunks thrown into the channel by Montefik tribesmen.

That evening the *Euphrates* anchored off Suk el-Shuyuk, the capital and main trading centre of the Montefik tribe. The tide from the Persian Gulf had already been felt some fifty miles upstream and the next day, as the majestic river broadened into the vast sheet of the Hammar Lake, one of the crew thought they had already reached the sea. The rushy banks were barely visible from the main channel and wood-cutting was out of the question. The steamer arrived without incident at Korna, where the Euphrates and Tigris rivers meet. A decrepit Turkish man-of-war lay there at anchor, serving as a custom-house. The *Euphrates* fired a gun to honour the Sultan's flag and, after a long delay, the Turkish ship returned the salute.

Arab legends identify Korna as the seat of the Garden of Eden. 'It is certainly not a paradise now', Estcourt wrote. 'It is covered with Palm trees, but the Musquitoes defy the heaviest sleeper. We were glad to leave it before day break.'[20]

On 19 June 1836, ninety-one days after leaving Bir, the expedition steamed down the broad Shatt el-Arab waterway at half speed, using crates and barrels to eke out their fuel supply. Around noon the *Euphrates* anchored at the roadstead in the river where Basra is connected by a short canal.

Besides an ancient Turkish warship, two East Indiamen lay in the roads; one of them, the 372-ton *Cavendish Bentinck*, was preparing to depart. Salutes were exchanged and Chesney celebrated one of the greatest days in his tortured life by ordering the chronometers to be placed on one of the steamer's boats, hoisting the royal standard and firing off a gun for every year of the King's life. (William IV was at that time in his seventy-first year.)

The *Cavendish Bentinck* was taking a cargo of horses to Calcutta and planned to stop at Bushire to pick up more horses. The captain was glad to accommodate the Helfers if they were prepared to leave at once. Pauline Helfer records their departure:

> There was no time for sad thoughts and feelings. With a shake
> of the hand, and a laconic 'Good bye,' which, with the
> monosyllabic English, expresses all that other nations use many
> words for, we took leave of our comrades.[21]

Meanwhile Chesney had contacted the agent of the East India Company, an Armenian named Johannes Parseigh, and had learned that there were no despatches awaiting him from Bombay. At that moment, while gunsmoke still clouded the sultry air, the Euphrates expedition began to fall apart.

Chapter 11
Waiting for the Indian Mails

Sir Robert Grant, the Governor of Bombay, was the younger brother of Charles Grant, who had been President of the India Board from November 1830 to December 1834 and was now Colonial Secretary with the title of Lord Glenelg. Only a year apart in age, they had been born in Bengal and came to Britain in 1790 in their early teens.

Backed by the wealth and connections of their father, an important East India Company director, 'the Grant twins', as they were called, helped each other climb the ladders of political success. When Charles Grant was appointed President of the Board of Control, his brother Robert joined the board as one of the commissioners and later served on the House of Commons Select Committee that considered the Euphrates river project.

Both of them were intelligent and deeply religious. Robert Grant wrote hymns in his leisure hours, among others 'O worship the King, all glorious above'. But their temperaments were very different. As Chesney had discovered, Charles Grant was a weak, diffident introvert. His brother, on the other hand, a pleasant, sensible man with many friends, was long remembered as 'the good governor' of Bombay.[1] A contemporary poet wrote of Charles and Robert Grant:

> He has a very good berth,
> He does nothing at all on the face of the earth,
> But his brother Bob beyond the sea
> Is a far sprightlier chimpanzee.[2]

Robert Grant had resigned his post at the Board of Control when he was appointed governor of Bombay and had sailed for India in September 1834.

107

He understood the political objectives of the Euphrates expedition and he knew that upon completion or abandonment of the project the two vessels would be turned over to the East India Company for possible patrol work on the river Indus. He also knew that the Company and the British government were working on a plan to develop a regular service between Bombay and Suez to connect with the new Admiralty packet from Malta to Alexandria. But he could not know how the planning work had developed on these two projects while he was at sea.

In May 1835, two months after Grant had been sworn in as governor, the *Hugh Lindsay*, returning from Suez, had brought Chesney's letter of 17 March from Malta (see p. 49), which predicted that the Euphrates expedition would arrive at Basra 'about the end of June', ready to take a mail from Bombay up the Euphrates for delivery to an Admiralty packet on the Syrian coast 'about the middle of July'.

The Select Committee, on which Grant had served (with his brother as chairman), had recognized that the carriage of mail would be a useful offset against the substantial expense of a regular steamship service between Britain and India. It was contemplated that, if the experimental river voyage proved the Euphrates to be navigable, the service would use the Persian Gulf/Euphrates route between June and September, when the south-west monsoon prevented navigation by the Red Sea route. After hearing testimony from a retired officer of the Indian Navy, the committee concluded that steam navigation 'would be practicable between Bombay and Bussora during every month of the year'.[3] (The witness had been referring to a modern steamer, able to develop a speed of nine miles an hour in still water; he had warned the committee that even with such a vessel the 1,587-mile voyage from Bombay to Basra might take a month in July or August.)

The idea that the Indian Navy should send a vessel with mail from Bombay to connect at Basra with Chesney's experimental voyage was totally new. Chesney may have developed the idea when he learned that the March 1835 mail from England was going to India for the first time by steam, using the Malta-Alexandria packet and the *Hugh Lindsay* from Suez to Bombay. At that moment he may have decided that his name should go down in history as the man who had pioneered a similar service on the Euphrates route by receiving mail from India at Basra, carrying it up the river in his steamboats and delivering it on the coast of Syria to a steam packet bound for home.

Chesney's idea, which obsessed him more and more as time went on, had a fatal flaw that was obvious to the authorities in Bombay and should have been perceived by Peacock at the East India House and by Cabell at the Board of Control. The Indian Navy did not possess a vessel capable of making the voyage from Bombay to Basra against the south-west monsoon. After receiving Chesney's March 1835 letter from Malta, Grant noted in an official minute that 'as we have no steamer big enough to carry enough coal to "force a passage" during the monsoon, and sailing vessels can't make headway, I propose that Chesney be told to employ this [monsoon] season in surveying the Tigris & Karoon.'⁴ Captain Hennell, the Resident at Bushire, was instructed to send sailing vessels periodically to Basra to make contact with Chesney if he should appear.

(Grant's remark about steamers reflected the Indian Navy's experience in 1834, when Lord Clare was still governor of Bombay. Orders had been received from Calcutta that the *Hugh Lindsay*, recently returned from Suez, should take some important despatches from Bombay to Bassadore [Basidu], a port in the Strait of Hormuz off Bandar Abbas which was the base of the Persian Gulf squadron. From there they would be forwarded by sailing ship to Basra and thence overland to Aleppo.

Bassadore was 1,100 miles from Bombay, there had been no time to set up a coal depot, and the monsoon season was approaching. However, the captain was willing and on 31 May, a week after leaving Bombay, the *Hugh Lindsay* reached Bassadore with two days' supply of coal remaining. After delivering the mail to the squadron commander, the steamer managed to limp back to Bombay using sail as well as steam and eking out her coals with wood procured at Bassadore.)

In his letter of 21 July 1835 to Grant, Chesney had offered to pick up a mail at Basra not later than 1 October and take it upstream to Syria (see pp. 60 and 67). This would have required a vessel to leave Bombay toward the end of the monsoon season. Fortunately, this letter was delayed in delivery and was superseded by Chesney's third and final letter of that year (see p. 66), which notified Grant that the expedition was detained at Bir and that he would advise the governor when it would be ready to move. Consequently, Grant had made no plans for the *Hugh Lindsay* to go to Basra and no coal depots had been set up in the Persian Gulf. The steamer made two return voyages between Bombay and Suez (November 1835/January 1836 and March/June 1836); on the second voyage she brought news that Chesney had started down the Euphrates. Grant, who was staying at a hill station south of Bombay, received this information on 3 June 1836.⁵

Assuming correctly that Chesney would reach Basra some time in June, Grant urged Sir Charles Malcolm to send off a fast vessel to Basra with despatches for Chesney to take to Syria. In place of the *Hugh Lindsay*, unavailable due to lack of coaling depots, and after all alternatives had been reviewed, the task was assigned to the *Shannon* schooner. But this vessel was still in Bombay harbour on 20 June, when a sloop arrived from the Persian

Gulf bearing Chesney's letter of 17 March from Bir (see p. 77) with the list of stores required from India for the return voyage – quantities far greater than the little *Shannon* could carry. A week later, as his colleagues debated new arrangements in the shadow of the approaching monsoon, Grant placed on record his 'deep mortification at the wavering that has delayed the despatch of the *Shannon*, which should be in the Persian Gulf by now.'

Chesney's plans had always allowed for a period of three or four weeks' stay at Basra to refit the steamers before going back up the river. There was now only one vessel to be refitted, but her paddle boxes had been damaged during the passage of the Lemlum marshes. Repairs of any kind would be difficult, since most of the essential tools had been lost when the *Tigris* went down.

Unfortunately, the once thriving port of Basra that Chesney remembered from his brief visit in April 1831 had been wasted by plague and civil disorder. He had assured the Select Committee of the House of Commons that there were 'very great facilities' for repairing an iron steamboat at Basra,[6] but he looked in vain for craftsmen and when the Turkish admiral courteously offered him the use of the dockyard, Chesney found that there was no paint there and 'not a plank nor a rope was to be obtained.'[7]

The only alternatives were to sit and wait in the sweltering heat for a vessel to arrive from India; or to attempt to reach the port of Bushire and refit there with the aid of Captain Hennell, whom Chesney had met in 1831. The naval officers argued strongly against exposing a flat-bottomed river steamer to the open sea, but as they had often seen at Amelia and Port William, a challenge merely helped Chesney to make up his mind. Estcourt records that two days after their arrival at Basra 'Colonel Chesney, always in a hurry and always impatient of remaining at rest, it is a disease with him, weighed anchor, leaving Murphy and myself, and went to Bushire.'[8] Estcourt, who was suffering from malaria, had chosen to stay with Murphy and Corporal Greenhill at Basra to help them with their survey work.

The guns and other heavy weights were stowed below for greater stability. Deadlights secured the portholes, while the cabin windows, which were two feet square and only a foot above the water, were blocked with planking. Aided by two experienced pilots, the *Euphrates* steamed down the last seventy miles below Basra to anchor at the mouth of the river.

The next morning they crossed the sandbar that marks the entrance to the Persian Gulf and made ready for the 200-mile voyage to Bushire. For the first part of the journey offshore shoals and sandbars obliged the steamer to lay its course out of sight of the low, marshy coast. The pilots were of little help; in Charlewood's words, 'it was all guess work how we were to steer, the compasses being useless, not having been corrected for the attraction of the iron hull.'[9] The vessel rolled constantly and the boiler pipes needed frequent desalting, but she faced the waves well and made good headway until towards evening Charlewood noticed something unusual. He recalled that:

> Whilst walking the deck, it occurred to me that the water was looking very thick, and the sea breaking rather ominously. I put the lead over the side, and to my amazement found that we were in 6 feet water; the vessel drawing about 4½ feet. The helm was instantly put down, and now, as we turned towards the sea a wave burst in the planking of one of the foremost windows, and the water rushed in in a deluge. The men went down below, and at last succeeded in forcing hammocks into the aperture and so stopping the rush of water. In the course of time the damage was repaired, and we succeeded in getting into deep water. We passed a most anxious and uncomfortable night, steering as well as we could by the stars. The stoke-hole was so intensely hot, the men could not be induced to remain in it. I, with others, had occasionally to go down and put coals on the fires.

There was a fresh wind that night, but the weather moderated as they passed Kharg Island at daybreak and steamed on through smooth water to Bushire. Arriving late that evening, they were greeted with surprise and admiration by the Resident, who had received no instructions from Bombay. The next morning the steamer was saluted by the five ships that were anchored in the roadstead: two Indian Navy warships, the eighteen-gun *Elphinstone* sloop of war and the little *Cyrene* schooner; a frigate owned by an Arab prince; and two merchantmen. One of the merchantmen was the *Cavendish Bentinck*, which was expecting to depart for Calcutta with Dr and Madame Helfer on board.

The crowded, unhealthy town of Bushire, built on the rocky tip of a peninsula that juts out from the Persian coast, was in those days a busy port with a roadstead sheltered by the peninsula and nearby Kharg Island. The East India Company residency, where the Helfers stayed as guests of Captain Hennell, lay outside the town. After a few days in Bushire, the Helfers decided that they did not like the place. Dr Helfer went out into the country in search of insects, but when his wife left the compound to do some sketching, she was pursued by a crowd of men to the edge of a cliff, where she had to be rescued by the Residency guard.

The Helfers discussed their plans with Captain Hennell, who urged them to give up the idea of staying in Persia. Since the *Cavendish Bentinck* was still in the roadstead, loading horses for the Indian army, the Helfers decided to sail on her to Calcutta and seek a new life there.

While at Bushire the Helfers discovered the identity of their former companions, the self-proclaimed Afghan princes who had taken their money in exchange for imitation jewels. Hennell had not met them but he knew a lot about them. They were the sons of a European indigo planter in the Lucknow district and his Indian wife. After stealing a chest of gold coins from their father, they had made their way to Europe and lived there for a long time under various names. Somehow the Indian police had learned that after spending all their money, the two men were coming home. They had been recognized when they disembarked at Bombay and had been arrested and jailed in Lucknow. (One of their last dupes was Victor Fontanier, the French vice-consul at Basra. When the two imposters arrived there, they had announced that they were the advance guard of the Euphrates Expedition bearing important despatches for India. Fontanier, who had been assigned to find out all he could about the project, had listened eagerly to their stories although he had been surprised that they did not recognize the names of several well known European Orientalists. They had left after a few days, but not before 'Mr Brown' had managed to touch the vice-consul for 'un petit emprunt', repayable in Bombay.)[10]

Since the *Cavendish Bentinck* was sailing direct to Calcutta and there was no vessel going to Bombay, Chesney sent off a letter from Bushire, dated 30 June, addressed to Lord Auckland, the new Governor-General, with enclosures for Sir Robert Grant.[11] After describing the events of the voyage down the Euphrates and the object of his trip to Bushire, Chesney explained that there were two reasons why he must ascend the Euphrates before the end of July, even if the mail from India did not arrive in time. The first reason was that he had promised to pick up the mail from England, which should reach the Syrian coast by 27 July. The second, more compelling reason was a message Chesney had received at Ana from Lord Ponsonby, who was convinced that war between the Sultan and Mehemet Ali was inevitable. Chesney gathered from the ambassador that a voyage to Beles and back might be possible in July, but that 'the Ascent cannot be made safely at a later period on account of the political World, or rather what it is likely to be on our immediate route'.

As he scanned the horizon vainly for the missing *Hugh Lindsay*, Chesney began to assess the difficulties he must face. The situation of the Euphrates expedition was not good. The steamer, already buffeted in the Lemlum passage, had suffered further damage in crossing over from Basra. Charlewood recalls that 'our poor vessel was in a sad plight; the decks opened out and let the water pour down into the cabins, the iron of the sides had also begun to crack abaft the paddle-boxes.'[12] Refitting at Bushire would take time, since some items would have to be brought from Bassadore. The deck needed caulking, while the paddle floats and boxes and some of the iron plates had to be repaired. In addition, the engines needed to be inspected and overhauled. More smiths and carpenters were hired and the entire vessel was emptied to allow room for the work. Hennell arranged for the ship's company – other than Chesney, who stayed at the Residency – to be accommodated on *The Sovereign of the Seas*, a 300-ton Arab ship that had been converted into a hulk.

After refitting, the *Euphrates* would face the perils of the open sea voyage to Basra, to be followed by the uncertainties of the journey up the river. Chesney recognized that the *Euphrates* was too large for the bends in the Lemlum marshes and claimed in his reports[13] that after the initial survey voyage was completed he had intended to use her only in the upper part of the river and to rely on the smaller *Tigris* for the Lemlum segment and the lower stretch. This may have been his plan, but now he had only the one steamer, too slow in answering the helm and liable to be grounded in the swamps among mosquitos and hostile Arabs, an easy prize for Mehemet Ali and his son in the event of war.

(Mehemet Ali revealed his feelings about Chesney and his project when he learned about the wreck of the *Tigris*. 'This is a good beginning,' he told the Russian consul, 'but for me the loss of one of the steamers is not enough; most of all I wish Colonel Chesney had been drowned, for he is the sole author of this wretched expedition that has caused me so much trouble.'[14])

The Helfers were not the only ones for whom the merchant ships riding easily at anchor offered an escape from hot, unfriendly Bushire. Unlike the gunners and sappers, who were governed by army discipline, the seamen served on the *Euphrates* under the terms of a contract. On 4 July Cleaveland reported to Chesney that the seamen were claiming to be discharged; even some of the gunners were asking to be sent home.

Many years later Chesney's biographers observed that 'perhaps the better course would have been to have dismissed the expedition at this point, and transferred the gallant little vessel, when renovated, to the Indus, her ultimate destination.'[15] But Chesney was more than the commander of an expeditionary force. He was the promoter of a new route to India and had just proved its feasibility by completing, against all odds, the voyage from

Bir to the mouth of the Euphrates. His confidence was reinforced by sealed reports on the voyage that he had asked each of the officers to draw up, together with suggestions as to how a regular steam service might operate. Chesney sent them to the India Board unread, but he assured Peacock that 'they are all you could have desired & twice as favorable as either you or myself had dared even to hope . . . At any rate *your child* has matured & the problem solved.'[16]

Chesney acted promptly to restore the expedition's morale. Hennell agreed that when the *Euphrates* was ready to leave, the *Elphinstone* would tow her across the open sea and would carry the entire expedition except for a skeleton crew on board the steamer. This procedure would reduce the risks of the voyage, but some of the seamen still wanted to be gone. Finally Chesney granted them a dishonourable discharge after arranging with Hennell to replace them with Indian Navy volunteers from the *Elphinstone* and the *Amherst*, a sister cruiser.

When the *Cavendish Bentinck* finally sailed on 7 July with the Helfers and a full cargo of horses, Chesney sent Auckland and Grant a more sombre update of his previous letters.[17] After relating his troubles with the seamen, he stated that if the *Hugh Lindsay* did not arrive in time to permit an ascent of the river by 15 July, he would be guided by Ponsonby's warning and stay at Bushire with the *Euphrates* awaiting further orders.

The hot, wearisome month of July passed with no news from India. Since the refit of the steamer was proceeding slowly, Ainsworth gained permission to make a tour of southern Persia. Estcourt, now recovered from malaria, sent periodic reports by boat from Basra and forwarded the May mail from England, along with a note from Hector that the *Tigris* had been found. There was little of importance for the expedition in the despatches from London, since they had been sent three weeks before the India Board learned that it had even left Bir. A duplicate of Hobhouse's previous letter reminded Chesney of the 31 July termination date. Among the private mail was a letter to Cleaveland from a friend at the Admiralty urging him 'to get clear of the business as soon as might be, as his extra time would not be allowed'.[18] (Cleaveland quickly reassured Chesney that he planned to stay.)

Once the possibility of a July voyage up and down the Euphrates was gone, Chesney needed to make arrangements for bringing down the mail from England for India, which he had expected to pick up in Aleppo at the end of the month. Chesney had learned from Hennell that the authorities in Bombay were considering re-activating the 'Great Desert Route', by which despatches from Basra had at one time been sent directly across the desert to Aleppo. Hennell had been in touch with Sheikh Jaber ben Abdallah el-Sabah, the ruler of Kuwait (then known as Grane), who offered to provide dromedaries and riders that would make the journey in fifteen days each way. Chesney realized at once that here was an ideal means of bringing down the mail from Aleppo. Accompanied by Cleaveland, Charlewood and Ainsworth, he left Bushire on 19 July on the *Cyrene* schooner for Kuwait.

Five days later they anchored in deep water off Kuwait, which Ainsworth described as 'a group of mud houses with flat roofs, a port with a Sheikh's house, and a trifle of life and bustle, but by far the greater part of the town uninhabited or in ruin'.[19] The sheikh quickly agreed to provide dromedaries and Chesney handed him a fat bundle of letters and reports to be delivered to Nathaniel Werry, the British vice-consul in Aleppo, who would send them on to the India Board. The British mail for India would be brought back by dromedary to Kuwait.

The tenor of Chesney's letters from Kuwait recalls his confused state of mind a year earlier at Port William. In a letter to Werry, a trusted friend who had helped the expedition to solve many problems in Syria, Chesney wrote: 'I confess I fear we may be detained long enough without any kind of news negative or affirmative, to make it too late to attempt anything in the way of an ascent now more important than ever to overcome our Enemies.'[20] (Cleaveland commented to Werry that if the mail from Bombay did not arrive by 31 July, 'really I suppose Sir J. H.'s orders for breaking up the Exp. at that time, must be carried into effect – and really the blackened state of the Political Horizon at home will make it a happy release for most of us.')[21]

Werry relayed these remarks to the Foreign Office, observing that the Russians would rejoice at 'the Contrariety of this Enterprize'.[22] He did not know that the package from Kuwait also contained a letter from Chesney to Sir John Hobhouse dated 24 July with an altogether different tone. After reviewing his reasons for having carried on with the expedition (one of which was the possibility of salvaging the *Tigris*), Chesney wrote:

Therefore – after much anxious thought, and, with more hesitation than I ever felt before, I have determined to proceed up the River, even if the Mail does not come – but this step must be taken immediately, on account of the falling water, which, at best, will give us but little time with our vessel (never intended for the low season). Unless – therefore – I hear

115

something decided about hostilities, your reply* will, in all probability find me in the upper Euphrates and most likely near the *Tigris*.[23]

This change of plan was already in Chesney's mind before he left Bushire, for he attached a copy of a letter of 19 July to Sir Robert Grant that stated: 'I propose to proceed up the River, about the 25th *with* or *without* the Mail.'[24]

Chesney's contradictory signals from Kuwait reflect his swings of mood between wishful thinking and calm analysis. Cleaveland, Charlewood and Fitzjames sympathized with his plight but found it hard to carry out unrealistic orders or put up with his anger when they were not fulfilled. When Chesney and his companions returned to Bushire at the end of July, they found the *Euphrates* not yet ready to leave. Fitzjames, who had been left in charge, reported that there was some repair work still to do and that he was still awaiting coals and written authority from Bassadore for the volunteer seamen to serve with the expedition.

The bold plan outlined in Chesney's letter to Hobhouse had assumed an immediate departure from Bushire. Bitterly discouraged, Chesney allowed Hennell and the Residency doctor to take him away from the heat of Bushire to rest for two weeks at Hennell's palm-tree cottage at the foot of the nearby hills.

Basra, where Estcourt, Murphy and Corporal Greenhill had been stationed since 21 June, is not a pleasant place in the summer. Ainsworth remarked that the ancient city, surrounded by canals and date groves, was largely in ruins and that 'a death-like silence pervaded the streets and city generally'.[25] During the day the townspeople sheltered in their cellars from the burning sun and the hot, sandy wind that blows in from the Arabian desert during the south-west monsoon.

The East India Company Residency, a riverfront compound at Maqil, outside the city, was spacious and well provided. But once Estcourt had regained his health, he grew fretful. The French vice-consul Victor Fontanier, rated by Hobhouse as 'very clever, very amusing, very injudicious',[26] provided some company, but much of the time Estcourt was alone with Murphy. A peevish letter to his father describes their existence:

---

* Chesney's expectation of an early reply from Hobhouse was a flight of fancy. Delivery times for despatches between Aleppo and London averaged from one to two months each way. In fact, the 24 July package from Kuwait took thirty-three days to get to to Aleppo and did not reach the India Board until late October.

We are, Murphy and I as before, still at Bussora. I am heartily tired of it: To walk to one of the parts of the town before breakfast and the heat: to pass the day in a state of filtration, longing for the night: to be bored all the time by one of the best tempered and excellent men in the world, gives you some idea of my life. Murphy deserves all that I have said: he is excellent in every way, but his calculating and precise mind, with the argumentative disposition of his countrymen, bores me exceedingly. The weather (101° of Farenheit) is too hot for such a companion.[27]

A few days after these words were written, Murphy came back from a midday swim with a fever that rapidly grew worse. A boat was sent to Bushire to fetch Ainsworth, since there was no European doctor in Basra. Estcourt tried various remedies suggested by Fontanier and Parseigh, but nothing would work. After a week of restless days and restless nights Murphy died on 9 August. Estcourt reproached himself for not having nursed Murphy more skilfully, but felt better when Ainsworth (who arrived after Murphy died) told him that this type of fever was always fatal.

On 13 August – the same day that Ainsworth had left Bushire on his futile errand – a three-masted clipper barque, the 350-ton *Sir Herbert Compton*, sailed into the roadstead with supplies for the expedition and 150 tons of coal. She had left Bombay on 16 July and had picked up the long-awaited permits for the Indian Navy seamen at Bassadore. Most important of all, she brought copies of despatches from the government of Bombay.

In atonement for the lost weeks of wavering, the Bombay government moved promptly and on a grand scale after receiving Chesney's letter towards the end of June. Subject to approval from Calcutta, it was decided that the *Hugh Lindsay* should make a pioneer voyage up the Persian Gulf at the close of the monsoon season in mid-September. The *Sir Herbert Compton* was specially chartered to establish coal depots for the steamer and deliver the stores Chesney had ordered for his expedition.

In an official despatch dated 28 June the governor's secretary congratulated Chesney on his achievement and explained that it would be impossible to send a steamer to Basra against the south-west monsoon; however, the *Shannon* schooner would sail shortly for the Persian Gulf with despatches and some Bombay mail for England.[28] (The captain of the clipper ship confirmed that the *Shannon* had left Bombay on 5 July.) Mail from all three presidencies would be assembled in Bombay to be put on board the *Hugh Lindsay*, which would expect to rendezvous with Chesney at Korna by the end of September, thereby enabling him to take the mail up to Syria by 24 October and pick up there the October mail from England. Chesney was requested to make arrangements through the India Board for Admiralty packet steamers to carry the westbound and eastbound mails.

The merchantman unloaded the expedition's stores and sailed on to Basra, carrying a letter form Chesney to Hobhouse dated 14 August, reporting Murphy's death.[29] A second letter, sent off the next day by courier through Persia, notified the minister that Chesney was looking forward to an early ascent of the Euphrates with the *Shannon* mail. He assured Hobhouse that he would be cautious in the ascent of the river and that 'if the water decidedly fails, I shall put about without hesitation'. Chesney added that he was lightening the vessel and would leave her library at Bushire.[30]

A few days later the *Euphrates* lay alongside the *Elphinstone*, ready to be towed across the sea. Once again the deadlights were fixed over the portholes and the guns and heavy items stowed below. But this time the lower paddle floats were taken off and the funnel was put on board the *Elphinstone*, along with most of the expedition. Chesney, Cleaveland, Charlewood and eight volunteers manned the steamer, a forlorn object with chains lashed tightly around her hull to keep it together.

The weather had now changed and a strong north-west wind was blowing. The *Elphinstone* was continually obliged to tack or wear, difficult manoeuvres for a towing vessel. After six days of hard navigation the two vessels brought up inside the bar of the Shatt el-Arab on 31 August. The next morning the *Euphrates* was once more fully manned, except that Corporal Black was in charge of the engine room, replacing John Caldow from Lairds who was ill. The funnel was mounted and the paddle wheels made ready. At first the breeze was so light that the steamer had to tow the sailing ship, but after a while the wind picked up, the tow rope was cast off and the two vessels ran up the river to anchor off Mohammerah (now known as Khorramshahr) on the left bank of the waterway where the Karun river flows in from the north-east.

Chapter 12

The Ascent

For over two hundred years the navigation rights on the Shatt el-Arab and on its eastern tributary, the Karun river, which is also navigable for ocean-going ships, have been the objects of disputes and wars. During the eighteenth century the decline of the Ottoman empire and civil war in Persia enabled the local Arab tribes to establish an autonomous state in Khuzistan, the nominally Persian province on the left bank of the Shatt el-Arab. In 1812 the chief of the Muhaisen tribe (whose family ruled the province until 1924) built a fortress at Mohammerah, where the two waterways joined, and established a free port that prospered in competition with Basra and its heavy harbour dues. In 1831 Chesney reported that the town contained about 800 houses; five years later Ainsworth termed it 'busy and lively'.[1] The East India Company had shown interest in the Karun river, which Sir Robert Grant had suggested as a secondary survey project for the Euphrates expedition.

Upon arrival at Mohammerah, Chesney's first task was to reassemble his forces. The *Euphrates* steamed up to Basra to pick up Estcourt and Corporal Greenhill, who had also suffered from a fever but had come through with the help of Estcourt's attention. Ainsworth reappeared on 5 September after three weeks of wasted effort. He had left Bushire on the *Cyrene* on 13 August; reached Basra too late to save Murphy; met the *Sir Herbert Compton* off Mohammerah with a letter from Charlewood requesting the *Cyrene* to proceed to Kuwait to collect the dromedary mail from Aleppo; found no mail there; crossed over to Bushire, where he discovered that the *Euphrates* had just left; and finally beat his way up to Mohammerah in a hired Arab boat.

Since the *Shannon* had still not arrived, Chesney decided to work out his new crew by ascending the Karun. The steamer went seventy-five miles up the river before encountering shallow water and returning to her anchorage. A brief survey was also made of the Bahmanshir river, another channel in the Karun delta. Estcourt noted that the *Euphrates* 'has lost speed since going to Bushiere from some cause, which as yet we have been unable to discern: and she steers exceedingly wild from the shape of her bow'.[2] But Corporal Black worked the engines well and the Indian Navy crew became, in Chesney's words, 'now quite another cast of men, thanks to a little judicious management in our discipline'.[3]

The *Shannon* arrived off Mohammerah on 13 September, seventy days after leaving Bombay. The captain of the 87-ton schooner (one quarter of the size of the *Sir Herbert Compton*) had judged that she could not sail direct to the Persian Gulf against the south-west monsoon and had taken the long southern route down to the coast of Africa and from there north to Socotra and around the south-eastern tip of Arabia. Estcourt may well have been echoing the opinions of his naval colleagues when he wrote indignantly and perhaps unjustly to his father: 'It is a great disgrace to the Indian Navy to have such a bad sailor in this service.'[4]

While the *Euphrates* was at Mohammerah, Chesney had been in touch with Colonel Taylor in Baghdad and had learned that the life of the expedition had been extended to 31 January 1837. Chesney had not yet received Hobhouse's official despatch to that effect, which was dated 1 June 1836, and had been written in response to Chesney's optimistic letters from Bir and Beles, some time before the India Board knew about the loss of the *Tigris* and the delays in the Persian Gulf.[5] Hobhouse commended Chesney for his achievement in getting the expedition under way and added that, since Chesney was planning to ascend the Euphrates in July, 'I am not willing to bring the expedition to a close, until you have completed the enterprize.' This letter, along with other mail for the expedition, had reached Baghdad in August and had been sent on to Hilla for delivery to Chesney as he steamed up the Euphrates.

But Chesney had other plans for the expedition. He had heard no more from Ponsonby about the likelihood of war, but when he was in Kuwait there were rumours of troop movements in Syria and efforts by Mehemet Ali to induce the Arab tribes to support a planned invasion of Iraq. Chesney had met some of Mehemet Ali's emissaries near Kuwait and reported later that 'I thought from their manner altogether that their object was to ascertain whether we were acting a part, by assisting *underhand* the Pacha's projects'.[6] When Estcourt confirmed that Basra was full of warlike rumours from Syria, which he attributed to Russian agents, Chesney began to fear that an ascent of the Euphrates might expose the vessel to attack. In any case, there was scarcely enough time to make a return voyage to Beles between 13 September, when the *Shannon* brought the Bombay mail, and the end of the month, when the *Hugh Lindsay* was expected.

As the *Euphrates* steamed away from Mohammerah, a bare three hours after receiving the mail from Bombay, Chesney made the startling announcement that, after stopping at Basra and Korna for coal, she would ascend the Tigris as far as it was navigable and return to Korna by 30 September to pick up the *Hugh Lindsay* mail. The vessel would then go up the Euphrates to Beles, where the expedition's horses were still waiting to take the mail to the Syrian coast, and would return to Basra in time to meet the 31 January 1837 deadline. Chesney added that M. Fontanier, the French vice-consul who had helped Estcourt and Murphy and was now himself suffering from the Basra climate, would be invited to travel with the expedition to and from Baghdad.

The journey started sadly with the death of John Caldow, the engineer, from an abscessed liver. He had come from the Laird shipyard to Beles with his colleague, John Struthers, who was drowned when the *Tigris* went down.

The 426-mile ascent of the Tigris from Korna to Baghdad in fifteen days was a triumph of skilful navigation and a masterpiece of bad planning. No depots of coal or wood had been established, since Chesney had expected that after the initial supply of coal was exhausted the *Euphrates* could rely on purchases from wood boats that supplied Baghdad. At Kut el-Amara the coal was used up but there were no wood boats there. For some distance above Kut the river banks, twenty feet above the water, were covered with a dense jungle of vegetation alive with birds, hyenas and lions. But it was impossible to persuade the river Arabs to cut wood; terrified by the sight of this roaring, smoking monster in their river, they fled into the bush. The steamer was obliged to stop each day for 'wooding' and to burn the wood green, which reduced her speed.

Closer to Baghdad they entered the area where wood boats were reported to be operating. But at one point, Estcourt records:

> We brought up mid stream all standing: we had steamed on
> and on, very improvidently depending upon the reports of the
> Arabs, who always declared, that the woodboats from Bagdad
> were loading in the jungle not far ahead – thus we continued
> our course until every atom of fuel was exhausted, and we came
> to a full stop in the middle of the channel.[7]

The *Euphrates* boats rowed up the stream until the wood boats were located, while Estcourt went ashore to hunt jackals.

At this time of the year the Tigris was at its lowest level. In shallow places the channel wound between sandy shoals, often at right angles to the river banks. The two pilots waded or swam ahead of the steamer, marking the course of the channel with sticks and willow branches, but sometimes her stern would be caught at one bend before her bow was clear of the next one.

Fontanier's health improved as the weather became more pleasant. He spent most of his time reading* or observing the human and animal life along the river. He was impressed by the efficient operation of the vessel, with Chesney perched at the bows with his watch and compass, entering elevations and soundings in his notebook, while Cleaveland sat on a paddle box, sheltered by an awning, calling out orders to the helmsman.[8] He also approved of his hosts' calm and fair conduct towards the Arabs and imagined the scenes that might have occurred if an Arab steamboat had been the first to navigate the Seine or the Thames. The vice consul talked to Chesney about the Euphrates route to India and was relieved to learn that it was not intended to be a British monopoly.

On 27 September they anchored a few miles below Ctesiphon. Early the next morning the Residency boat arrived from Baghdad, with Dr Ross aboard, bringing new pilots. A dragoman led Chesney and a few others around the ruined palace of the Persian kings. Its north wing was then still standing and Charlewood recalled later that he climbed 'sailor-like' to the top of the famous arch.[9] The *Euphrates* then picked up the sightseers and steamed up the river to a point nine miles short of Baghdad, where she grounded on a clay shoal and could not be moved. Ainsworth recorded that the shoal was 'said by the pilot, who is a quiz, to be newly formed!'[10]

Chesney, Estcourt, Fontanier and Fitzjames decided to walk to the city, but arrived after sunset and found the gates closed. The dragoman located someone to take a message to Colonel Taylor and a boat was sent to take them to the Residency.

The next morning Chesney and Estcourt sat down with Taylor to examine the mail retrieved from Hilla and review their plans. Hobhouse's letter of 1 June extending the life of the expedition to the end of January informed Chesney that the British government did not anticipate a war between the Sultan and Mehemet Ali; three more recent letters from Lord Ponsonby in Istanbul confirmed this opinion. Werry in Aleppo wrote that two mails had arrived from England; despite some reports of troop movements between Deir and Ana, he had forwarded the mails by dromedary to Kuwait.

* Fontanier's reference to 'la bibliothèque si bien choisie qu'on avait à bord' suggests that not all of the books were left behind at Bushire.

Fontanier learned that Ali Riza Pasha, the governor of Baghdad, was in Kurdistan making new arrangements following the surrender of the rebel chief. The vice-consul accordingly paid his respects to the deputy governor Ashker Pasha, a shrewd bureaucrat from Istanbul whom Estcourt had met in June. Tall and thin, Ashker Pasha was said to have been brought up as a slave in the Sultan's harem; after years of grovelling to his sovereign his legs had become so deformed that he was unable to stand up for long.[11]

As the junior officer of the expedition, Fitzjames had leisure to look around. His diary entries describe the buildings and grounds of the Residency and conclude as follows:

> Colonel Taylor keeps a capital table and lives in a fine style;
> he has some good horses, and an ostrich, a lion, and a leopard.
> Mrs.Taylor appeared at times.[12]

Meanwhile the steamer remained stuck fast for two days. During this time one of the gunners died after a long illness and was buried on the river bank. Cables finally freed the vessel, enabling her to make a triumphant entry into Baghdad in the afternoon of 30 September. Taylor and Chesney were received on board with an eleven-gun salute, the bridge of boats was opened and thousands of onlookers watched the *Euphrates* steam up to the citadel. After saluting the Sultan's representative, she turned around and anchored opposite the Residency. Taylor invited the members of the expedition to join him for a cup of tea on his roof. Ainsworth and Corporal Greenhill (who was still ill) came ashore in a tarred wicker coracle with Dr Ross and his pet lion.

The evening ended with a display of rockets and blue lights and was followed by two days of open house on board the *Euphrates*. Some of the visitors had seen steamers in the Mediterranean, but none made of iron; it was generally believed that this vessel had a wooden hull to which iron plates had been attached. Special times were arranged for the wives of Moslem notables to inspect the steamer from behind their veils. In addition, Mrs Taylor brought a group of fifty well dressed Armenian ladies who removed their veils and joined the officers for lunch in the state cabin.

Ashker Pasha, who did not share Ali Riza's love for the British, took umbrage at the gun salute and refused to go on board the *Euphrates*, although he did condescend to watch her perform various manoeuvres in his honour.[13] (Charlewood asserts that the Pasha arrived unexpectedly while Mrs Taylor's luncheon party was going on and that the refreshments were whisked out of sight while her friends hid in the side cabins. This was allegedly done for two reasons: Turks were supposed not to look at food during the Ramadan fast, and also 'this old Pacha of Bagdad was a notorious old rascal, and it was not desirable that Armenian ladies should be on board with him'.[14] The story is amusing but dubious; in that year Ramadan fell in December, and in view of his upbringing Ashker Pasha was no threat to females.)

Due to the delays in the ascent, Chesney had to abandon his idea of surveying the Tigris above Baghdad. He did, however, arrange for Corporal Greenhill and a small party to survey a possible canal route between the Tigris near Baghdad and the Euphrates; this project, promoted by Colonel Taylor and his brother in Daud Pasha's time, was one of Ali Riza's dreams. Before leaving Baghdad on 5 October, Chesney delivered the *Shannon* mail from Bombay to Colonel Taylor, to be sent on to London by way of Aleppo together with a package of reports to Hobhouse and the East India Company and personal letters to Cabell and Peacock. (All of this material finally reached London at the beginning of February 1837).

Chesney expected the descent of the Tigris to be quicker than the ascent, since he had left orders for coal boats from Basra to lay down depots along the river. But the trip down to Korna took eleven days, of which two were spent grounded on a sandbank and the remainder were shortened by other groundings and delays for wooding. (There was no news of the coal boats.)

Finally, the helmsman's reassuring cry, 'Five fathoms and no bottom!' told them that the steamer was approaching Korna.[15] But, as they contemplated the impending challenge of ascending the Euphrates, emotions among the expedition were very mixed.

Chesney was pleased by the steamer's performance up and down the difficult, uncharted Tigris at its low season and he hoped to do better on the Euphrates, which usually rises and falls a month later. He knew that it would be hard to get her around the sharp turns in the Lemlum channel against a strong current, but he counted on Arab trackers to ease the helmsman's work. In one of his letters to Hobhouse from Baghdad he summed up as follows:

> I have just received satisfactory news not only from the Arabs, where we had a bloodless affair on both sides;* but also of the state of the water, which is quite as good as I ventured to anticipate. The ascent of the Euphrates will be easy compared to what has been just overcome, and which has demonstrated that both rivers are navigable at all times with ease.[16]

In another letter Chesney had reported to Hobhouse that his old pilot

* Chesney was referring to the confrontation at Hilla (see pp. 100–1).

'Getgood' had just arrived from Ana and Felluja with news that 'there is still water for us to ascend'.[17]

Chesney's optimism was not shared by Estcourt or by the naval officers, who were all convinced it was futile to try to go up the Euphrates because the vessel would never get past the Lemlum marshes. Estcourt even hoped that the news of the *Tigris* wreck might have caused Sir Robert Grant to cancel the *Hugh Lindsay* voyage, so that everyone might go home.[18]

But when the *Euphrates* reached Korna on 16 October, the *Hugh Lindsay* was waiting for them there and had been waiting since 3 October. Her four gun crews were at their action stations, ready to fire at an unruly crowd of Arabs on the river bank or, if so ordered, at a Turkish man-of-war.

Several blunders had brought about this unhappy state of affairs. When Chesney had made his sudden decision to steam up the Tigris and order boats from Basra to bring coal up the river, he had not realized that Korna was a customs point and that the sheikh of the Montefik Arabs considered himself the collector. Unable or unwilling to pay duty, the coal boats had returned to Basra.

A few days later the *Hugh Lindsay*, a previously unknown vessel, even larger and more menacing than the *Euphrates*, had steamed up from Basra and had anchored off Korna. The Arabs there had shown great hostility and refused to sell provisions. A delegation from the village had gone aboard with a message from the sheikh of the Montefiks ordering the vessel to go away. The *Hugh Lindsay*'s captain, Commander J. H. Rowband, had replied that she could take care of herself if attacked and passed word to the Turks that if their man-of-war did not help him fight off an Arab attack, he would sink her too. The villagers had then offered to sell provisions but the captain had forbidden his men to go ashore.

Incidents of this type were commonplace in those days. But in this instance a more serious event had occurred in Basra that accounted for the truculence of the sheikh, who had generally been friendly to the British. In addition to the mail and despatches, the *Hugh Lindsay* had brought three passengers from Bombay, two of whom planned to travel with Chesney to Syria. The third was a Protestant missionary named Jacob Samuel, formerly a Prussian Jew, who had been expelled from Iraq in October 1835 after causing a riot in Baghdad by distributing anti-Islamic tracts in the bazaar.[19]

On this occasion, when the *Hugh Lindsay* arrived at Basra, Samuel had disembarked and moved into the East India Company Residency with the avowed purpose of converting Jews to Christianity. After attempting vainly to make a speech in the local synagogue, he had gone into the bazaar and begun distributing his tracts. A riot had been about to start when the

Residency guards had hustled the missionary back on board the *Hugh Lindsay*.

Word spread among the Arab tribes that the infidel steamers had come to take over the country and destroy the faith of Islam. The villagers at Korna, already perturbed by the coal boat incident, were particularly alarmed by Samuel's presence on the vessel. When the Montefik Sheikh Isa was shown one of the tracts, he swore that he would burn any steamer that tried to go up the Euphrates.

Chesney was not worried by this threat, which Estcourt termed 'Arab bravado'.[20] But enmity with the Montefik could jeopardize the ascent of the Euphrates. Chesney had been relying on Sheikh Isa to punish his Beni Hucheyim vassals for their attack on the vessel in June and to dissuade them from seeking revenge. Even more important, Chesney was expecting the sheikh to provide trackers for pulling the *Euphrates* around the bends in the Lemlum channel.

A showdown with Sheikh Isa was clearly necessary. A messenger was sent to Suk el-Shuyuk, the Montefik market town where one of the expedition's coal depots was located; he carried an official communication from Chesney to the Sheikh that 'we intended decidedly to ascend the river, if possible on a friendly footing with him and his people, but quite prepared to resist and signally punish anything like hostility on their part.'[21]

Meanwhile provisions and a new pilot were brought up from Basra. Chesney's biographers record that Commander Rowband, who at first was 'no little displeased at his forced detention of a whole fortnight' under trying circumstances, proved most co-operative.[22] The steamboat's engines were overhauled by the *Hugh Lindsay*'s skilled engineers, one of whom was loaned to Chesney to replace Caldow. Smiths repaired her damaged anchor and several tons of coal were put on board for the trip.

Sixteen boxes of letters from Bombay, Madras and Calcutta were transferred to the *Euphrates*, together with a packet of despatches from the Bombay authorities to the Secret Committee of the East India Company Court of Directors. The contents of this packet were so sensitive that the bearer was instructed to destroy it 'in the event of danger from an enemy, or of its falling into other hands'.[23] In addition, two British merchants from Bombay, one of them a young man in poor health, came on board with an inordinate amount of luggage. Estcourt learned with relief that ten other prospective passengers had been deterred by the news of the loss of the *Tigris*.[24]

The *Hugh Lindsay* left Korna on 18 October, taking the French vice-consul back to Basra, where the steamer would await the mail from England. (The controversial missionary appears to have been sent back to India.)

The *Euphrates*, drawing four feet with her full load, weighed anchor early in the morning of 20 October. There was still plenty of water in the lower part of the river, which was filled with heavy date barges and numerous small craft. The vessel steamed seventy miles upstream to refuel at Suk el-Shuyuk. Chesney's letter to the sheikh had not yet arrived, but the expedition was cordially received. The interpreter Seyid Ali rejoined them here; he had travelled overland from Baghdad and reported that the Arab tribes were in a state of uproar. Chesney was concerned by this news, for he had encountered no hostility along the river except at one place near Suk el-Shuyuk, where the Arabs 'evinced their animosity against us, by pelting the vessel with sticks and pieces of hard mud. The women also showed their anger by exposing their persons in a very indecent manner'.[25]

The next morning the steamer brought up alongside Sheikh Isa's encampment at Kut el-Muammir. Estcourt, accompanied by Seyid Ali, went ashore and made his way through a crowd of onlookers to the sheikh's tent, where they were informed that Sheikh Isa was in his private quarters and could not see anyone. At that moment a Turkish officer who was there on an errand from Baghdad offered to convey a message from Estcourt to the sheikh. The message repeated Chesney's complaint about the coal boats, demanded that the Beni Hucheyim should be punished for their attack on the vessel and asked for a hundred trackers to be supplied. The message also stated emphatically that the Euphrates expedition was 'altogether unconnected with Mr. Samuel and his operations'.[26]

After a long wait an aged mullah, reported to be a close advisor to the sheikh, emerged. He boarded the steamer and announced that the sheikh was satisfied by Estcourt's message. Chesney was invited to come ashore and sign a treaty of friendship and mutual advantage. The *Euphrates* fired a seven-gun salute as Chesney, Estcourt, Cleaveland, Ainsworth and Seyid Ali were ushered into Sheikh Isa's vast circular tent. There were four hundred tribesmen inside, with their chiefs seated in front and an open space in the middle for the visitors. But there was no sheikh. Estcourt recorded what followed:

> The Colonel therefore seeing that he was absent, and supposing
> that it was an Arab trick of slight turned about and walked
> away with his party, leaving the assembled Arabs confounded.
> It was declared, the sheik was at prayers, that he would be
> instantly there, and the Beg was entreated to return; but that
> the Beg would not do, he walked off to the Turkish officer to
> whom he related the treacherous indignity offered to him, and
> the course he should pursue.

Seyid Ali was following Chesney and Estcourt out of the tent when Sheikh Isa came in. The sheikh called to the interpreter and protested that no offence was meant; he had really been at prayers and would do anything to please the Beg. It was sunset before matters were patched up and it was agreed that a Montefik chief would accompany the expedition to punish the Beni Hucheyim. A pilot was provided to guide the vessel through the marshes and it was promised that trackers would be supplied. As regards the coal boats, Sheikh Isa revealed that the attempt to block Colonel Taylor's boats had been instigated by M. Fontanier.

Two days later they reached El Khidr, where the conflict with the Arabs had taken place in June. The village was deserted, as if expecting an attack; no women, children or cattle were in sight, while the men were back in the sacred wood with their muskets at the ready. But this time there was no shooting. When the villagers heard the sound of a bugle and saw a boat being lowered into the water, they returned peaceably to their huts. Rassam went ashore with the Montefik chief, who called the tribesmen ignorant dogs who deserved to be put to death. However, he added, the British were merciful, as was Sheikh Isa; their lives would be spared and the incident would be closed.

Upstream from El Khidr navigation became more difficult. There were many shallow places where the vessel was unresponsive to her helm. As they entered the winding stretch of river through the Lemlum marshes the channel narrowed and the current flowed more swiftly around the bends. Finally, on 24 October, Estcourt recorded that 'we have now this moment anchored at a narrow winding, past which we cannot get'.[27]

Seyid Ali had already gone to Samawa, a nearby town, to hire trackers. But as the members of the expedition sat waiting for a group of illiterate Arabs to help the immobilized steamboat overcome the forces of nature, a mood of pessimism settled on them. Even Chesney's self-control began to give way. 'The Colonel', Estcourt wrote, 'is getting exceedingly disagreeable', adding that he personally had nothing to complain about and that 'much allowance is to be made for the very trying positions in which he [Chesney] is continually placed'.

The interpreter returned with eighty trackers from the Khezail tribe, none of whom had worked with or even seen a steamer before. After forty trackers had been stationed on each bank, the vessel started at half-steam. Fitzjames describes the scene:

> We worked, tracked, anchored, weighed, grounded, backed,
> hove, yelled and screeched at times, till 12.30, when we

anchored to dine, and the vessel had advanced two miles! We
found that the trackers were of no use, as it was impossible to
check her head in when the current took her at the sharp
turnings, or even in the straight parts. We got 500 yards by
evening, heaving hawsers and steam.[28]

Chesney was convinced that the trackers were trying to prevent the steamer
from going up the river; at one moment they almost overturned the vessel,
but she was saved by a hawser parting. Ainsworth compared them to 'a
parcel of schoolboys just let loose from their lessons'. They would pull for
a minute, then dance, then sing a song. 'But quiet and steady they could
not be.'[29]

Next day the steamer made half a mile in the morning and only a few
yards in the afternoon, At that point, Fitzjames records, the trackers were
discharged, having begun to be 'very insolent and troublesome'.[30]

In the midst of these exertions a man was seen on the river bank, waving
at the steamer. It was a messenger from Baghdad, bringing despatches and
mail from another world and almost from another age. A letter from Hobhouse conveyed King William's 'deep and heartfelt concern' upon learning
of the loss of the *Tigris*.[31] Another letter requested Chesney to inform the
minister about his quarrel with Lynch at Beles.[32] (Lynch, Eden and the
other *Tigris* survivors had returned home by various routes in August and
September 1836.)

Chesney had ample time to attend to his correspondence. The fuel was
now exhausted. After unshipping the paddles, the crew tried to warp the
vessel up the river. As many as four hawsers were anchored to the bank
and hauled in by means of pulleys. This was hard work against a three-
knot current; after several hours of warping, the vessel had gained only
twice her length.

Estcourt now joined the naval officers in pleading with Chesney to abandon the ascent. Forty more miles of winding channel lay ahead before the
river broadened again above New Lemlum. They pointed out that the
project would not be doomed just because one vessel was unsuited to its
task. On the other hand, the miserable rate of progress was delaying the
mail and some important despatches. The supporters of the Euphrates route
might well become disillusioned if it were to be associated in their minds
with difficulties and delays.

Chesney could not be moved. Ainsworth well described him as 'a staunch
adherent of the doctrine that nothing was antecedently impossible.'[33] He
was determined to go on until he had to stop. Wood was collected and the
ascent continued on the following day with a combination of warping and

steam. Fitzjames recorded in his journal: '28th. – Worked all day steaming and heaving at the hawsers. Got 800 yards ahead.'[34]

The next entry in Fitzjames's diary reads simply: '29th. – In cleaning the engines, found that the cross-head of the air pump of the larboard engine was broken, which stops us for the present.'

In fact, the cross head was merely cracked, due to some gravel having been sucked in at the bottom of the pump. But the engineer from the *Hugh Lindsay* explained that if the engine were to be re-started, the rod would break and most of the engine machinery would be destroyed. His recommendation, which Chesney reluctantly accepted, was to drop down the river using the remaining good engine and await a replacement part from England.

Chesney had already prepared a contingency plan for the mail and despatches. The day after the accident they were loaded on an Arab river boat under the care of Fitzjames, along with the two passengers and their luggage, the interpreter Seyid Ali and two servants. The boat was bound for Hilla, where Seyid Ali would escort the passengers to Baghdad, while Fitzjames would go on by dromedary to Aleppo and Iskenderun. If a packet steamer was at Iskenderun with a mail for India, Fitzjames was instructed to deliver the mail and despatches for England and bring back the India mail. If there were no steamer there or at Suedia, he was to take the mail and despatches to London as best he could. At the time he received this important assignment, Fitzjames was twenty-two years old.

Upon arrival at New Lemlum the group was greeted hospitably by the local Khezail sheikh. In the morning, however, while the sheikh was at prayer, they were surrounded by armed tribesmen who spent the next two days looting the passengers' heavy luggage, which contained valuable jewels and curios from India but had been reported by the boatmen to be full of gold. The mail boxes were not touched, because the Arabs treated Fitzjames and Seyid Ali as mere tartars. Fitzjames did nothing to undeceive them and courteously declined their offer to give him half the plunder if he would reveal where the passengers had hidden their gold.

After a week's detention by the Khezail, Fitzjames's party managed to hire a boat by selling some of their clothes. They reached Diwaniya, a town loyal to the Turks but at that moment besieged by rebellious tribes; as a result Fitzjames and his companions did not reach Hilla until 19 November. Finding no dromedaries available, they went on to Baghdad, where a caravan was about to leave for Damascus. Four camels were needed to carry Fitzjames, Seyid Ali, two guides and the sixteen boxes of mail. They went by way of Ana and Palmyra, where, like many other travellers, they inscribed their names and the date of their visit at the entrance to Iamlichu's tower tomb.[35] At Beirut Fitzjames boarded an Admiralty steam packet that took him to Malta in time for the mail and despatches to be fumigated and put aboard another packet, which arrived at Falmouth on 8 February 1837, five months after they had left India and six weeks after an East India-man had brought the duplicates that had been sent by way of the Cape. (Fitzjames himself was delayed by quarantine and did not reach England until March.)

Chapter 13

The End of the Expedition

After Fitzjames and Seyid Ali had departed with the passengers, mail and despatches from the crippled *Euphrates*, the remaining members of the expedition – Chesney, Estcourt, Cleaveland, Charlewood, Ainsworth and Rassam – made ready to take the steamer back to Basra. The first, most difficult task was to release the vessel from her cramped position in the shallow Lemlum channel and drop down to the open part of the river where she could be turned around.

The descent began on 31 October. After unshipping the paddles to avoid their being damaged at the river bends, they took in the warps that had secured the vessel to the banks. Then, trusting in the strength of their anchor cables, they floated cautiously downstream, unable to prevent the strong current from banging her from side to side against the banks.

Finally, the *Euphrates* reached open water where she could reship her paddles, get up steam and turn around. Chesney was pleased to see 'the Vessel making so well with one Engine'.[1] Ainsworth adds a piquant detail: 'When we got into the more open channel beyond the marshes we assisted ourselves with sails.'[2]

In contrast with Fitzjames's experiences, the steamer had no trouble with the Arabs. When she lay immobilized in the Lemlum channel, the discharged trackers watched sullenly, perhaps waiting for a chance to loot, but made no move to attack. Farther downstream, the Beni Hucheyim tribesmen fired a couple of shots as the vessel steamed by, but quietened after she rounded up and came close to the village. Chesney records that Sheikh Isa of the Montefik greeted him cordially and 'even went so far as to express his readiness, on any future occasion, to go with us himself, in order to make sure that his dependents conducted themselves properly.'[3]

132

Arriving at Basra on 8 November, Chesney found the *Hugh Lindsay* anchored in the roads, awaiting a third mail from England that had been sent overland from Syria. By great good fortune that cruiser's engineers were able to repair the cracked cross head in their forge, so that the *Euphrates* was fit for duty again.

The next decision to be made was what the expedition should do during the ten weeks that remained until 31 January 1837, the scheduled break-up date. There were no fresh orders from England or from India. The most recent despatches from Bombay were those brought by the *Hugh Lindsay* that had been delivered to Chesney at Korna with the mail. In a letter dated 16 September the Bombay government had enclosed a warm personal letter from Lord Auckland, the Governor-General, together with an official letter suggesting that he should survey the Karun and the Tigris if he could not get up the Euphrates.*[4] The expedition had now been up and down the Tigris as far as Baghdad, but the Karun river delta had hardly been surveyed at all.

For Chesney the major issue was to learn what the authorities in India planned to do after 31 January: whether they would continue a steamer service from Bombay to the Mediterranean by way of the Persian Gulf and the rivers of Iraq, or whether they intended to use the *Euphrates* in an expedition up the river Indus; and what role Chesney might play in furthering their projects. He knew that he would have to go to India to get answers to these questions, but he was reluctant to leave the companions with whom he had shared so much triumph and tragedy; in addition, as he wrote Grant, he did not want to set 'the example of a chief leaving his post'.[5]

By this time the mail from England had arrived at Basra, having left home at the beginning of September (together with the packages delivered to the *Euphrates* in the Lemlum channel), and the *Hugh Lindsay* prepared to weigh anchor for Bombay. Chesney made up his mind to go to India, leaving Estcourt in charge of the expedition. A long letter of instructions authorized Estcourt to survey the Karun and the Tigris, after which he should turn over the steamer and the Indian crew to Colonel Taylor in Baghdad and return to England with the rest of the expedition.[6] Chesney was planning to be in Bombay for only three weeks; the letter of instructions stated that he expected to be back in Iraq before the end of January.

'On November 14', Ainsworth relates, 'we bade adieu to our gallant commander with three hearty cheers and a salute of eleven guns.'[7] The

* Auckland thanked Chesney for a letter of 18 April from Beles and two letters dated 30 June and 7 July from Bushire, which the *Cavendish Bentinck* had brought to Calcutta on 23 August. Such was the speed of communication in the days of sail.

Euphrates was bound for Mohammerah to start the survey of the Karun. The *Hugh Lindsay* left Basra soon afterwards, stopped at Bushire to pick up the dromedary mail Werry had sent from Aleppo, and reached Bombay on 1 December.

Sir John Hobhouse's letter of 29 July and a letter from Cabell dated 1 September were the last communications Chesney received from the India Board before he left Basra. At the time when those letters were written, Hobhouse and Cabell had heard no news from Chesney since learning in late July that the *Tigris* had been sunk and that the expedition was regrouping at Ana.

With some difficulty Hobhouse had arranged for the Admiralty to send a special steam packet to Iskenderun,[8] which had arrived there on 30 July with a mail from England. For several days the captain of the packet had waited vainly for the mail from India and then steamed away after handing the India-bound mail to Werry, who had no information about Chesney's plans to ascend the river.

August and September had passed with no news reaching the India Board about the expedition, other than a report from Werry that Hector had found the sunken *Tigris*. A second mail was sent to Iskenderun; it was delivered to Werry, but the steamer left with no mail from India. Meanwhile London periodicals had started printing accounts by Ainsworth and others, describing the horrors of the winter at Port William, the duplicity of Mehemet Ali and his son, and the apparent inability of the British government to protect the expedition.

(Lord Palmerston was annoyed by these allegations and also by a warning Chesney had sent to Patrick Campbell, the British consul in Egypt, that all the official correspondence with Mehemet Ali would one day be published and everyone would know of the viceroy's bad faith. Chesney later apologized to Hobhouse and assured him he had never planned to release official papers to the press.)

The India Board received three mails from the expedition in October. The first one, sent from Basra in June, reported the stages of the descent from Ana. The second was the dromedary mail from Kuwait, in which Chesney announced that he would go up the Euphrates with or without the Bombay mail, while Cleaveland declared that if it did not arrive by 31 July there would be no ascent. The third was a brief note from Chesney written in Bushire in mid-August, reporting Murphy's death but giving no hint of the expedition's plans. This letter, which the *Sir Herbert Compton* had taken to Basra, reached London ahead of a fourth letter Chesney had sent at the same time by way of Persia that set forth his plans to take the *Euphrates* back across the Gulf and carry the *Shannon* and *Hugh Lindsay* mails upstream. This last letter did not reach London until November.

Hobhouse was troubled by the tenor of the letters he received in October. (For some reason Chesney had reported next to nothing about the need to refit the *Euphrates*, the scanty facilities at Basra and Bushire, the lack of supplies from India, or the discharge of the British crew – each a valid reason for delay in going up the river). Hobhouse could not make out whether Chesney still planned an ascent or had given up the idea. Only three things were certain: the expedition had reached Basra on 19 June and on 15 August it was still at Bushire; the level of the Euphrates was falling; and Chesney was spending a lot of time worrying about eastbound and westbound mails.

As President of the Board of Control, Hobhouse had the power to direct the government of India to continue or suspend the work of the expedition beyond 31 January 1837. But unless funds were provided by Parliament or by the East India Company, the expense would fall on the Indian budget and the authorities in Calcutta and Bombay would have to be persuaded to fit it into their plans. Hobhouse began to prepare a contingency plan to be put into effect in case the expedition failed to ascend the Euphrates in 1836.

The arrival of Chesney's fourth letter, in which he tied the date of an ascent to the arrival of the *Shannon* and the *Hugh Lindsay*, was the last straw for Hobhouse. In a scathing despatch to Chesney, written on 30 November (long before the India Board learned about Chesney's Baghdad escapade or the Lemlum channel fiasco), Hobhouse expressed his gratification that Chesney still planned to ascend the Euphrates, at least with the *Shannon* mail, but added:

> I regret that you should have thought it necessary to wait for the Bombay mail longer than the day which you had had fixed for commencing the ascent of the river – namely the 9th July – your principal object was not the mere conveyance of a letter from Bassora to the Coast of Syria, but the practical proof by actual experiment, that your Steamer could safely, and with due speed make the ascent at the period which you contemplated; and I certainly shall be exceedingly disappointed if, by waiting for Sir R. Grant's dispatches, you should have lost the opportunity of performing that which is generally, though perhaps unjustly, considered as being the most important and most difficult part of the enterprize.

Hobhouse reminded Chesney that the East India Company grant of £8,000 towards the continuation of the project had been expressly conditioned on Chesney making the ascent of the river, so that if Chesney failed, Hobhouse would have to go back to Parliament for the deficiency. He urged Chesney to submit promptly the accounts of the expedition expenses, which Cabell had estimated at £42,000 through 31 January 1837.

Hobhouse then turned to a subject that still vexes governments in a democratic society – the unauthorized leakage of confidential information. Chesney was reminded that regulations required the commander of an expedition to collect all journals and other documents written by its members. This precaution was all the more necessary in this case, owing to the delicate nature of Chesney's mission and 'the very indiscreet use, to say the least of it, which has been made already of the intelligence obtained by more than one person of the expedition'. Hobhouse's despatch continued:

> The remarks to which I allude, conveying censures on the authorities in Syria, on Russian agents, and more imprudently still, on the Indian Govt., must be calculated to throw additional obstacles in the way of any continued attempt to establish the projected line of communication through the heart of a country where such an arrangement can be made only on sufferance; and I must request you to impress upon your Officers the expediency and propriety of much reserve in their future communications even with their friends. As to corresponding with public journalists during the actual performance of their service, such a practise is entirely at variance with the rules prescribed for officers engaged in duties similar to those of your expedition.

Hobhouse concluded this stinging letter by notifying Chesney, whose colonelcy was only for the duration of the expedition, that he was being promoted from captain to the rank of major.[9]

By the time Hobhouse's letter reached Iraq, Chesney had already left for India and the expedition was under Estcourt's command. In compliance with Chesney's instructions the first three weeks after his departure were spent surveying the Karun river delta by steamer, by sailboat and on foot: the Karun was found to be navigable as far up as Ahwaz, where the channel was blocked by a ridge of rocks and a ruined bridge.

After completing the Karun survey, the *Euphrates* refuelled at Basra, leaving on 12 December on her second ascent of the Tigris. On this occasion coal boats were sent on ahead. The steamer overtook them above Korna, where despite Chesney's agreement with Sheikh Isa the boats had been detained by local tribesmen demanding tolls. To the amazement of the Arabs, the steamer took the two boats in tow and proceeded up the river. One boat was dropped off empty at Kut el-Amara, but the second was towed all the way to Baghdad, where the expedition arrived on 26 December.

At the beginning of January 1837 Estcourt attempted to ascend the upper part of the Tigris above Baghdad. But the river, which had favoured their ascent from Basra, had fallen again. Fifty miles upstream the vessel grounded so violently that one of the rudder rings was broken and she limped back to Baghdad to be repaired and also to lengthen her rudder for better steering.

The time had now come to break up the expedition. Hector was recalled from Ana to take custody of the vessel. The Indian Navy crew was sent back to the Persian Gulf. Ainsworth and Rassam planned to ride up the Tigris valley to Mosul (Rassam's home town) and on through Kurdistan, prospecting for coal. A camel caravan was organized to take Estcourt, Cleaveland, Charlewood and the rest of the expedition across the desert from Baghdad to Damascus.

Two days before the caravan was due to leave, Estcourt received a despatch from the Bombay government dated 21 December (three weeks after Chesney had arrived in Bombay), announcing that the survey would be continued and that the *Euphrates* should be kept in a state of readiness.[10]

'At so great a distance', Estcourt wrote a few weeks later, 'one must judge as well as one can and run all chances.' If the crew had been still available and the survey team up to strength, he might had disregarded Hobhouse's orders, even though they had been repeated in triplicate to ensure compliance. Under the circumstances, 'we could not fulfill the wishes of our Indian masters. The course therefore left, was to obey our masters in England.'[11] Events proved that his judgment was sound.

Estcourt's caravan left Baghdad on 23 January and reached Beirut a month later.* An Admiralty steam packet took them to Malta after stopping at Alexandria to pick up Thomas Waghorn, who was travelling to England to receive his appointment as Deputy Agent of the East India Company in Egypt. Estcourt noted that 'as he is a vulgar sort of fellow, he saw in us, his opponents, & with no very friendly feelings. He was civil however; tho' there was always a lurking disinclination towards us.'[12]

In Malta Estcourt arranged for Cleaveland, Charlewood and thirteen

---

* At Palmyra Charlewood added his name to those of Fitzjames and Seyid Ali. Following recent restoration of Iamlichu's tomb the names are no longer visible.

others of the expedition to sail back to England on board a 74-gun man of war that brought them to Plymouth on 14 May. Estcourt himself returned home through Italy and France.

Waghorn's belated appointment by the East India Company as its authorized agent for conveying passengers and mail between Alexandria and Suez was part of the grand plan, developed by the Company and the British government in 1835, for a regular steam service between Britain and India by the Overland Route. The Admiralty steam packets had been serving Alexandria and Beirut for almost two years, but completion of the two new wooden-hulled steamers being built for the Company in London and Glasgow had been delayed.

The engines that powered these two new vessels, rated at 210 hp and 230 hp respectively, enabled them to steam all the way from England to India, drawing on coal depots laid down at various ports. On 29 December 1836 the first of the new steamers, the 617-ton *Atalanta*, left Falmouth on her maiden voyage around the Cape to Bombay, where she arrived on 13 April 1837. A second ship, the 664-ton *Berenice*, reached Bombay two months later. It was planned that these two steamers, together with the *Hugh Lindsay*, would maintain a monthly service between Bombay and Suez during the period when the south-west monsoon was not blowing. During the monsoon season it was expected that the new steamers would be able to get through to the Persian Gulf with the mail for England. A dromedary post was established to carry mail and despatches between Mohammerah, Baghdad and the Syrian coast.

Details of these plans were still being worked out when Chesney arrived in Bombay and was warmly greeted by Sir Robert Grant, whom he had known in 1834 when Grant had been a member of the House of Commons Select Committee which had endorsed the Euphrates expedition project. Chesney received a hero's welcome in Bombay. The Chamber of Commerce voted to present him with a gold-mounted sword. At first Chesney declined the offer, suggesting that the funds might be better used to erect a monument at Ana in memory of the *Tigris* victims. Eventually, however, the Bombay government agreed to pay for the monument,* a public subscription raised £500 for the bereaved families, and Chesney accepted the sword.

But the main purpose of Chesney's visit to Bombay had been to learn what the authorities intended to do with the expedition after 31 January

---

* The monument was finally erected in the Residency compound at Maqil, near Basra. Over the next hundred years it was re-discovered and repaired several times. Its present location and condition is unknown.

1837. Disappointed to find that there was no role for river transportation in the East India Company's mail plans, he developed the idea of building two small steamers, half the length of the *Euphrates* and quite capable of navigating the Lemlum channel. Alone and suffering from intense head-aches, Chesney urged his views on Sir Robert Grant and his officials, finally persuading them to issue orders to keep the expedition in being and to put Hector in charge of a dromedary post that would run directly between Mohammerah and Damascus every other month. Chesney's main purpose, which would be assisted by these steps, was to modify the Company's plans by providing that the new ocean-going steamers should use the Red Sea and Persian Gulf routes in alternate months, with the dromedary post carrying the mails from Mohammerah until the small river steamers were ready to go into service. Grant forwarded this proposal to the East India House in London with a copy to the Governor-General in Calcutta, whose concurrence would be required.[13] Chesney also sent a personal note to Peacock, pleading for him to support the new proposals and ending: 'Do not desert us at the 11th hour therefore if you would be useful to India and England.'[14]

Despite their admiration for Chesney's courage and determination, the Bombay merchants' attitude to his ideas was mixed. Several offered money to build the proposed river steamers, but others preferred the proven Cape route and the promising Red Sea route to his new Euphrates scheme. One local satirist wrote:

> Let us set up three lines instead of one
> Ere the Red Sea line has fairly begun;
> O! weep by the waters of Babylon
> O'er two lakhs [£20,000] spent and still more to pay,
> Besides a few mails that have gone astray.[15]

Lord Auckland, a diffident bachelor described by a colleague as 'much wanting in decision', delayed answering Grant's letter. At the end of February Grant allowed the impatient Chesney to go to Calcutta to present his case. He took the route followed by the overland mail, stopping at government rest houses. At one of these he encountered a runner bearing the Governor-General's reply. The *Euphrates* steamer was now not required for the Indus; as regards the opening of a route between Mohammerah and Syria, a decision on this matter was being postponed. Recognizing that it would be useless to go on to Calcutta, Chesney decided to rejoin his expedition. On 18 April he was back in Bombay, where further unwelcome news awaited him.

A letter from Estcourt notified Chesney that it had not been possible to carry out the instructions from Bombay and that the expedition was on its way home.[16] The same mail probably brought Hobhouse's letter of 30 November, which had been sent by the Malta packet to be delivered to Chesney in Iraq.

A week before Chesney returned from his fruitless trip, the new *Atalanta* steamship had docked in Bombay harbour, bringing the Christmas mail from home. She also brought letters from Hobhouse to Auckland and Grant setting forth his views regarding future survey work on the Euphrates and Tigris rivers.

The Board of Control and the directors of the East India Company were discussing a new project, to be entitled 'The Expedition to the Euphrates and Tigris Rivers', which would take charge of the *Euphrates* steamer and the *Tigris*, if recoverable, as well as any other steamers that might be employed in the future on the two rivers. The stated purpose of the project was to complete the survey work that had been already commenced. The officers and crews would be supplied by the Indian Navy and all expenses would be covered from India. The commander of the expedition would be an Indian Navy officer, who would report directly to the Board of Control through the Secret Committee of the Company's court of directors, while keeping the Indian authorities informed. Hobhouse suggested that Lieutenant Henry Blosse Lynch be appointed to this command. In these and subsequent letters Hobhouse expressed his strong desire that Chesney should not be associated with the new expedition in any capacity.

Chesney left Bombay on 28 April for England. He travelled on the *Hugh Lindsay* to Basra, where he determined to cross the desert to Damascus by the 'Great Desert Route'. Lieutenant Charles Duane Campbell, a young Indian Navy officer, laid out the route for him and taught him how to navigate by compass and by the stars. After hiring four light camels for himself and two Arab guides, the forty-eight-year-old Chesney accomplished the 958-mile journey to Damascus in twenty-two days. The fatigue and monotony of his journey was relieved by occasional views of the Euphrates river, thirty miles away, reflected clearly above the horizon by a refraction of the light, and a pause at Palmyra to rest the weary camels.

From Damascus Chesney went on to Beirut and sailed to Alexandria, where he took a French steamer to Marseilles. At Leghorn, noticing many vessels flying their flags at half mast, he learned that King William IV, his warm sponsor and according to one newspaper 'the only person really interested in the expedition',[17] had died on 20 June. A few weeks before his death, the king had ordered his secretary to write to Bombay that 'the King cannot for a moment hesitate in sanctioning Colonel Chesney's accepting and wearing the sword which the Bombay Chamber of Commerce has presented to him'.[18]

After performing quarantine in Marseilles, Chesney crossed France and arrived in London on 8 August. Three weeks earlier Hobhouse had submitted to Parliament a carefully edited set of despatches, letters and reports dealing with the Euphrates expedition. Among them was a memorandum from Cabell estimating its total cost at £43,197. By including extracts from his 30 November 1836 letter to Chesney the minister made it clear that he was washing his hands of the whole matter.[19]

The new expedition, like its predecessor, was more than an exercise in geographical research. Although the British government no longer feared a Russian invasion of Iraq, Mehemet Ali's designs were still obscure. In 1834 the viceroy had been warned indirectly by Tsar Nicholas, that, if he were to attack the Sultan's forces in Anatolia, Russia would intervene; but the Tsar had also said 'that he would not object to see Mehemet Ali Caliph of Arabia'.[20] Recent troop movements in the Euphrates valley and the presence of Egyptian agents in Kuwait and among the desert Arabs suggested that Mehemet Ali might now be contemplating a move against Iraq or perhaps against the Arab sheikhdoms along the Persian Gulf.

Hobhouse's plan was to form a steam flotilla that would patrol the Euphrates and Tigris rivers, conduct surveys and, when needed, carry mail between Basra and Baghdad. But its real function (and the reason why it would report directly to London) would be to safeguard one of Britain's routes to India by gaining friendship and respect from the Arab tribes. The flotilla would start with only the *Euphrates* (and possibly the *Tigris*) but Hobhouse hoped to add more vessels as required.

Lynch was well qualified to command the flotilla, possessing diplomatic skills, a knowledge of the Arabs and experience in steam navigation – fields in which Chesney had been shown to be deficient. He received his official appointment on 18 April 1837 and reported to Colonel Taylor in Baghdad in July.

The spring floods had washed the *Euphrates* on to a sandbank sixty miles below Baghdad. But she had suffered little damage; after hiring an engineer and a skeleton Arab crew, Lynch was able to get her off the sandbank and return to her anchorage by the Residency in March 1838. She was now ready to descend the Tigris to Basra, where a crew from India was expected, and then carry out Lynch's first assignment: to test the navigability of the Euphrates by steaming up to Beles and back again.

Lynch's plans were well executed. The voyage from Baghdad to Basra in the spring high water was completed in just four days. Three weeks later the Indian Navy sloop-of-war *Clive* sailed over from Bushire with the new crew, armament and supplies. Her captain, Commander Hawkins, quickly decided that his ship should remain at anchor while he would take several of his officers and most of his crew on board the *Euphrates* to help Lynch's men navigate the steamer up and down the great river.

The stream was in full force and the steamer steered well. Dr Winchester of the *Clive* wrote home proudly:

> We left Bussorah on the 17th [of May], at 2 o'clock p.m. and reached Babylon on the 24th, at the same hour, after a most arduous but highly successful passage through the Lumtoome and Babylonian marshes – thus removing the great barrier to the upward navigation of this noble river, and thus accomplishing, for the first time, an achievement of the highest national importance.[21]

Lynch wrote Peacock that the *Euphrates* passed the Lemlum marshes in twelve hours 'with only a little trouble, and some risk to our unfortunate paddles; but by playing a bold game, and dashing her bow whenever I feared her paddles would go, we got through.'[22] His despatch to the Secret Committee explains how it was done:

> Navigation of the Lemlum marshes difficult, but we steamed through them without any warping or external aid, merely using our anchors to swing the vessel when the helm was rendered powerless by the narrow turnings and force of the current; and when they failed grounding her bow on the bank, until the current brought her stern round, and her head fell off in a direction up the Stream when full power of Steam was found sufficient to force her up the rapids, which ran in places six knots.[23]

There is no record of how the naval officers of Chesney's expedition reacted to this achievement, which they had declared to be impossible. However, the last laugh went to the Royal Navy, for when the *Euphrates* reached Hit on 2 June, she found her passage blocked four miles upstream by a wall of water that rushed between two large dams on either side of the river. Her engines could not overcome the compressed force of the current, which Fitzjames had remarked on in one of his reports to Chesney. Lynch considered using trackers, but felt that the Arabs would regard this as a sign of weakness. The river was beginning to drop, but rather than wait for lower water and risk being grounded on an obstruction farther up, Lynch decided to go back.

A week later Colonel Taylor, looking out across the Tigris from his Residency in Baghdad, noticed the smoke of a large steamer approaching from the west. It was the *Euphrates*, fulfilling his dead brother's dream of travelling from one river to the other by the ancient Saklawiya canal. The steamer had been obliged to navigate the first few miles stern foremost, aided by trackers who pulled her around the bends; but farther down the canal became broader and straighter, enabling her to finish the four-day transit in proper position. (This was the first and last time that a paddle-wheel steamer navigated this waterway. Ali Riza Pasha, who had once supported the use of a canal between the two great rivers, was so dismayed by this proof of Baghdad's vulnerability that he blocked off the western entrance to the Saklawiya canal, thereby causing the Euphrates to change its course over the years and drying up the Lemlum marshes.) The steamer then took the borrowed portion of her complement back to Basra and returned to Baghdad in time for the celebration of Lynch's marriage to Caroline Taylor, the Resident's daughter, in August 1838.*

The war clouds that Chesney had so often apprehended were now gathering in earnest. Mehemet Ali, approaching the age of seventy, decided that now or never was the time when Egypt and his other provinces should become an independent state. Sultan Mahmud, although younger, was a sick man and was determined to crush the rebellious viceroy before he died. Orders were given to assemble a large army in Anatolia that would subdue Mehemet Ali once for all.

In May 1838 Mehemet Ali informed the British, French, Austrian and Russian consuls in Egypt that he intended to declare his independence from the Sultan. British reaction was swift. While Palmerston strove by diplomatic means to preserve the integrity of the Ottoman empire, Hobhouse ordered Auckland to seize the strategic port of Aden and to have Indian troops ready to defend Basra in case the Egyptians should attack.

Aden was taken in January 1839, but in the Persian Gulf British power was stretched too thin to prevent an Egyptian force from Riyadh crossing the Arabian desert and occupying Qatif and two other fishing ports opposite the island of Bahrein. Egyptian agents were sent off to procure supplies

* Her sister, Harriet Taylor, married Henry Lynch's younger brother, Thomas Kerr Lynch.

from Bahrein, Kuwait and the Montefik tribe of Arabs in the Euphrates valley.

It was now high time to augment Lynch's one-vessel steam flotilla. Working in great secrecy through Peacock at the East India House, the India Board ordered three iron river steamers from the Laird shipyard, to be delivered in frame for assembly at destination. In June 1838 the *Urania*, a merchantman bound ostensibly for Montevideo, sailed with the crates and a group of skilled craftsmen who would put the vessels together.

In Iraq 1839 was a year of tension. In February and March Lynch surveyed the Tigris above Baghdad. The *Euphrates* was able to ascend as far as Sultan Abdallah, a shallow point thirty miles below Mosul. Lynch rode on to Mosul, where he learned that the Turkish army in Anatolia was moving down to Bir, close to the Syrian border. Sensing that the long-expected war between the Sultan and Mehemet Ali was imminent, Lynch steamed quickly down the river to Baghdad.

Sultan Mahmud died on 1 July 1839, unaware that a week earlier Ibrahim Pasha had decisively defeated the Turkish army at Nisib, across the Euphrates from Bir. (Ainsworth and Rassam, who were on a geographical expedition to Kurdistan, observed this battle as guests of the Turkish commander and lost all their baggage when his headquarters was overrun.)[24] Mehemet Ali's triumph was completed when the Turkish fleet deserted Mahmud's sixteen-year-old successor and sailed into Alexandria harbour.

This time Mehemet Ali did not advance into Anatolia, for he believed he had won his game. But when Britain, Russia and Austria made common cause to support the new Sultan, a lengthy period of bargaining began.

When the news of Mehemet Ali's triumph reached Iraq and the Persian Gulf, some Arab sheikhs made ready to switch their allegiance to him. But the Indian Navy still patrolled the gulf and could at any time blockade the Egyptian garrisons near Bahrein.

The *Urania* finally reached Basra in December, having been obliged to put in at Bombay for water. The iron steamers were assembled at Maqil, where Lynch had built a pier, barracks, slips and a dock on the Residency grounds. Three weeks after the crates had been discharged, the *Nimrod* was in the water, followed by the *Nitocris** in February 1840 and the *Assyria* in March. By May the craftsmen had left, the crews for the new vessels had arrived from India, and the 'Euphrates Steam Flotilla' (which included the *Euphrates*, now commanded by Henry Lynch's younger brother Michael)

---

* Peacock's influence may be detected here. The Greek historian Herodotus states that Queen Nitocris of Babylon constructed large engineering works along the Euphrates.

was ready to start a mail shuttle service on the Tigris between Basra and Baghdad.

The new steamers, identical in size and power, embodied lessons learned from the mishaps of the *Euphrates*. Their length was the same as hers, but they had been designed with flatter bottoms to provide lighter draught; they were also slightly narrower in the beam. They each measured 153 tons, compared with the *Euphrates*' 179 tons, and had 40 hp engines, compared with the older vessel's 50 hp (the *Tigris* had measured 109 tons with 20 hp engines.) Lynch had long believed that only a small, high-powered steamer could navigate the entire Euphrates, but such a vessel would require many fuel depots and an assured supply of wood from the river Arabs. In the present situation, where the tribes might be unfriendly, a steamer needed range; the *Euphrates* had been modified to hold five days' supply of fuel. A steamer also needed room to carry troops and needed to be well armed. Each of the new steamers was equipped with 2 nine-pounder guns and 6 one-pounder swivel guns.

The swift assembly, launching and fitting out of the three steamers at Maqil seemed at first to vindicate Peacock's opinion that Chesney should have started at the mouth of the river instead of at Port William. But Lynch's success was achieved at a cost. When the summer heat and humidity came to Basra, fever attacked the vessel crews and Lynch himself fell ill and was invalided home.

Lieutenant Campbell, aged twenty-six, was put in command of the flotilla until Lynch should return. Throughout the summer of 1840 the vessels lay at anchor below Baghdad, immobilized by sickness. The shuttle service was suspended; several deaths occurred among the crews and at one point only one of the six engineers was fit for duty. Hobhouse's long planned steam flotilla could thus play only a passive role in the last act of Mehemet Ali's career.

Negotiations dragged on for months between Mehemet Ali and the Sultan's government, now backed by Britain, Russia, Austria and Prussia. The ageing viceroy, encouraged by French support, kept a tight hold on the Turkish fleet and strengthened his forces in Syria by withdrawing troops from Arabia, including the garrisons along the Persian Gulf. The end came in September 1840, when a *firman* from the Sultan dismissed Mehemet Ali from all his posts. Simultaneously, the British Mediterranean fleet landed British, Austrian and Turkish troops on the Syrian coast. The Egyptian army was defeated and forced to withdraw to Egypt, where British ships blockaded Alexandria. In November Mehemet Ali sued for peace. The final settlement, signed in June 1842, allowed him to keep Egypt as a hereditary fief and restored all his other provinces to the Sultan. The viceroy's spirit was broken and after a long period of senility he died in 1849.

The end was also approaching for the Euphrates steam flotilla. With the Sultan's authority re-established in Syria and Arabia, the tribesmen relapsed into their old feuding ways and no longer jeopardized Turkish rule in Iraq. Since Russia had co-operated with Britain in supporting the Sultan's government against Mehemet Ali, the threat of a Russian invasion through Anatolia into Iraq seemed hardly likely now.

On the other hand, this was a good time to complete the survey of the Euphrates river by ascending all the way to Beles. The steam flotilla had now recovered its health and vigour, except for Michael Lynch, who took sick leave and died on his way home. Before starting the ascent, Campbell, a cautious man, surveyed the Euphrates valley on horseback from Hit, where Henry Lynch had been blocked in 1838, as far as Ana, returning by river boat.

On 1 April 1841, Campbell left Basra with the *Nitocris* and the *Nimrod* on the third and final attempt to steam up and down the Euphrates. The stream was full and the vessels went through the Lemlum marshes without serious difficulty, making the voyage to Felluja in ten days. Leaving Felluja on 19 April, they easily overcame the rushing water above Hit (although in other places Campbell had to resort to warping or the use of trackers). After passing the wreck of the *Tigris*, submerged at this season, the two steamers reached Deir ez-Zor on 22 May. Two days later, on Queen Victoria's birthday, they passed the ruins of Zenobia. No further incidents are recorded until 31 May, when the *Nitocris* and the *Nimrod* anchored below Beles and Campbell ordered 'a royal Salute to be fired in honor of our own "Most Gracious Queen" '.[25]

The vessels had suffered some damage on the way up; the cross head of one air pump was bent (but not cracked). Time was needed to rest, refit, close down the Port William storehouse and obtain supplies from Aleppo. The river was now falling, but the two steamers did not weigh anchor until 23 August. Twelve miles from their starting point the *Nimrod* grounded on a sandbank, requiring three days to get her off. At Kalat Jaber Campbell was told that the clearances downstream were barely three feet, whereas the fully laden vessels needed almost six feet of water to pass. After consulting with his brother officers, Campbell ordered the steamers back to Beles to wait for the river to rise.

Returning from England at the end of August to resume command, Lynch landed at Beirut to find the captains of his two steamers about to leave for Malta to buy supplies. He ordered them at once to return with him to Aleppo. After listening to Campbell's excuses, Lynch, recently promoted to the rank of commander, decided that the survey should proceed despite the low water. The steamers left Beles for the second time on 16 October with supplies for three months.

The descent of the river was a nightmare. Fifteen miles below Kalat Jaber the steamers came to a ford where there was only two feet of water. They stayed there until late November vainly awaiting the river's brief winter rise. Finally, Lynch reported:

> the vessels were grounded on the bar, and gradually made their
> way through it, sometimes heaving, and sometimes allowing the
> stream to eat away the pebbles. The operation of eating away
> the pebbles occupied nearly a month (23 days.)[26]

From this point the steamers made slow progress until they were beyond Rakka. On 16 February 1842, as the *Nimrod* was passing a narrow stretch eight miles below Rakka, a sunken tree pierced her iron hull. The captain quickly grounded her on a shoal, which proved to be a quicksand, and she rapidly filled with water; the engine room was fortunately sealed off with bulkheads. The next morning, as she began to settle by the head, the entire engine and all other heavy objects were taken out of the vessel. Her head then rose a little above the water and, after three days of heaving and baling, she was brought to safety against the river bank. By the end of March the *Nimrod* had been repaired and the two steamers continued their descent, reaching Ana on 29 April, 195 days after leaving Beles.

Lynch and Campbell went straight to Baghdad from Ana, since orders had been received to break up the flotilla and send three of the four steamers to India. The two captains took the *Nitocris* and the *Nimrod* down to Basra, where in September 1842 the *Euphrates*, the *Nimrod* and the *Assyria* were towed by an ocean-going steamship to Bombay.

The cost of the 'Expedition to the Euphrates and Tigris Rivers', excluding the cost of the vessels, was 350,000 rupees (£35,000). Its principal achievement was summarized in Lynch's despatch to the Secret Committee:

> I regret much that the result of the experiment on the
> Euphrates, and a careful survey of that River, between Hit
> and Beles, obliges me to report to your Honorable Board, that
> it is not well adapted for the purposes of Steam Navigation.[27]

In a personal letter to Peacock, Lynch expressed his sorrow that his conclusion should have been negative.[28] Peacock's reply has not been preserved, but he had learned to mask his feelings and he left no record of the pain he suffered when his thirteen-year dream was laid to rest.

Chapter 14
Epilogue

Peacock was fifty-seven when the Euphrates flotilla was broken up, leaving only the *Nitocris* in Iraq to be employed by the East India Company for survey and other work. He had been appointed Examiner at the India House in 1836 and held that post until his retirement in 1856, one year before the outbreak of the Indian Mutiny that led to the transfer of authority from the Company to the British government in 1858.

Shortly after the three small steamboats were ordered for the Euphrates flotilla, Peacock became involved in the design and construction of six large iron steamers for service along the coasts and rivers of India. These vessels were fitted with sliding wooden keels, operated by windlasses, which enabled them to navigate in open water as well as in rivers.

When the Opium War broke out with China, the India Board decided to send four of these vessels out from England, two under steam and two in frame, to serve with the British squadron in the China Sea. On her maiden voyage from the Laird shipyard to London in January 1840, the first steamer of this class, which carried Peacock as a passenger, struck a rock while rounding the Lizard in foggy weather. One of her iron plates was broken, but the bulkheads held fast and the vessel was able to reach Portsmouth for repairs.[1] Subsequently, all four of these heavily armed steamers, which Peacock called 'my iron chickens', were used in penetrating the shallow estuaries of the China coast.

Peacock resumed writing essays and reviews after his wife died in 1851. In his years of retirement he wrote his reminiscences of Shelley and his last novel, *Gryll Grange*, which was published in 1861. He died in 1866 at the age of eighty.

In June 1841 a short, factual synopsis of the Euphrates expedition was prepared under Peacock's direction for a magazine editor who was writing an article about Chesney.[2] With this exception, Peacock is not known to have written anything about the project he had conceived, promoted and watched from its beginning to its end.

The task of writing the history of the Euphrates expedition was assigned to Chesney, who was promised £1,500 by the Treasury and smaller sums by the East India Company and the Board of Control. Unfortunately this project took on a life of its own in Chesney's mind. Only two out of the projected four volumes were published, after much delay, in 1850. They contain all of his maps and some useful illustrations, but the text deals only with the geography and history of the Near East, which Chesney had intended to serve as a background for subsequent volumes covering the events of the expedition. Years later, Chesney was persuaded to write a one-volume 'Narrative', which contains a good account of the expedition, with some omissions but useful appendices and many illustrations.

Having returned to England under a cloud of official displeasure, Major Chesney (as he now ranked) found it hard to pick up the threads of his career. He spent much time putting together the scattered records of the expedition's expenditures and ensuring that his officers received their promised promotions. In 1841 Chesney was instructed to return to regimental duty. Two years later he was appointed to command the artillery at the newly acquired colony of Hong Kong, but his tour of duty there was marred by a petty dispute with the commanding general. Chesney's last military post was in Ireland, where he commanded the Cork district from 1847 to 1852. He rose by steps to the rank of Major-General in 1855, at which point despite his age he was considered for the command of a Foreign Legion to serve with the British forces in the Crimean war. For various reasons the project was abandoned. Consequently, when Chesney died at Packolet in 1872 in his eighty-third year with the rank of full General, his only active service had been the brief skirmish with the Beni Hucheyim Arabs in June 1836.

In his later years Chesney became associated with abortive projects to build a railway along the Euphrates valley; on one occasion he revisited Iskenderun, Suedia and Antioch with a surveying party. Ironically, Chesney received great acclaim in connection with the opening of the Suez Canal in 1869. Ferdinand de Lesseps, the builder of the canal that ensured the triumph of the Red Sea route, hailed Chesney as 'Le Père du Canal', because his 1830 report had proved the feasibility of a sea-level canal.[3]

In April 1839 Chesney married Everilda Fraser. It was a sad ceremony, for the forty-six-year-old bride was so ill she could barely stand. Chesney records that he wore full-dress uniform with his Bombay sword and the shoes he had worn when the *Tigris* went down. Eighteen months later she was dead.

Chesney married again in his sixtieth year and had five children by his third wife, Louisa Fletcher. One of their children, named Everilda, married the son of Midshipman (later Admiral) Edward Charlewood.

It is difficult to pass judgment on Francis Rawdon Chesney. Behind the mask of authority – a French-speaking visitor to Port William described him as 'froid et sévère'[4] – seethed an intense personality Chesney sought to control and direct to a worthy purpose. At the end of each year his diary chronicled the number of occasions when he lost his temper or showed 'decided Anger'[5] and registered his determination to exert better self-control. A psychiatrist could best judge whether fear of this bottled-up inferno deterred Everilda Fraser from marrying him until she was able to dominate him from her sickbed.

Chesney was a visionary. Unlike young men, who can shed their enthusiasm as easily as a snake shakes off his skin, Chesney was well into middle age when the vision of Euphrates first appeared to him and it obsessed him for the remainder of his life. Ellenborough may have sensed this when he referred to Chesney as a 'red-hot Irishman, likely to lead others to serious danger'. But although Chesney pushed his men hard, he never demanded anything he was not prepared to do himself. Perhaps Estcourt, a frequent critic who remained a lifelong friend, understood Chesney best when he wrote home that 'I never in my life met with a man so little able to exercise a rational judgement in any calculation.'[6]

Chesney was not the first commander who disregarded the principles of military science when he smelled the whiff of fame. In the early stages of the expedition Chesney may be blamed for the faulty survey of the Orontes and the inadequate winter quarters at Port William. These omissions were made good by improvisation – one of Chesney's greatest skills – and the main purpose of completing the steamers was achieved. In 1836, however, he showed poor judgment in risking his one remaining ship in a needless trip up the uncharted Tigris and subsequently on the attempted ascent of the Euphrates in the low-water season – all for the glory of carrying a mail that could have been expedited more cheaply overland.

Yet Chesney's vision and his determination to bring it to life provided the spark that inspired the young men in the expedition to overcome so many obstacles. (Only Estcourt and Murphy were over thirty when the expedition was organized.) Unfortunately, Chesney's leadership capacity deserted him when he became absorbed in carrying the mails; towards the end of the expedition he was becoming a lonely, embittered man.

To his admirers, like Ainsworth and Charlewood, Chesney was a hero unjustly robbed of recognition for all he had done. To his friends, like Estcourt and perhaps Peacock also, he was a tragic, in retrospect pre-destined, victim of forces beyond his control. Posterity, bereft of all but a few of Chesney's personal papers, can only wonder at the inner drive that impelled this man so far.

Estcourt, promoted to the rank of Lieutenant-Colonel on his return from the Euphrates expedition, retired from active duty in 1843. For three years he represented Great Britain on a boundary commission that surveyed and marked the frontier between the United States and eastern Canada. On the outbreak of the Crimean war in 1854, he was recalled to the army and sent out as Adjutant-General of the British forces. He died of cholera in June 1855 during the siege of Sevastopol at the age of fifty-two.

Cleaveland went back to active service with the Navy after his return to England and was promoted to the rank of commander. But his health was impaired; Estcourt's report on their journey from Baghdad to Damascus at the end of the expedition noted that 'he has suffered considerably by his services in this country, and has become subject to frequent and severe spitting of blood, with a bad cough'.[7] Cleaveland was placed on half pay in 1839 and died in South America in 1842.

Eden was promoted to lieutenant soon after his return to England after the wreck of the *Tigris*. He served on the *Beagle* survey vessel for some years (at a later period than Darwin's voyage) and subsequently in various home and overseas stations. After promotion to commander in 1846, he remained on half pay until he retired in 1864 with the rank of captain. He died in 1880.

Fitzjames had a short but brilliant naval career. Promoted to lieutenant in 1838, he served off the coast of Syria in 1840 in the brief war against Mehemet Ali; on one occasion he landed secretly outside Beirut to distribute leaflets among the Egyptian troops. His ship took part in the subsequent bombardment of the town and in the blockade of Alexandria. In 1842 he distinguished himself as commander of a rocket brigade in several actions during the war with China. At the end of that war Fitzjames was promoted to commander and given command of a sixteen-gun sloop, on which he revisited Basra and Korna, subdued a mutiny aboard some merchant ships off West Africa and returned to England in October 1844.

At that moment the Admiralty was preparing an Arctic expedition designed to discover the North-West Passage off the shores of northern

Canada. Barrow, still the senior civil servant, had hoped that Fitzjames and Charlewood would be appointed to command the *Erebus* and the *Terror*, the two sailing ships selected for the survey. However, Sir John Franklin and another officer with greater seniority were finally appointed. Fitzjames sailed on the *Erebus* as second in command to Franklin, while Charlewood was not picked to join the expedition.

The two ships sailed from England in May 1845 and became icebound in September 1846. Franklin died in June 1847 and Fitzjames succeeded to the command of the *Erebus*. In April 1848, when the vessels seemed close to breaking up, Fitzjames and the captain of the *Terror* led their crews on a hopeless march overland on which everyone died. Fitzjames' last letter, found years later beside a cairn, records the abandonment of the ships and the start of the tragic march across the ice and snow.

Charlewood was promoted lieutenant a week before Fitzjames. He also served with distinction in the Syrian war and was promoted again to commander. In 1841 and 1842, while on half pay, Charlewood commanded the *Guadelupe*, a four-gun iron steam frigate built by Lairds for the Mexican Navy. He took her across the Atlantic from Liverpool – at that time quite an achievement for a 788-ton vessel – and took part in the storming of Campeche, a port controlled by Yucatan secessionists. In 1845 Charlewood missed being picked for the North-West Passage expedition. From 1848 to 1861 he was employed on coast guard service. He retired in 1861, attained the rank of admiral in 1884 and died in 1894. His son Edward married Chesney's daughter Everilda.

When the expedition broke up, Ainsworth and Rassam travelled to Istanbul by way of Mosul and Trebizond. On his return to England Ainsworth published his geological notes from the expedition.[8] In 1838 and 1839 he and Rassam went on an expedition to Kurdistan, which was a financial disaster for its sponsors. From 1841 until 1879 Ainsworth published a magazine of general interest in association with his novelist cousin. Ainsworth's *Personal Narrative of the Euphrates Expedition*, published in 1888, is a mine of information in which the nuggets of his own experiences lie between heavy layers of antiquarian dross. Ainsworth died in 1896, the last survivor of Chesney's expedition.

Dr Charles Staunton continued his service with the Royal Artillery until 1857, when he was placed on half pay. He died in 1884.

His brother Andrew Staunton was appointed an assistant surgeon in the

Ordnance Department upon his return to England. He later emigrated to Canada, where he died around 1860.

Thomson, who played a small part in the survey but was fortunate to escape from the wreck of the *Tigris*, changed his career after returning to England. He entered the Foreign Office and served in Persia and Chile. He retired in 1879 with a knighthood and died in 1883.

Alexander Hector was disappointed in his hopes of salvaging the *Tigris*, but he stayed on in Baghdad after the expedition broke up, first as custodian of the *Euphrates* and later as the proprietor of a successful import-export firm.

John Bell, the interpreter who waited so long at Beles for the steamer that never returned, joined a British expedition to Ethiopia in 1843 and became the trusted bodyguard and advisor to the Emperor Theodore. In 1860, when the British consul was kidnapped by a rebel chief, Bell arranged his ransom but the consul died from wounds suffered in captivity. Leading a punitive expedition against the rebels, Theodore and Bell were ambushed in a wood. Bell saved Theodore's life by shooting the rebel chieftain, but was slain by another rebel, who in turn was shot dead by the emperor.

Christian Rassam had a more placid life. On his arrival in England with Ainsworth, he made a good impression among influential people by his intelligence and manners. In 1839 he was appointed British Vice-Consul at Mosul, a post he occupied until his death in 1872. By that time he had become one of the richest men in the city. His brother Hormuzd was a noted but controversial archaeologist.

William Elliot (Dervish Ali) vanished from the chronicle of the expedition after the wreck of the *Tigris*, when he went back to Aleppo with Thomson. Sadly, his long string of escapes and escapades was drawing to its end. In August 1837, while travelling with a caravan from Damascus to Baghdad, he was taken ill and died. As a devout Moslem, he was buried in the desert where he died. Pauline Helfer's appraisal provides a fitting epitaph for the wandering dervish: 'He was one of those people who, richly endowed by nature but outcasts from society, live in perpetual conflict with it, and either conquer or perish.'[9]

Dr and Madame Helfer acquired a plantation in southern Burma, where they raised coconut and areca palms. Much of the field labour was done by convicts from a nearby penal settlement, among whom the Helfers recognized their false friends 'Mr Hunter' and 'Mr Brown'. But the doctor spent many months on exploration trips, leaving his wife to take care of the plantation. In 1840 he was killed by a poisoned arrow in the Andaman Islands. His widow returned to Europe and married Count Joseph Dittmar von Nostitz-Rokitnitz, an Austrian landowner. In 1873 she published an account of her travels with Dr Helfer in the Near East, India and Burma, which includes a colourful description of their experiences on the Euphrates expedition. She died in 1881.

After the disbandment of the Euphrates Flotilla, Henry Blosse Lynch received an Indian Navy staff appointment in Bombay and was promoted captain in 1847. He commanded a squadron in the 1851–3 war with Burma and was the senior officer in the Indian Navy when he retired in 1856. His last years were spent in Paris, where he died in 1873.

Throughout the two expeditions, Lynch remains an elusive, contradictory character. Most of the published and unpublished accounts of him come from Chesney, who bore Lynch little love. Ainsworth and Charlewood hardly mention him in their books, while Estcourt's letters are strangely silent about a man he must have known well at Port William. Pauline Helfer provides a good description of her meeting with Lynch in Aleppo and the journey from there to Port William when the Helfers and their Afghan friends were escorted by Lynch. But after their arrival at Port William she likewise seldom mentions Lynch.

The historian of the Indian Navy (which was abolished in 1866) recalled Lynch as a man who 'possessed that happy mixture of the *fortiter in re*, which enabled him, by dint of energy and resolution, to carry an enterprise to a successful issue, with the *suaviter in modo*', which eased his relations with Royal Navy officers.[10] In Paris he was remembered for 'his ready Irish wit, untempered by cynicism, and his exuberant geniality'.[11]

Henry Lynch's only son died young and the Partry property in Mayo passed to his brother Edward, a general in the Indian Army, and his descendants.

Curiously, the name of Lynch was remembered longer in Iraq than that of Chesney or anyone else on the expedition. In 1841 Thomas and Stephen Lynch, brothers of Henry Lynch, started a trading firm in Baghdad, importing goods on convoys of teak rafts, dragged by trackers up the Tigris from the Persian Gulf. In 1861, they formed the Euphrates and Tigris Steam Navigation Company, which took over the defunct East India Company's vessels in Iraq, and obtained from the Sultan a renewal of the navigation rights granted to the original Euphrates expedition in 1834. The company was owned and managed by members of the Lynch family for close to a century. At the end of the Second World War the prospect of keener competition from highway, rail and air transport persuaded the proprietors to sell their fleet and put the company into voluntary liquidation.

The *Euphrates* steamer served the Indian Navy until 1847, when she was retired and scrapped.

Source References

Source material on the Euphrates expedition is surprisingly scarce.

Parliamentary committee hearings, reports and a selection of relevant official documents, many of them carefully edited, may be found in Parliamentary Papers published between 1832 and 1838, viz:

> PP 1831–2 No. 735. Minutes of Evidence taken before the Select Committee on the Affairs of the East India Company: Vol. 2, Finance.
>
> PP 1834 No. 478. Report from the Select Committee on Steam Navigation to India.
>
> PP 1837 No. 540. Euphrates Expedition: Copy of Instructions to Colonel Chesney, together with Abstract of Correspondence and Accounts of Expenditure.
>
> PP 1838 No. 356. Euphrates Expedition: Copies of Extracts from additional Communications or Despatches.

The latter two papers contain the *General Statement of the Labours and Proceedings of the Expedition to the Euphrates* compiled by Ainsworth and submitted by Chesney and Estcourt to the India Board. The text of this report with minor editorial changes appeared in the *Journal of the Royal Geographical Society*, Vol. 7, 1837.

The archives of the India Office Library and Records contain the bulk of the official files on the expedition. Most of them are collected in L/MAR/C/573 and 574. The files of Lynch's 1837–42 Euphrates Flotilla are in L/P&S/9/106–121 and L/P&S/9/13. The Broughton Papers for 1835 and 1836 (MSS Eur F 213/4 and 5) contain Hobhouse's correspondence regarding the expedition.

Foreign Office file FO 78 (Turkey) at the Public Record Office contains relevant despatches from the British Embassy at Istanbul and from consular posts at Alexandria, Damascus and Aleppo, together with drafts of correspondence from the Foreign Office to Istanbul and Alexandria.

References to the Euphrates expedition also appear in the French diplomatic archives (Correspondance politique des consuls, Turquie, Consulats divers, vols 5 and 7) and in the archives of the Russian consulate in Alexandria published by René Cattaui between 1931 and 1936.

Chesney's *Narrative of the Euphrates Expedition*, published in 1868, lacks much of the detail found in other accounts, but includes valuable reports by Lynch, Estcourt, Cleaveland, Charlewood and Fitzjames on the initial phases of the expedition. It also contains a wealth of illustrations, many of them based on drawings by the participants.

As noted previously, only the first two volumes of Chesney's projected four-volume work entitled *The Expedition for the Survey of the Rivers Euphrates and Tigris* were ever published. Apart from a few illustrations and a complete set of Chesney's maps, they contain little about the expedition, which the author had planned to cover in the third and fourth volumes.

Chesney's official biography, *The Life of the late General F. R. Chesney*, by his widow Louisa and his daughter Jane O'Donnell, edited by his nephew Stanley Lane-Poole and published in 1885, is the primary source for Chesney's life. The authors had access to Chesney's personal papers, including his diary and his letters to his father. A second edition was published in 1893.

The location of Chesney's voluminous papers is a mystery. The Public Record Office of Northern Ireland holds one section of his diary for the period from July 1829 to March 1831 and letter books covering the years 1823–9, 1838–42, 1846–7 and 1850–71. Information regarding the remainder of his papers, which were used and in places cited by his biographers in 1885 and 1893, would be welcome.

As regards the participants, Lynch's letters home have not survived. Fortunately, Estcourt's letters to his family were preserved and are now in the Gloucestershire Records Office. Charlewood published privately in 1869 *Passages from the Life of a Naval Officer*, a short book which contains anecdotal material about the Euphrates expedition.

In contrast, two civilian members of the expedition published full-length accounts of their experiences. In 1873 and 1877 Pauline Helfer (by that time Countess Nostitz) published *J. W. Helfer's Reisen in Vorderasien und Indien*;

an English translation, which contained ten additional chapters describing her life after Dr Helfer's death, appeared in 1878 under the title *Travels of Doctor and Madame Helfer in Syria, Mesopotamia, Burmah and other Lands*. In 1888 Ainsworth published *A Personal Narrative of the Euphrates Expedition*.

A poem entitled *The Loss of the Tigris* by Henry Richardson, published in 1840, contains some details not mentioned elsewhere and also a good print of the *Tigris* under construction based on a drawing by Estcourt.

The Times, the *Athenaeum* and the *Literary Gazette* covered the expedition in varying degrees, the last named carrying unsigned letters from Ainsworth. The *Asiatic Journal*, though hostile to the project, is a valuable source for steam navigation events and also for arrival and departure dates of vessels at Indian ports.

Abbreviations

AE/CPC	Ministère des Affaires Étrangères (Paris), Archives Diplomatiques, Correspondance Politique des Consuls.
AP	William [Francis] Ainsworth, *A Personal Narrative of the Euphrates Expedition*, 2 vols, London, 1888.
CE	Lieut-Colonel [Francis Rawdon] Chesney, RA, *The Expedition for the Survey of the Rivers Euphrates and Tigris . . . 1835, 1836 and 1837*, 2 vols, London, 1850.
CL	Louisa Chesney and Jane O'Donnell, *The Life of the late General F. R. Chesney*, ed. Stanley Lane-Poole, London, 1885.
CN	General Francis Rawdon Chesney, RA, *Narrative of the Euphrates Expedition*, London, 1868.
EP	Papers of General J. B. Estcourt, Gloucestershire Records Office (D 1571).
FO	Foreign Office (London).
IO L/MAR	India Office (London), Marine Dept Records.
IO L/P&S	India Office (London), Political and Secret Dept Records.
IOR MSS Eur	India Office Records, European Manuscripts.
NH	Countess Pauline Nostitz, *Travels of Doctor and Madame Helfer in Syria, Mesopotamia, Burmah and other Lands*, trans. Mrs. G. Sturge, 2 vols, London, 1878.
PP	Parliamentary Papers.
PRONI	Public Record Office of Northern Ireland (Belfast).

The Euphrates Expedition

Source Reference Notes

Introduction

1   EP, Estcourt to Father, 25 October 1835.

Chapter 1 Peacock's Dream

1   Carl Dawson, *His Fine Wit*, p. 288.
2   *The Letters of Percy Bysshe Shelley*, ed. Frederick L. Jones, vol. 1, p. 325.
3   *The Works of Thomas Love Peacock*, ed. Henry Cole, vol. 1, p. xxxi.
4   Edward Law, 1st Earl of Ellenborough, *A Political Diary, 1828–1830*, ed. Lord Colchester, vol. 2, p. 77.
5   Peacock's *Memorandum* was printed in PP 1834 No. 478, Appendix, pp. 2–10.
6   PP 1834 No. 478, p. 130, Sir Harford Jones Brydges, Bart. evidence, 27 June 1834.
7   James Hingston Tuckey, *Maritime Geography and Statistics*, vol. 3, p. 69.

Chapter 2 The State of the Art

1   PP 1834 No. 478, Appendix, p. 10.
2   *Ibid.*, p. 5.
3   G. A. Prinsep, *An Account of Steam Vessels and of proceedings connected with Steam Navigation in British India*, p. 6.
4   *Ibid.*, p. 15.
5   [Philip E. Clunn], *Sketch of the Life of Lieutenant Waghorn, R.N.*, p. 3.
6   George W. Smith, 'In the Early Forties', *The Cornhill Magazine*, vol. 9 (N.S.), 1900, p. 578.
7   Boyd Cable [E. A. Ewart], *A Hundred Year History of the P. & O.*, p. 50.
8   Ellenborough, *A Political Diary 1828–1830*, vol. 2, p. 262.
9   PP 1834 No. 478, p. 1.
10 Felix Felton, *Thomas Love Peacock*, p. 237.
11 PP 1837 No. 539, *Report from the Select Committee on Steam Communication with India*, p. 55, Peacock evidence, 26 June 1837.

Chapter 3 The Chesney Reconnaissance

1   Bowater's memorandum, dated 17 June 1830 and signed 'J. Bowater', was printed in PP 1831–2 No. 735, vol. 2, pp. 737–41.
2   Thomas Waghorn, *Particulars of an Overland Journey from London to Bombay, by way of the Continent, Egypt, and the Red Sea*.
3   PRONI D.3480/52/12 (copy in IOR Neg. 1881), Caroline Lady Estcourt, undated memorandum included in manuscript of CL but cut out by editor. Cf. CL, pp. 405–10 for a fuller discussion of Chesney's personality.

4 PRONI D.3480/52/1, p. 38 (copy in IOR Neg. 1874), Chesney diary, 5 April 1830.

5 *Ibid.*, p. 43, 7 May 1830.

6 Chesney's report to Gordon on the Red Sea route, dated 2 September 1830, was printed in PP 1834 No. 478, Appendix, pp. 88–91. Extracts had been printed in PP 1831–2 No. 735, vol. 2, pp. 753–6.

7 PRONI D.3480/52/1 p. 78, Chesney diary, 19 December 1830.

8 *Ibid.*, p. 79, 27 December 1830.

9 *Ibid.*, p. 78, 26 December 1830.

10 *Ibid.*, p. 87, 3 January 1831.

11 PP 1834 No. 478, Appendix, p. 67, Chesney to Gordon, 25 January 1831.

12 F. W. Newman, *Personal Narrative, in Letters, principally from Turkey, in the Years 1830–3*, pp. 98–9.

13 J. R. Wellsted, *Travels to the City of the Caliphs*, vol. 1, p. v.

14 PP 1834 No. 478, Appendix, p. 53, Chesney to Gordon, 3 June 1831.

15 Chesney's *Memoir on the Euphrates*, dated 3 June 1831, was published privately in 1833 and reprinted in PP 1834 No. 478, Appendix, pp. 53–93.

16 IO L/P&S/5/327, Governor in Council Bombay to Secret Committee, No. 8, 23 October 1833.

17 Chesney's survey of northern Syria, entitled *Additional Memoir on the Euphrates* and dated 11 May 1832, was addressed to Sir Stratford Canning and was printed in PP 1834 No. 478, Appendix, pp. 93–8.

Chapter 4 The Balance of Power

1 PP 1831–2 No. 735, vol 2, pp. 119–30, Peacock evidence, 17 March 1832.

2 CL, p. 261.

3 PP 1834 No. 478, p. 22, Chesney evidence, 11 June 1834.

4 *Ibid.*, p. 7, Peacock evidence, 9 June 1834.

5 *Quarterly Review*, vol. 49, 1833, pp. 212–28.

6 *The Correspondence of Lord William Cavendish Bentinck*, ed. C. H. Philips, [vol. 2], p. 1300, Auber to Bentinck, 10 June 1834.

7 PP 1834 No. 478, pp. 1–13, 95, Peacock evidence, 9 and 20 June 1834; *ibid.*, pp. 13–56, 75, 126, 147, Chesney evidence, 9, 11, 20, 25, 27 June 1834.

8 *Ibid.*, pp. 56–74, 95, 184–9, MacGregor Laird evidence, 16 and 23 June, 2 July 1834; *ibid.*, pp. 75–87, 94–5, Field evidence, 20 June 1834.

9 *Ibid.*, pp. 208–16, 229–32, Waghorn evidence, 7 and 9 July 1834.

Chapter 5 Getting Ready

1 NH, vol. 1, p. 123.

2 Sir Henry C. Rawlinson's address, *Journal of the Royal Geographical Society*, vol. 43, 1873, p. clxviii.

3 George Ryan, *The Life of Major-General Estcourt*, p. 4.

4   EP, Estcourt to Elly, 6 March 1835.
5   [Edward Philips Charlewood], *Passages from the Life of a Naval Officer*, p. 28.
6   *Byron's Letters and Journals*, ed. Leslie A. Marchand, vol. 5, p. 222, Journal entry, 26 November 1813.
7   AP, vol. 1, p. 396.
8   Sir John Barrow, Bart., *Voyages of Discovery and Research within the Arctic Regions*, pp. ix-x.
9   Sir Clements Markham, *Life of Admiral Sir Leopold McClintock*, pp. 36–7.
10 EP, Estcourt to Tom, 23 April 1835.
11 *Ibid.*, Estcourt to Elly, 6 March 1835.
12 IO L/MAR/C/571, Sabine to Chesney, 8 October 1834.
13 *Ibid.*, Chesney to Palmerston, 8 September 1834.
14 *Ibid.*, MacGregor Laird to Peacock, 27 November 1834.
15 *Ibid.*, MacGregor Laird to Peacock, 2 December 1834.
16 FO 78/234, Palmerston to Ponsonby, No. 42, 23 August 1834.
17 FO 78/244, Palmerston to Campbell, Nos 8 and 9, 1 and 16 September 1834.
18 *Ibid.*, Palmerston to Campbell, No. 11, 1 October 1834.
19 *Ibid.*, Palmerston to Campbell, No. 14, 26 October 1834.
20 FO 78/247, Campbell to Palmerston, No. 63, 8 December 1834, and Private, 11 December 1834.
21 IOR MSS Eur F 213/5, p. 311, Chesney to Hobhouse, 10 November 1836.
22 CL, p. 282.
23 FO 78/240, Ponsonby to Palmerston, No. 179, 17 November 1834.
24 *Ibid.*, Ponsonby to Palmerston, No. 211, 17 December 1834. Ref. also FO 78/252, Ponsonby to Wellington, No. 1, 12 January 1835, enclosing text of *firman*.
25 PP 1837 No. 540, p. 6, Ellenborough to Chesney, 24 January 1835.
26 EP, Estcourt to Elly, 6 March 1835.
27 IO L/MAR/C/573, Grant minute, 29 May 1835.

Chapter 6 *Disappointments and Delays*

1   EP, Estcourt to Elly, 3 April 1835.
2   *Ibid.*
3   CL, p. 291, Fitzjames diary, 6 April 1835.
4   IO L/MAR/C/573, Farren to Chesney, 9 March 1835.
5   CN, pp. 173–4.
6   AP, vol. 1, p. 6.
7   CN, p. 384, Estcourt diary, 5 April 1835.
8   IO L/MAR/C/573, Chesney to Ellenborough, 2 May 1835.
9   EP, Estcourt to Elly, 3 April 1835.
10 CN, p. 405, Estcourt diary 28 April 1835.
11 FO 78/257, Campbell to Wellington Nos 12 and 15, 22 April and 26 May 1835.
12 IO L/MAR/C/573, Lynch to Clarke, 20 June 1835.
13 *Athenaeum*, No. 406, 8 August 1835, p. 603, Chesney letter, 4 June 1835.

14   CN, p. 460, Cleaveland dairy, 30 June 1835.
15   *Ibid.*, p. 479, Charlewood diary, 5 August 1835.
16   EP, Estcourt to Father, 23 May 1835.
17   IO L/MAR/C/573, Lynch to Clarke, 20 June 1835.
18   *Ibid.*, Chesney to Hobhouse, 19 July 1835.
19   Ref. *ibid.*, Chesney to Grant, 4 October 1835.
20   EP, Estcourt to Father, 4 August 1835.
21   CN, p. 200.

Chapter 7 New Faces and Old Problems

1   IO Bengal Christenings, vol. 7, p. 247; IO L/P&S/3/122, James Elliot to India
     Board Secretary, 27 September 1836; AP, vol. 1, pp. 87–9; EP, Estcourt to Elly,
     1 January 1836; NH, vol. 1, p. 122; Charles Rathbone Low, *History of the Indian
     Navy*, vol. 2, p. 32. For Elliot's travels with Ormsby see Wellsted, *Travels to the
     City of the Caliphs*, vol. 1, pp. 209 ff. and 309 ff; the diary of his journey back
     from Syria is summarized in J. Baillie Fraser, *Mesopotamia and Assyria*, pp.
     304–10.
2   NH, vol. 1, p. 122.
3   EP, Estcourt to Elly, 1 January 1836.
4   CN, p. 479, Charlewood diary, [25 August 1835].
5   *Ibid.*, pp. 202–3.
6   *Ibid.*, p. 191.
7   IO L/MAR/C/573, Chesney to Cabell, 20 September 1835.
8   *Ibid.*, Chesney to Hobhouse, 6 October 1835; Chesney to Grant, 4 October 1835.
9   Ref. *ibid.*, Ponsonby to Taylor, 10 June 1835. Ref. FO 78/258, Campbell to
     Palmerston, No. 35, 28 September 1835, for text of Sultan's letter to Mehemet
     Ali, 18 June 1835.
10   NH, vol. 1, p. 138.
11   *Ibid.*, p. 123.
12   EP, Estcourt to Elly, 1 January 1836.
13   PP 1837 No. 540, p. 70, *General Statement*; ref. also AP, vol. 1, pp. 82–4.
14   EP, Estcourt to Father, 26 December 1835.
15   IO L/MAR/C/574, Chesney to Hobhouse, 18 March 1836.
16   AE/CPC, vol. 5, f. 179r, Vannier to Ministry, No. 14, 7 February 1836.
17   Henry Richardson, *The Loss of the Tigris*, p. 29.
18   EP, Estcourt to Tom, 25 January 1836.
19   *Ibid.*, Estcourt to Elly, 1 January 1836.
20   AP, vol. 1, p. 97.
21   EP, Estcourt to Elly, 1 January 1836.
22   [Charlewood], *Passages*, p. 32.
23   NH, vol. 1, p. 143.
24   PP 1834 No. 478, p. 42, Chesney evidence, 11 June 1834.
25   FO 78/257, Palmerston to Campbell, No. 5, 2 November 1835.

26 EP, Willy Estcourt to Tom, 14 March 1836.
27 Ref. IO L/MAR/C/574, Chesney to Cabell, 10 April 1836.
28 NH, vol. 1, p. 218, Dr Helfer diary, 19 April 1836.
29 *Ibid.*, p. 181, Dr Helfer diary, 14 March 1836.

Chapter 8 Steaming down the Great River

1 PP 1837 No. 540, p. 7, Hobhouse to Chesney, 2 November 1835.
2 IO L/MAR/C/574, Peacock to Court of Directors, 13 January 1836.
3 NH, vol. 1, pp. 183–4, Dr Helfer diary, 16 March 1836.
4 PP 1837 No. 540, p. 61, Estcourt to Hobhouse, 31 March 1837.
5 CL, p. 312.
6 IO L/MAR/C/574, Chesney to Grant, 17 March 1836.
7 *Ibid.*, Chesney to Hobhouse, 18 March 1836.
8 *Ibid.*, Chesney to Rowley, 20 March 1836.
9 AP, vol. 1, p. 219.
10 *Ibid.*, p. 249.
11 EP, Estcourt to Father, 22 April 1836.
12 AP, vol. 1, pp. 258–63.
13 NH, vol. 1, pp. 218–19, Dr Helfer diary, 20 April 1836.
14 IO L/MAR/C/574, Chesney to Cabell, 22 April 1836.
15 *Ibid.*, Chesney to Cabell, 2 May 1836.
16 IOR MSS Eur F 213/5, pp. 236–7, Chesney to Hobhouse, 26 October 1836.
17 IO L/MAR/C/574, Chesney to Cabell, 30 April 1836.
18 EP, Estcourt to Minnie, 16 December 1836.
19 CN, pp. 240–1. Cf. NH, vol. 1, p. 228, Dr Helfer diary, 29 April 1836, and AP, vol. 1, p. 267.
20 Ref. IO L/MAR/C/574, Chesney to Cabell, 2 May 1836.

Chapter 9 The Wreck of the Tigris

1 IO L/MAR/C/574, Chesney to Cabell, 17 May 1836.
2 Fraser, *Mesopotamia and Assyria*, p. 308.
3 [Charlewood], *Passages*, p. 32.
4 Gasparo Balbi, *Voyage to Pegu*, translated in Samuel Purchas, *His Pilgrimes*, vol. 2, p. 1722, reprinted in PP 1834 No. 478, Appendix, p. 14.
5 1837 No. 540, pp. 8–9, Hobhouse to Chesney, 31 March 1836.
6 IO L/MAR/C/574, Lynch to Cabell, 5 February 1836.
7 *Ibid.*, Chesney to Cabell, 17 May 1836; ref. also IO MSS Eur F 213/4, pp. 95–6, Hobhouse to Sir Herbert Taylor, 21 March 1836.
8 CN, p. 248.
9 *Ibid.*, p. 251.
10 *Ibid.*, p. 252.
11 CL, pp. 327–8.

12 CN, p. 252.
13 *Ibid.*
14 PP 1837 No. 540, p. 21, Chesney to Hobhouse, 21 May 1836.
15 CL, p. 330, Chesney to sister, 25 May 1836.
16 IO L/MAR/C/574, Cleaveland to Chesney, 28 May 1836.
17 AP, vol. 1, p. 391.
18 CL, p. 330, Chesney to sister, 25 May 1836.
19 *Ibid.*, p. 328.
20 CN, p. 254.
21 *Ibid.*, p. 253.
22 NH, vol. 1, p. 248, Dr Helfer diary, 21 May 1836.
23 CN, p. 256.
24 Richardson, *Loss*, p. 29.
25 CL, p. 328.
26 *The Times*, 29 July 1836.
27 AP, vol. 1, p. 90.
28 CN, p. 257.
29 [Charlewood], *Passages*, p. 36.
30 CN, p. 258.
31 AP, vol. 1, p. 396.
32 CN, p. 260.

Chapter 10 Down to the Persian Gulf

1 CN, p. 277.
2 *Ibid.*, p. 278.
3 AP, vol. 1, pp. 419–30.
4 [Charlewood], *Passages*, p. 32.
5 *Ibid.*
6 EP, Estcourt to Minnie, 4 June 1836.
7 NH, vol. 1, p. 258.
8 *Ibid.*, pp. 260–1.
9 AP, vol. 2, p. 284.
10 EP, Estcourt to Father, 19 June 1836.
11 AP, vol. 2, p. 20.
12 *Ibid.*, p. 43.
13 *Ibid.*, p. 42.
14 *Ibid.*, pp. 46–7.
15 NH, vol. 1, p. 283.
16 [Charlewood], *Passages*, pp. 33–4.
17 AP, vol. 2, p. 64.
18 *Ibid.*, pp. 67–8.
19 *Ibid.*, p. 69.
20 EP, Estcourt to Father, 19 June 1836.

21   NH, vol. 1, p. 291.

Chapter 11 Waiting for the Indian Mails

1   James Douglas, *Bombay and Western India*, vol. 1, p. 198.
2   Theodore Hook, cited in Lord Teignmouth, *Reminiscences of Many Years*, vol. 1,
    p. 297.
3   PP 1834 No. 478, pp. 189–95, James Jeakes evidence, 4 July 1834.
4   IO L/MAR/C/573, Grant minute, 29 May 1835.
5   IO P/412/52, Grant minute, 30 June 1836.
6   PP 1834 No. 478, p. 47, Chesney evidence, 11 June 1834.
7   PP 1837 No. 540, p. 75, *General Statement*.
8   EP, Estcourt to Father, 30 June 1836.
9   [Charlewood], *Passages*, p. 37.
10 V. Fontanier, *Voyage dans l'Inde et dans le Golfe Persique*, vol. 1, pp. 289–91.
11 IO L/MAR/C/574, Chesney to Auckland, 30 June 1836; Chesney to Grant, 14
    and 30 June 1836.
12 [Charlewood], *Passages*, p. 38.
13 IO L/MAR/C/574, Chesney to Grant, 30 June 1836.
14 *Le règne de Mohamed Aly d'après les archives russes en Égypte*, ed. René Cattaui Bey,
    vol. 2, part 2, p. 96, Duhamel to Nesselrode, 27 June 1836.
15 CL, p. 337.
16 IO L/MAR/C/574, Chesney to Peacock, 18 July 1836.
17 IOR MSS Eur F 213/5, pp. 62–5, Chesney to Auckland, 7 July 1836, and
    Chesney to Grant, 7 July 1836.
18 CL, p. 339.
19 AP, vol. 2, p. 168.
20 FO 78/293, Chesney to Werry, 24 July 1836.
21 *Ibid.*, Cleaveland to Werry, 24 July 1836.
22 *Ibid.*, Werry to Bidwell, 26 August 1836.
23 IOR MSS Eur F 213/5, pp. 15–17, Chesney to Hobhouse, 24 July 1836.
24 *Ibid.*, pp. 20–1, Chesney to Grant, 19 July 1836.
25 AP, vol. 2, p. 93.
26 IO Board's Collections, vol. 1797, Colln 73816, Farish minute, 10 November
    1838, cited by J. B. Kelly, *Britain and the Persian Gulf 1795–1880*, p. 434.
27 EP, Estcourt to Father, 30 June 1836.
28 IO L/MAR/C/574, Bombay Govt Secretary to Chesney, 28 June 1836.
29 IOR MSS Eur F 213/5, Chesney to Hobhouse, 14 August 1836.
30 IO L/MAR/C/574, Chesney to Hobhouse, 15 August 1836.

Chapter 12 The Ascent

1   AP, vol. 2, p. 171.
2   EP, Estcourt to Father, 14 October 1836.

3   IO L/MAR/C/574, Chesney to Cabell, 26 September 1836.
4   EP, Estcourt to Father, 12 September 1836.
5   IOR MSS Eur F 213/4, pp. 175–6, Hobhouse to Chesney, 1 June 1836.
6   IOR MSS Eur F 213/5, pp. 219–20, Chesney to Hobhouse, 27 September 1836.
7   EP, Estcourt to Father, 12 September 1836.
8   Fontanier, *Voyage dans l'Inde*, vol. 1, pp. 313–17.
9   [Charlewood], *Passages*, p. 42.
10 *Literary Gazette*, 11 February 1837, p. 95.
11 Fontanier, *Voyage dans l'Inde*, vol. 1, pp. 319–22.
12 CL, pp. 349–50.
13 Fontanier, *Voyage dans l'Inde*, vol. 1, p. 319.
14 [Charlewood], *Passages*, p. 41.
15 EP, Estcourt to Father, 14 October 1836.
16 IOR MSS Eur F 213/5, p. 225, Chesney to Hobhouse, 1 October 1836.
17 *Ibid.*, p. 228, Chesney to Hobhouse, 3 October 1836.
18 EP, Estcourt to Father, 14 October 1836.
19 *Asiatic Journal*, vol. 21 (NS), 1836, p. 36; Fontanier, *Voyage dans l'Inde*, vol. 1, pp. 156–9.
20 EP, Estcourt to Father, 22 October 1836.
21 CN, pp. 312–13.
22 CL, p. 352.
23 IOR MSS Eur F 213/5, p. 268, Bombay Govt Secretary to Chesney, 16 September 1836.
24 EP, Estcourt to Father, 14 October 1836.
25 CN, p. 316.
26 EP, Estcourt to Father, 22 October 1836.
27 *Ibid.*
28 CL, p. 354.
29 AP, vol. 2, p. 200.
30 CL, p. 354.
31 PP 1837 No. 540, p. 10, Hobhouse to Chesney, 29 July 1836.
32 Ref. IOR MSS Eur F 213/5, pp. 235–8, Chesney to Hobhouse, 26 October 1836.
33 CN, p. 353.
34 *Ibid.*, p. 354.
35 [Charlewood], *Passages*, p. 56.

Chapter 13 The End of the Expedition

1   IO L/MAR/C/574, Chesney to Cabell, 4 November 1836.
2   AP, vol. 2, p. 201.
3   CN, p. 321.
4   IOR MSS Eur F 213/5, p. 269, Bombay Govt Secretary to Chesney, 16 Septem-

ber 1836; *ibid.*, pp. 270–3, India Govt Secretary to Bombay Govt, [29 August 1836].

5   IO L/MAR/C/574, Chesney to Bombay Govt Secretary, 30 October 1836.
6   PP 1837 No. 540, pp. 43–6, Chesney to Estcourt, 8 November 1836.
7   AP, vol. 2, p. 204.
8   Ref. FO 78/293, Werry to Bidwell, 1 and 6 August 1836.
9   IOR MSS Eur F 213/5, pp. 101–4, Hobhouse to Chesney, 30 November 1836.
10 Ref. PP 1837 No. 540, pp. 58–9, Estcourt to Hobhouse, 21 January 1837.
11 EP, Estcourt to Father, 7 May 1837.
12 *Ibid.*
13 IO L/MAR/C/574, Bombay Govt to Court of Directors, 17 December 1836.
14 *Ibid.*, Chesney to Peacock, 16 December 1836.
15 Douglas, *Glimpses of Old Bombay*, p. 134.
16 CN, p. 332.
17 *Athenaeum*, 7 October 1837, p. 738.
18 Richardson, *Loss*, p. 58.
19 PP 1837 No. 540, 17 July 1837; ref. pp. 63–7 for financial details.
20 FO 78/247, Campbell to Palmerston, 10 November 1834.
21 *The Times*, 25 July 1838.
22 IO L/MAR/C/574, Lynch to Peacock, 31 May 1838.
23 IO L/P&S/9/106, Lynch to Secret Committee, 24 May 1838.
24 Ainsworth, *Travels and Researches in Asia Minor, Mesopotamia, Chaldea, and Armenia*, vol. 1, pp. 289–364.
25 IO L/P&S/9/120, Campbell to Hobhouse, 1 June 1841.
26 Lynch, 'Memoir, in three parts, of the River Euphrates', *Transactions of the Bombay Geographical Society*, vol. 6, 1844, p. 182.
27 IO L/P&S/9/13, Lynch to Secret Committee, 25 June 1842.
28 *Ibid.*, Lynch to Peacock, 27 July 1842.

Chapter 14 Epilogue

1   W. D. Bernard, *Narrative of the Voyages and Services of the* Nemesis, *from 1840 to 1843*, vol. 1, pp. 10–13; Augustin F. B. Creuze, 'On the *Nemesis* Private Armed Steamer', *United Services Journal*, vol. 33, 1840, pp. 90–100.
2   IO L/MAR/C/574, [Peacock], *Memoir of Col. Chesney*, June 1841. Ref. also 'Our Portrait Gallery. – No. 24', *Dublin University Magazine*, vol. 18, 1841, pp. 574–80.
3   CL, pp. 466–7.
4   AE/CPC, vol. 5, f. 130r, Charles Jouannin, Renseignements sur l'expédition Anglaise sur l'Euphrate, 3 November 1835.
5   PRONI D.3480/52/1, p. 83, Chesney diary, 31 December 1830.
6   EP, Estcourt to Father, 12 September 1836.
7   PP 1837 No. 540, p. 59, Estcourt to Hobhouse, 23 February 1837.
8   Ainsworth, *Researches in Assyria, Babylonia, and Chaldaea*.
9   NH, vol. 1, p. 122.

10   Low, *History of the Indian Navy*, vol. 2, p. 257.
11   *Ibid.*, p. 289.

Bibliography

[Ainsworth, William Francis], unsigned letters to Editor dated 21 March 1836 to 31 January 1837, published in *Literary Gazette*, 1836, pp. 443–4, 522–3, 713–14 and 1837, pp. 95–6, 288–9.

Ainsworth, William [Francis], *Researches in Assyria, Babylonia, and Chaldaea; forming part of the Labours of the Euphrates Expedition*, London, 1838.

Ainsworth, William [Francis], *Travels and Researches in Asia Minor, Mesopotamia, Chaldea, and Armenia*, 2 vols, London, 1842.

Ainsworth, William [Francis], *A Personal Narrative of the Euphrates Expedition*, 2 vols, London, 1888.

Anon, 'Our Portrait Gallery – No. 24. Lieutenant-Colonel F. R. Chesney, R.A.', *Dublin University Magazine*, vol. 18, 1841, pp. 574–80.

Anon, 'The Story of the Euphrates Company', *The Near East and India*, 24 November 1932, pp. 948–54.

Balbi, Gasparo, *His Voyage to Pegu*, included in Samuel Purchas, *Hakluytus Posthumus or Purchas his Pilgrimes*, London, 1625, vol. 2, pp. 1722–9 (reprinted Glasgow, 1905, vol. 10, pp. 143–64).

Barker, Edward B. B. (ed.), *Syria and Egypt under the last five Sultans of Turkey*, 2 vols, London, 1876.

Barker, William Burkhardt, *Lares and Penates: or, Cilicia and its Governors*, ed. William Francis Ainsworth, London, 1853.

[Barrow, John], review of Captain Chesney, RA, *Reports on the Navigation of the Euphrates*, London, 1833, in *Quarterly Review*, vol. 49, 1833, pp. 212–28.

Barrow, Sir John, Bart, *Voyages of Discovery and Research within the Arctic Regions*, London, 1846.

Bentinck, Lord William Cavendish, *Correspondence*, ed. C. H. Philips, 2 vols, Oxford, 1977.

Bernard, W. D., *Narrative of the Voyages and Services of the* Nemesis, *from 1840 to 1843; . . . from Notes of Commander W. H. Hall, R.N.*, 2 vols, London, 1844.

Bernstein, Henry T., *Steamboats on the Ganges*, Bombay, [1960].

Blanc, Dr Henry, *Narrative of Captivity in Abyssinia*, London, 1864.

Butler, Marilyn, *Peacock Displayed*, London, Routledge & Kegan Paul, 1979.

Byron, George Gordon, Lord, *Byron's Letters and Journals*, ed. Leslie A. Marchand, 12 vols, Cambridge (Mass.), 1973–82.

Cable, Boyd: ref. Ernest Andrew Ewart.

Carruthers, Douglas, 'The Great Desert Caravan Route, Aleppo to Basra', *Geographical Journal*, vol. 52, 1918, pp. 157–84.

Carruthers, Douglas, *The Desert Route to India*, London, 1928 (Hakluyt Society, series 2, vol. 63).

Carruthers, Douglas, *Arabian Adventure to the Great Nafud in quest of the Oryx*, London, 1935.

Cattaui Bey, René (ed.), *Le règne de Mohamed Aly d'après les archives russes en Égypte*, 3 vols, Cairo/Rome, 1931–6.

[Charlewood, Captain Edward Philips, RN], *Passages from the Life of a Naval Officer*, Manchester, 1869.

Chesney, Alexander, 'The Journal of a South Carolina Loyalist in the Revolution and After', ed. E. Alfred Jones, *The Ohio State University Bulletin*, vol. 26, 1921, no. 4.

Chesney, Captain [Francis Rawdon], RA, *Reports on the Navigation of the Euphrates*, London, [1833].

Chesney, Lieutenant-Colonel [Francis Rawdon], RA, 'On the Bay of Antioch, and the Ruins of Seleucia Pieria', *Journal of the Royal Geographical Society*, vol. 8, 1838, pp. 228–34.

Chesney, Lieutenant-Colonel [Francis Rawdon], RA, *The Expedition for the Survey of the Rivers Euphrates and Tigris . . . 1835, 1836, and 1837*, 2 vols, London, 1850.

Chesney, Colonel [Francis Rawdon], RA, *Observations on the Past and Present State of Fire-Arms, and on the Probable Effects in War of the New Musket*, London, 1852.

Chesney, Colonel [Francis Rawdon], RA, 'Observations on the Euphrates Line of Communications with India', *British Association for the Advancement of Science*, 1852 Report.

Chesney, Colonel [Francis Rawdon], RA, *The Russo-Turkish Campaigns of 1828 and 1829*, London, 1854.

Chesney, General Francis Rawdon, RA, *Narrative of the Euphrates Expedition*, London, 1868.

Chesney, Louisa and O'Donnell, Jane, *The Life of the late General F. R. Chesney*, ed. Stanley Lane-Poole, London 1885.

[Clunn, Philip E.], *Sketch of the Life of Lieutenant Waghorn, R.N.*, [London], 1894.

Creuze, Augustin, F. B., 'On the *Nemesis* Private Armed Steamer', *United Services Journal*, vol. 33, 1840, pp. 90–100.

Cyriax, Richard J., *Sir John Franklin's Last Arctic Expedition*, London, 1919.

Dawson, Carl, *His Fine Wit*, London, Routledge & Kegan Paul, [1973].

Dodwell, Henry, *The Founder of Modern Egypt*, Cambridge, 1931.

Douglas, James, *Bombay and Western India*, 2 vols, London, 1893.

Douglas, James, *Glimpses of Old Bombay and Western India*, London, 1900.

Ellenborough, Edward Law, 1st Earl of, *A Political Diary, 1828–1830*, ed. Lord Colchester, 2 vols, London, 1881.

[Ewart, Ernest Andrew] 'Boyd Cable', *A Hundred Year History of the P. & O.*, London, 1937.

Felton, Felix, *Thomas Love Peacock*, London, 1973.

Fontanier, Victor, *Voyage dans l'Inde et dans le golfe Persique par l'Égypte et la mer Rouge*, 3 vols, Paris, 1844–6.

Fraser, J. Baillie, *Mesopotamia and Assyria, from the earliest Ages to the Present Time*, Edinburgh, 1841.

Furber, Holden, 'The Overland Route to India in the Seventeenth and Eighteenth Centuries', *Journal of Indian History*, vol. 29, 1951, pp. 105–33.

Grant, Christina Phelps, *The Syrian Desert*, New York, 1938.

Grounds, Lieut. H. W., IN, 'A Memoir on the Country between Bagdad and the Hamreed Hills', *Transactions of the Bombay Geographical Society*, vol. 6, 1844, pp. 407–19.

Groves, Anthony Norris, *Journal . . . during a Journey from London to Baghdad, . . . also of Some Months Residence at Baghdad*, London, 1831.

Groves, Anthony Norris, *Journal of a Residence at Baghdad during the Years 1830 and 1831*, London, 1833.

[Groves, Harriet Baynes], *Memoir of the late Anthony Norris Groves, containing Extracts from his Letters and Journals*, London, 1856.

Groves, Henry, *'Not of the World': Memoir of Lord Congleton*, London, 1884.

Hachicho, Mohamed Ali, 'English Travel Books about the Arab Near East in the Eighteenth Century', *Die Welt des Islams*, vol. 9, 1964, pp. 1–206.

Harford, Frederic D., 'Old Caravan Routes and Overland Routes in Syria, Arabia, and Mesopotamia', *The Nineteenth Century*, vol. 84, 1918, pp. 97–113.

Hilprecht, H. V., *Explorations in Bible Lands*, Philadelphia, 1903.

Hoskins, Halford Lancaster, *British Routes to India*, London, 1928.

Ingram, Edward, *The Beginning of the Great Game in Asia 1828–1834*, Oxford, 1979.

Janka, Otto, *Flight of a Shy Magician* [a biography of Dr J. W. Helfer, written in Czech], Edition Karavana, vol. 222, Prague, 1989.

Jones, Dorsey D., 'Chesney Chose the Euphrates Route', *Phi Alpha Theta*, vol. 5, 1942–3, pp. 5–23. (Paper no. 761, Journal Series, University of Arkansas.)

Joukovsky, Nicholas A., 'Peacock before *Headlong Hall*: A New Look at his Early Years', *Keats-Shelley Memorial Bulletin*, vol. 36, 1985, pp. 1–40.

Joukovsky, Nicholas A., 'Peacock: Examiner of All Things East', paper read at Modern Language Association of America Convention, New Orleans, 1988.

Kaye, Sir John William, *The Life and Correspondence of Major-General Sir John Malcolm, G.C.B.*, 2 vols, London, 1856.

Kelly, J. B., 'Mehemet Ali's Expedition to the Persian Gulf 1837–1840', *Middle Eastern Studies*, vol. 1, 1964–5, pp. 350–81; vol. 2, 1965–6, pp. 31–65.

Kelly, J. B. *Britain and the Persian Gulf 1795–1880*, Oxford, 1968.

Khan, Muhammad Golam Idris, 'British Policy in Iraq, 1828–43', PhD dissertation, British School of Oriental and African Studies, London University, 1967.

Laird, John; John Laird, Sons & Co., and Laird Brothers, *List of Iron and Wood Vessels built at the Birkenhead Iron Works from 1829 to 1889*, Liverpool and Birkenhead, 1893.

Layard, Sir Austen Henry, *Autobiography and Letters*, ed. Hon. William Bruce, 2 vols, London, 1903.

Longrigg, Stephen Hemsley, *Four Centuries of Modern Iraq*, Oxford, 1925.

Longrigg, Stephen Hemsley, '*Iraq, 1900 to 1950*, Oxford, 1953.

Lorimer, J. G., *Gazetteer of the Persian Gulf, Oman, and Central Arabia*, 2 vols, Calcutta, 1908–15.

Low, Charles Rathbone, *History of the Indian Navy (1613–1863)*, 2 vols, London, 1877.

Lynch, Lieutenant H. Blosse, IN, 'Note accompanying a Survey of the Tigris between Ctesiphon and Mosul', *Journal of the Royal Geographical Society*, vol. 9, 1839, pp. 441–2.

Lynch, Lieutenant H. Blosse, IN, 'Note on a part of the river Tigris betwen Baghdad and Samarrah', *Ibid.*, pp. 471–6.

Lynch, Commander H. [Blosse], IN, 'Memoir, in three parts, of the River Euphrates', *Transactions of the Bombay Geographical Society*, vol, 6, 1844, pp. 169–86.

Lynch, T. K., *Across Mesopotamia to India by the Euphrates Valley*, London, 1879.

Markham, Clements R., *Memoir on the Indian Survey*, London, 1871.

Markham, Sir Clements [R.], *Life of Admiral Sir Leopold McClintock*, London, 1909.

Mitford, Edward Ledwich, *A Land March from England to Ceylon Forty Years Ago, through Dalmatia, Montenegro, Turkey, Asia Minor, Syria, Palestine, Assyria, Persia, Afghanistan, Scinde, and India, of which 7000 miles on horseback*, 2 vols, London, 1884.

Musil, Alois, *The Middle Euphrates*, New York, 1927. (American Geographical Society, Oriental Explorations and Studies No. 3.)

Newman, F. W., *Personal Narrative, in Letters, principally from Turkey, in the Years 1830–3*, London, 1856.

Nicholes, Eleanor L., article on Peacock in *Shelley and his Circle*, ed. Kenneth Neill Cameron, Cambridge (Mass.), 1961-, vol. 1, pp. 90–114.

Nostitz, Pauline, Countess, *Travels of Doctor and Madame Helfer in Syria, Mesopotamia, Burmah and other Lands*, trans. Mrs G. Sturge, 2 vols, London, 1878.

Oppenheim, Dr Max Freiherr von, *Die Beduinen*, 4 vols, Leipzig/Wiesbaden, 1939–67.

Ormsby, Lieut H. A., IN, 'Narrative of a Journey across the Syrian Desert', *Transactions of the Bombay Geographical Society*, vol. 2, 1838–9, pp. 18–33.

[Peacock, Thomas Love], 'Report from the Select Committee of the House of Commons, on Steam Navigation to India; with the Minutes of Evidence, Appendix, and Index. 1834', *Edinburgh Review*, vol. 60, 1835, pp. 445–82.

Peacock, Thomas Love, *Works*, ed. Henry Cole, 3 vols, London, 1875.

Philips, C. H., *The East India Company 1784–1834*, Manchester, 1961.

Prinsep, G. A., *An Account of Steam Vessels, and of proceedings connected with Steam Navigation in British India*, Calcutta, 1830.

Raff, Helene, *Deutsche Frauen ueber Meer*, Stuttgart, [1928].

Richardson, Henry, *The Loss of the Tigris*, London, 1840.

Robinson, George, *Travels in Palestine and Syria*, 2 vols, London, 1837.

Rosselli, John, *Lord William Bentinck: The Making of a Liberal Imperialist 1774–1839*, Berkeley, 1974.

Ryan, George, *The Life of Major-General Estcourt, Adjutant-General of the Army in the East*, London, 1856.

Sabry, M., *L'Empire Égyptien sous Mohamed-Ali et La question d'Orient (1811–1849)*, Paris, 1930.

Saldanha, J. A., *Precis of Turkish Arabia Affairs, 1801–1905*, Simla, 1906.

Sankey, Marjorie, *'Care of Mr. Waghorn'*, London, 1964. (The Postal History Society, Special Series No. 19.)

Shelley, Percy Bysshe, *Letters*, ed. Frederick L. Jones, 2 vols, Oxford, 1964.

Sidebottom, John K., *The Overland Mail*, London, 1948.

Smith, Charles Roach, *Retrospections, Social and Archaeological*, 3 vols, London, 1883.

Smith, George M., 'In the Early Forties', *The Cornhill Magazine*, vol. 9 (N.S.), 1900, pp. 577–85.

Stocqueler, J. H. a.k.a. J. H. Siddons, *Fifteen Months' Pilgrimage through untrodden tracts of Khuzistan and Persia, in a Journey from India to England, through parts of Turkish Arabia, Persia, Armenia, Russia, and Germany*, 2 vols, London, 1832.

Taylor, Major John, *Travels from England to India . . . 1789, by the way of the Tyrol, Venice, Scandaroon, Aleppo, and over the Great Desert to Bussora*, 2 vols, London, 1799.

Teignmouth, Charles John Shore, 2nd Baron, *Reminiscences of Many Years*, 2 vols, Edinburgh, 1878.

Texier, Ch., *Description de l'Arménie, la Perse et la Mésopotamie*, 2 vols, Paris, 1842–52.

Tresse, R., 'L'installation du premier consul d'Angleterre à Damas (1830–1834)', *Revue d'histoire des colonies françaises*, vol. 24, 1936, pp. 359–80.

Tuckey, James Hingston, *Maritime Geography and Statistics*, 4 vols, London, 1815.

Waghorn, Thomas, *Particulars of an Overland Journey from London to Bombay, by way of the Continent, Egypt, and the Red Sea*, London, 1831.

Webster, Sir Charles, *The Foreign Policy of Palmerston, 1830–1841*, 2 vols, London, 1951.

Wellsted, J. R., *Travels to the City of the Caliphs, along the Shores of the Persian Gulf and the Mediterranean*, 2 vols, London, 1840.

Wilson, Commander J. H., IN, *Facts connected with the Origin and Progress of Steam Communication between India and England*, London, 1850.

Winchester, James W., 'Memoir on the River Euphrates, &c. during the late Expedition of the H. C. Armed Cruiser, "*Euphrates*" ', *Transactions of the Bombay Geographical Society*, vol. 2, 1838–9, pp. 1–22.

Ziegler, Robert E., *John Cam Hobhouse: A Political Life 1819–1852*, Columbia (Mo.), 1973.

Index

175

'Tartars', mounted couriers, 3, 57, 67, 84, 130

Taylor, James W., promoter, 15–18, 21–2, 45n, 63, 97, 124, 143

Taylor, Maj. John, Indian Army, 8, 55

Taylor, Col. Robert, Indian Army, HEICo resident at Baghdad, 9, 15, 21, 27–8, 33, 40, 46, 62–3, 91n, 97–100, 105, 120, 122–4, 133, 141, 143

Taylor, Mrs Robert, 27, 99–100, 123–4

Thapsacus, 83–4

Theodore II, emperor of Ethiopia, 154

Thomson, William Taylour, draftsman, 43, 54, 56, 71, 73, 90, 92, 154

Tigris river, 8–10, 21, 26, 28, 33, 35, 45n, 97–8, 100, 105, 109, 121–6, 133, 136–7, 140–1, 143–5, 151, 155

Trabzon, *see* Trebizond

Trajan, Roman emperor, 10

Trebizond, 92, 153

Tripoli, Lebanon, 56

Tuckey, Cdr James Kingston, RN, 7

Urfa, 8, 29, 36, 46–7, 56, 62

Varna, 10, 63

Waghorn, Lt Thomas Fletcher, RN, 16–20, 22, 24, 32, 35, 75, 137–8

Wellington, Arthur Wellesley, 1st duke of, prime minister, later foreign secretary, 4, 10, 17, 20, 31, 42, 47

Werry, Nathaniel W., vice-consul at Aleppo, 115, 122, 134

William IV, king of England, 31, 35, 45, 47, 54, 57, 60, 76, 81, 84, 106, 129, 140–1

Winchester, Dr James Webster, Indian Army, 142

Xenophon, Greek traveller, 63, 91

Yusuf Sadr, interpreter, 72–3, 90

Zelebiye, 84

Zenobia, queen of Palmyra, 1, 59, 84, 146

Zenobia (place), *see* Halebiye

Zinnitz, Germany, 64

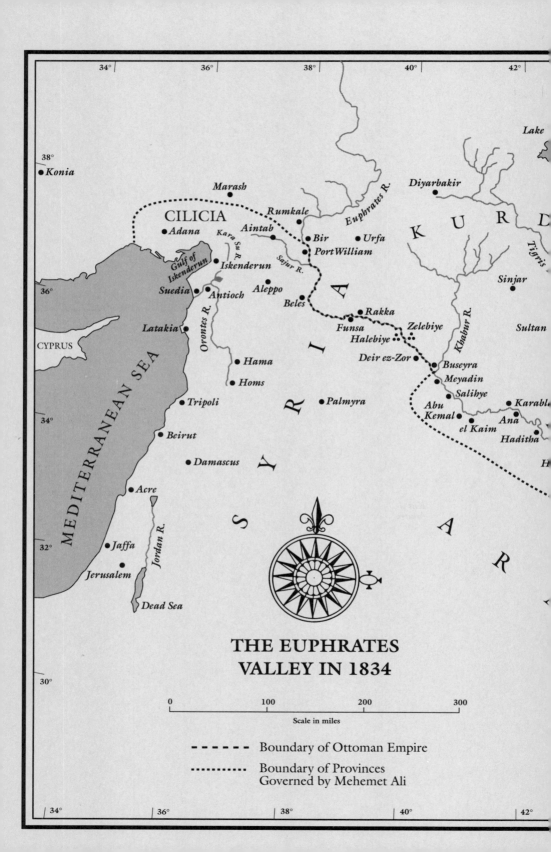

34° 36° 38° 40° 42°

Lake

38° ● *Konia*

Marash

Rumkale *Euphrates R.* *Diyarbakir*

CILICIA *Aintab*

● *Adana* *Kara Su R.* ● *Bir* ● *Urfa* K U R D

Port William

Iskenderun *Sajur R.* *Tigris*

Gulf of
Iskenderun

36° ● *Suedia* ● *Antioch* *Aleppo* ● *Sinjar*

Beles A *Sultan*

Orontes R. *Rakka*

● *Latakia* *Funsa* *Zelebiye* *Khabur R.*

CYPRUS *Halebiye*

Deir ez-Zor *Buseyra*

● *Hama* *Meyadin*

Salihye

● *Homs* *Abu* ● *Karabl*

34° ● *Tripoli* ● *Palmyra* *Kemal* *Ana*

el Kaim

Haditha

● *Beirut* H

M E D I T E R R A N E A N   S E A

● *Damascus* S

A

32° ● *Acre* R

● *Jaffa* *Jordan R.*

Jerusalem

Dead Sea

THE EUPHRATES
VALLEY IN 1834

0 100 200 300

Scale in miles

– – – – – – Boundary of Ottoman Empire

.... Boundary of Provinces
Governed by Mehemet Ali

34° 36° 38° 40° 42°